A CUTTING EDGE

Cabinet Diaries 1982-1987

Gemma Hussey

Gill and Macmillan

For Derry,
Rachel, Ruth and Andrew

Published in Ireland by
Gill and Macmillan Ltd
Goldenbridge
Dublin 8
with associated companies in
Auckland, Delhi, Gaborone, Hamburg, Harare,
Hong Kong, Johannesburg, Kuala Lumpur, Lagos, London,
Manzini, Melbourne, Mexico City, Nairobi
New York, Singapore, Tokyo
© Gemma Hussey, 1990
ISBN 0 7171 1764 2 (hardback)
ISBN 0 7171 1753 7 (paperback)

Designed by Fergus O'Keeffe
Print origination by Irish Typesetting and Publishing Co. Ltd,
Galway
Printed by Richard Clays, Suffolk

Contents

Acknowledgments

Dee Johnstone, my friend and secretary, was not only a constant support during my years in politics, but also gave invaluable help in first getting the diaries into typescript.

Ruairi Quinn kindly gave me permission to reproduce two of his cartoons drawn while at the Cabinet table.

To the very many people of my native Wicklow who worked with me, fought elections with me, and loyally put up with me when nobody else wanted to—my gratitude, respect, and continuing affection.

I also want to acknowledge the work of the Women's Political Association and countless individual women around the country who helped me from the beginning.

My special thanks to a circle of close friends whose help and encouragement were always generously given.

And finally, few people can fully understand the sacrifices which families make when a spouse and parent holds a demanding political job. My own family knows how grateful I am to them for their acceptance. This book is dedicated to them.

Preface

The Fine Gael–Labour Coalition Government in Ireland between 1982 and 1987 held office during a period which was both difficult and dramatic. There were moments of achievement and exhilaration, as well as moments of near-despair. The intense political pressures were felt most keenly by the Taoiseach and Tanaiste, Garret FitzGerald and Dick Spring, as well as by Ministers holding big-spending portfolios. Relations were often under severe strain, not only between the parties in Coalition, but inevitably between individual Ministers as well.

These diaries of my time as a Minister in that Government were written at home, in hastily-snatched half-hours, on a sporadic basis, as a private and personal record. They are part of a longer series of diaries which I have kept over many years.

They are now published in the hope that they will be of some value as part of the historical record of the country; they may also increase the citizens' knowledge of how Government actually works.

Apart from the omission of private family material, and paragraphs or entries which my publisher, Michael Gill, and myself felt were repetitious, inadvertently libellous, or had security implications, the words are exactly as they were written down over those four years.

The Government 1982–1987

On 14 December 1982 the appointed members of Government were as follows (FG = Fine Gael; L = Labour):
Garret FitzGerald (FG), *Taoiseach*
Dick Spring (L), *Tanaiste and Environment*
Peter Barry (FG), *Foreign Affairs*
Alan Dukes (FG), *Finance*
John Bruton (FG), *Industry and Energy*
Austin Deasy (FG), *Agriculture*
Michael Noonan (FG), *Justice*
Barry Desmond (L), *Health and Social Welfare*
Gemma Hussey (FG), *Education*
Frank Cluskey (L), *Trade, Commerce and Tourism*
Liam Kavanagh (L), *Labour*
Patrick Cooney (FG), *Defence*
Paddy O'Toole (FG), *Gaeltacht, Fisheries and Forestry*
John Boland (FG), *Public Service*
Jim Mitchell (FG), *Post and Telegraphs and Transport*
Peter Sutherland, *Attorney General*
Sean Barrett (FG), *Chief Whip*

Frank Cluskey resigned on 8 December 1983; Ruairi Quinn (L) replaced him in a minor reshuffle which moved Liam Kavanagh to Environment, Dick Spring to Energy and John Bruton to Trade, Commerce and Tourism. Ruairi Quinn became Minister for Labour.

On 13 February 1986 a major reorganisation of members of Government took place; the new responsibilities were as follows:

Garret FitzGerald (FG), *Taoiseach*
Dick Spring (L), *Tanaiste and Energy*
Peter Barry (FG), *Foreign Affairs*
Alan Dukes (FG), *Justice*
John Bruton (FG), *Finance*
Austin Deasy (FG), *Agriculture*
Michael Noonan (FG), *Industry and Commerce*
Barry Desmond (L), *Health*
Gemma Hussey (FG), *Social Welfare*
Liam Kavanagh (L), *Tourism, Fisheries and Forestry*
Patrick Cooney (FG), *Education*
Paddy O'Toole (FG), *Defence and the Gaeltacht*
John Boland (FG), *Environment*
Jim Mitchell (FG), *Communications*
Ruairi Quinn (L), *Labour and the Public Service*
John Rogers, *Attorney General*
Sean Barrett (FG), *Chief Whip*

Introduction

Garret FitzGerald's election as Taoiseach on 14 December 1982 marked the end of a prolonged period of political instability in Ireland. There had been three General Elections in eighteen months; the issues were mainly economic and there was the added twist of a serious personality conflict between the Fianna Fail leader Mr Haughey and Dr FitzGerald. H-Block hunger strikes and continuing murders kept the North of Ireland as a looming presence on the side-lines. Fine Gael had gained steadily in popularity at each election between June 1981 and November 1982 despite a failed (Coalition Government) budget in January 1982 and the unease and confusion caused by a proposed Constitutional Amendment on the subject of abortion. The Fine Gael share of the national vote went from 36% to 39% over this period.

The Government of Mr Haughey between March and November of 1982 gave rise to a new word in the Irish political vocabulary: GUBU. This word was coined by Conor Cruise O'Brien to describe a series of events ranging from the mysterious detention in Northern Ireland by the RUC of a man who was on his way to an Irish court to testify against the brother-in-law of the Minister for Justice, to the discovery of a murderer hiding in the apartment of the Attorney General. The letters stand for 'grotesque, unbelievable, bizarre and unprecedented' — words actually used by Mr Haughey as Taoiseach at a press briefing on the Attorney General affair.

During all this time the national debt soared and there was growing concern about the extent of Government borrowing and spending. It was clear that there was considerable internal dissension in the Fianna Fail Cabinet, as well as widespread rumours of illegal tapping of

1

journalists' telephones by order of a Government minister. Against this background and after a hard-fought and bitter election campaign in November 1982, the Coalition Government of Fine Gael and Labour came into office with Garret FitzGerald at the height of his popularity and Fine Gael holding 70 seats in the Dail.

When I joined Fine Gael in 1980 I became the Party's first spokesperson on Women's Affairs. In February 1982 on my election to the Dail I was appointed opposition spokesperson on Broadcasting, Arts and Culture. I had come into politics from a background of business (founding and directing a large language school for foreign students), the Irish women's movement, and university studies in economics and political science.

At the time of my appointment to the Cabinet on 14 December 1982 I had been just over five years in the Oireachtas, starting as a University Senator representing the National University of Ireland after my first election in 1977. I joined the Fine Gael Parliamentary Party in 1980 and ran for the Dail in my native Wicklow in June 1981. Having narrowly failed to get a seat on that occasion, I regained my NUI Senate seat and became Leader of the Upper House. At the next election in February 1982 I took a Dail seat in Wicklow and held it in the November 1982 election.

The Cabinet

During our four years in Government, I spent what must amount to several months shut up in the Cabinet room with the other members of the Government, plus the Attorney General and the Secretary to the Government. The meeting room is the 'Council Chamber', a large room on the first floor of Government Buildings in Merrion Street.

There were almost no changes in personnel in that time; Ruairi Quinn replaced Frank Cluskey in 1983 and John Rogers replaced Peter Sutherland after the post of Euro-Commissioner was given to Peter.

The seating arrangements at the Cabinet table were almost totally decided by a random choice made by each of us on that first morning in mid-December of 1982. The exceptions were that the Taoiseach automatically sat in the middle with his back to the windows, flanked by Dermot Nally (Secretary to the Government) and the Chief Whip (Sean Barrett), with the Attorney General beside the Chief Whip. Directly opposite the Taoiseach was the Tanaiste (Dick Spring) who had the Minister for Finance (Alan Dukes) on his right. The rest of us sat around the overcrowded but handsome oval mahogany table in that randomly chosen way, which had nothing to do with either seniority or party affiliation. During my four years there, the room needed a coat of paint and there were dull paintings on the wall.

Because my Ministerial baptism was so fiery and so public, I was thrown straight into endless Cabinet arguments about Education spending. Colleagues were, I think, taken aback by the strength of public reaction (whipped up relentlessly by Fianna Fail and the large interest groups) to school transport charges, and were extremely worried about the political consequences of further expenditure-cutting measures. But side by side with that worry went a feeling that we must stick firmly to our guns in order to make sure that the public got the message that we were going to practise what we had preached for so long. We knew that Fianna Fail, nationally and locally, would oppose any expenditure cut, that they would join forces with and encourage the Fianna Fail elements in the teachers' unions, the IVEA and every other large interest group. They were, therefore, a constant and predictably destructive force—but it was their effect on the constantly wavering Labour backbenchers which was the real worry.

At least twice a week we gathered in the Cabinet room and often it was more frequently. I would climb into the State car at home at about 10 a.m., with several large heavy black briefcases, and use the few minutes drive to Merrion Street to bone up once again on the arguments and figures surrounding the latest Education crisis or other urgent Government business. My private secretary, the always efficient and loyal Peter Baldwin, waited for me in the Communications Room directly across the corridor from the Cabinet room, with whatever urgent files he or the Department officials felt I must see before disappearing into Cabinet. I would have a list of messages, requests and requirements which had accumulated from whatever functions or meetings I'd been at the night before and from the stream of early morning phone calls at home. Finally, with Peter's assistance, I got myself and the several briefcases through the double doors into the Cabinet room. And I was usually the first or second to appear—no matter what punctuality resolutions had been made, my colleagues seemed to find it impossible to be on time. They took their lead from Garret, who would find himself running late from his early appointments. However, I have always had strong views about punctuality and lived in daily hope that others might develop it too.

Beside the large, airy and quite gracious Cabinet room in Merrion Street there was a private 'ante-room' where a tea-making and coffee pot arrangement were constantly in use. We gathered in there while waiting for Cabinet to begin and used it to refresh ourselves during very long sessions. I established quite quickly, without any announcements, that I didn't see any particular role for myself in boiling kettles or handing around tea. I felt that it was an area which might just become a symbol of some kind of distinction between me and all those men. So whoever happened to be available made the tea, whether it was Justice, Labour, Education or Foreign Affairs. Peter Barry was quite particular about the standard of the tea and made a good 'cuppa'.

We all dressed fairly formally for Cabinet, because it usually coincided with Dail sitting days—and Ministers would have a huge work schedule on any day, quite apart from Cabinet. It was only on the occasional foray to Barretstown (where I think we went four times in four years) that I saw my colleagues in sweaters and without ties. During some very long sessions when the night seemed endless, jackets would come off and ties were loosened. My own clothes followed the same pattern. I usually wore suits with a blouse which had a loose bow tie which became a sort of a trademark for cartoonists. I always envied the simplicity of dressing for my male Cabinet colleagues: not for me the possibility of wearing the same thing day after day, from breakfast through a hectic day, perhaps ending in a dinner dance in Aughrim, taking in *Today Tonight* en route. Women in politics have all sorts of extra criteria to cope with, extra dimensions of comment: it did one no good, politically, to be found on a 'worst-dressed' list (as I was once). If one looked tired or less than immaculate on television or in press photos, it was widely commented upon and seen as a black mark, a sign of weakness. That is another of the double standards women in public life face. The inevitable media comparisons of me with Thatcher were, to put it mildly, irksome; but I see why she dressed as she did (and does) and since she also started her Cabinet life as Minister for Education ('milk snatcher') I suppose it was inevitable.

Interestingly, one of the strongest and most attractive characters around the table for those first years was the person who was the most silent: Peter Sutherland. As Attorney General he hadn't the right to intervene in discussions unless asked for a legal opinion. However, Peter's expressive face and lively dark eyes spoke volumes when we were talking about something he was interested in (and that was most things). Frequently some Minister would, having watched the facial contortions, suggest to Garret that we should call on the Attorney General who would then speak clearly and incisively on the issue. I particularly rejoiced in Peter's discussions on the so-called Abortion Referendum, about which he felt passionately and spoke accordingly—and often with great humour. Peter's influence behind the scenes was considerable, he was respected and liked by all of us. I vehemently supported him for EEC Commissioner when it seemed for a while that Garret might wilt under pressure from Labour to appoint Justin Keating. It caused me a little difficulty because I'd known and liked Justin for a long time and regularly spent Christmas day in his company in Donard,

West Wicklow. However, my view was that Peter's formidable legal brain, extreme articulateness and indefatigable capacity for work were peculiarly suited for the EEC post. So I lobbied Garret incessantly on behalf of Peter, who was himself low-key and dignified during that period. And of course I'm delighted he proved his supporters right during four very distinguished years in Brussels.

Garret himself was described as 'an enigma' by Raymond Smith. And perhaps that's right. At the Cabinet table Garret was unfailingly gentlemanly. His attractive, concerned face regarded cross or recalcitrant Ministers with a mixture of incomprehension, anxiety and impatience. Since his encyclopaedic brain had assimilated huge chunks of knowledge about the portfolios of every Minister, he was frequently far ahead of Ministers when it came to anticipating problems. His lack of 'macho' characteristics had endeared him to me from the beginning — Garret never let slip a profanity or vulgar expletive, and was sensitive if that happened in mixed company. Since I was the only woman during all those Cabinet sessions over four years, when occasional tension quite naturally led to the odd robust verbal explosion, I always tried to convey to the apologetic colleague that I wasn't at all offended and hadn't been brought up in a glass case anyway. But it was unfailingly towards me those concerned blue eyes of Garret's would jump when the air thickened late in the night. His strongest word to convey disapproval of one's actions was 'unhelpful' — to be accused of that by Garret was upsetting because one knew he felt very strongly. His concern to reach consensus on the issues facing Government meant that our Cabinet meetings were much longer than was comfortable — and I often felt wearily that he could have been more impatient and less accommodating with, say, the verbose Barry Desmond or the cool, but often inflexible Alan Dukes.

Like myself, Garret had a continual weight problem all the time we were in Government. Like myself he enjoyed good food and wine but I often wondered if his weight gain, like my own, was directly related to the stresses of the job. To counteract all the unsociable hours and bad eating habits, I suggested to him that he might come with me on my four-mile walk in the early morning—to be greeted with a horrified refusal: Garret only walked to get from one place to another and didn't believe in taking exercise. He was a hard-working, brilliant man, but never 'one of the lads'—and didn't seem at ease if he joined a group of story-telling, relaxing Cabinet colleagues who had gathered in the Chief Whip's office after a very late night Cabinet session for a drink to unwind. His one great fault—and it's not surprising that I would say this—was to rush into some big decision without quietly working out the whole plan of campaign in advance. By contrast, the area where he demonstrated that he *was* capable of cool, calculated, clever advance planning was in the Anglo-Irish Agreement.

The Tanaiste, Dick Spring, was the complete opposite. He was, of course, suffering constantly from the severe back injury caused by a car crash when he was Junior Minister for Justice in 1981. Dick was quiet, almost brooding. He was capable of sharp and witty comments, but these were mostly delivered in informal sessions. All the time we were in Government I was conscious of two things: the affection and respect in which the Taoiseach and Tanaiste held each other, the almost fatherly concern of Garret for Dick, and the terrific burden Dick carried of acute worry about the malcontents on his backbenches who always threatened revolt when the heat of public hostility rose. The combination of his back problems, the crisis in public finances and the consequent strains in the Labour Party gave Dick a bad-tempered, often sulky demeanour which irritated many of us in Fine Gael (particularly people like myself who felt beleaguered by huge public hostility and felt we were the ones who were carrying the can for the whole Government). With hindsight I feel more benevolent towards him, but at the time it was difficult. And all the time Fianna Fail sought to destabilise the Government by taunting the Labour Party over every minor expenditure cut. Dick and Garret sorted out a great many potentially explosive items before they ever came to Cabinet, quite often in Garret's basement sitting room in Palmerston Road.

Alan Dukes was a workaholic, a calm Minister for Finance, whose command of his brief was astounding. He, like Garret, was not 'one of the lads' though never realised it. I found his cool style of argument, particularly about education, quite maddening — though preferable to that of John Bruton, a later Finance Minister who frequently went at things like a bull in a china shop. Alan, all 6'4" of him, smoked incessantly, smiled most of the time, seemed — as he still does — unmoved by anything I could throw at him. I quickly learned that I just had to be as tenacious, stubborn and inflexible as he was, though my internal stomach-churning had to be hidden under a veneer of calm. Alan suffered because of Garret's need to keep Dick and the Labour Party on side. I believe we all felt, despite some frustration, that a return to 'GUBU' and reckless Fianna Fail spending would be far worse for the country than our own efforts to put things financially right and to govern honourably. Alan's particular personality, calm as it was and apparently imperturbable, was just right for the difficult tightrope he had to walk between Garret and Dick and the Civil Service mandarins in Finance (whose conclusions Garret often questioned, and was often proved right). Alan's liberal attitudes on many social issues, which I shared, were a bond between us which helped to counteract the tensions we inevitably felt with each other because of my big spending portfolio of Education.

There were many strong characters around that table in 1982 — John Boland's acerbic brilliance when he was in form, Barry Desmond's air of injured outrage at any suggestion of health cuts and his interminable but very clever defence of his brief; Liam Kavanagh's solid, middle-of-the-road reliability and strength which Dick needed and appreciated (though I had my differences with Liam, largely because I felt he did not publicly support Government actions sufficiently in Co. Wicklow, our shared constituency). John Bruton, clever, untidy and hardworking, loud-voiced and boyish, frequently an original thinker but difficult in his over-reaction to opposition, and at the same time capable of immense charm when losing an argument — someone whose obvious patriotism is so attractive. Frank Cluskey who despite great personal charm and great Dublin humour never gave the impression of either being happy in Government, or capable of withstanding the frequently daunting pressures we were under. A sure sign of an impending obstructive outburst from Frank was a mannerism of repeated shoulder flexing as if ready to throw a punch, a tuneless whistle through his teeth and a strange recourse to a sort of nervous giggle. I liked Frank, and I think he liked me, but I felt much more comfortable with Ruairi Quinn his successor, who was prepared to work strenuously with all of us to keep the Government together and to undertake reform programmes energetically. He had a particularly acute understanding of women's issues — more than even Garret — which was useful to me when issues arose which particularly affected women and I was defending women specifically as Minister for Social Welfare. He also had a way of helping us to keep things in perspective when he drew lightning cartoons on some issue we were discussing which were passed around, distracted us, and so broke the tension of a difficult moment.

Peter Barry was absent a great deal, because of his Foreign Affairs commitments and mostly conveyed the impression of concerned uncle when he was present. His Cabinet input wasn't considerable; though his devotion to Northern Ireland affairs was great, it was done outside Cabinet. Also he suffered from the disadvantage that Garret himself was the authority on Northern Ireland and most other Foreign Affairs issues when they appeared on the Cabinet agenda. He was not burdened with liberal or progressive attitudes, but was a source of wisdom inside the Party and a major calming influence there in times of stress.

Jim Mitchell was a legendary hard worker and vote getter in his Dublin West Constituency. He brought energy and determination to his job as Transport and Communications Minister, and was very frustrated by the problems with Labour over the Radio legislation and the frustration boiled over sometimes, despite Garret's efforts to keep the temperature down around the Cabinet table. Jim's great boast—and it was justified—was that he brought a new sense of business and achievement to the semi-State bodies under his aegis, such as Aer Lingus and CIE. Of all of those men I sat with for all those days and months, Jim was the most emotional, something I found attractive but which is not appreciated by men on the whole. I was surprised to find him a conservative, however, on the role of women.

Pat Cooney, once considered to be a liberal young tiger, was a source of wonder; extremely astute, deeply conservative, capable of considerable charm and bonhomie. His dislike of Garret's (and my) position on social reform was palpable, and there were some difficult and tense times. We were at either ends of the spectrum on women's rights. It was a considerable shock when he was appointed Minister for education in my place in February 1986. That promotion from Defence came as a shock to him as well as to the education world.

Michael Noonan was catapulted into the national limelight as quickly as myself, but his area (Justice) was easier in that he didn't incur the wrath of the nation, only of Fianna Fail. As revelation followed revelation in January 1983 about the extraordinary behaviour of former Ministers Ray MacSharry and Sean Doherty, and the peculiar involvement of senior Gardai, the atmosphere became almost unreal. Michael dealt with the situation with admirable coolness, humour and considerable courage, because some of the confrontations he had to face were particularly nasty, if not dangerous. I was struck by his answer to a remark of mine congratulating him on his success and high public standing. He said: 'When you find yourself in my position all of a sudden, the only way is down'. And so it proved—he gradually became less popular. The rasping Limerick voice and 'cute hoor' reputation he gained were not helpful to him later.

Austin Deasy, blunt, straight-talking and impatient, sat beside me for a long time. He hated long Cabinet meetings and despite the marathon all night Brussels agricultural sessions, always said they were preferable to Cabinet. I think he found the 'star chamber' sessions of defending his Department against the onslaught of Finance as harrowing as I did. I always liked Austin—and he was, I believe, a good and respected Minister for Agriculture. I sometimes broke my rule and administered black coffee to him before Cabinet meetings when he seemed exhausted.

Paddy O'Toole, the quietest man in Cabinet, was one of the nicest people I met in politics. He was loyal, hard-working, and concerned for his colleagues and his country. It was a combination of his non-assertive personality and the enforced absences from Mayo East (where the thrusting young Senator Jim Higgins was beavering away) which lost him his Dail seat and subsequently scotched his Senate election chances. He was a casualty of our strange political system.

It was a Cabinet which had to deal with a massive financial crisis at a time when no political consensus existed; it was therefore tense and difficult as Labour came under fierce pressure from their left wing—who never gave, and still don't give the impression of being able or willing to undertake the responsibilities of Government. Those of us in high-spending Ministries were put under particular strain therefore, and faced weekly Dail storms from Fianna Fail as well as constituency unpopularity and continual public controversy in every county in Ireland. So sometimes the Cabinet room, understandably, represented a haven or place where at least we all understood why we were doing what we were doing and sympathised with whichever colleague was having a rough time (that frequently seemed to be me—and I often remarked as good-humouredly as I could that some public solidarity wouldn't go amiss either). We sometimes wryly referred to that room as the bunker—it was the only place where we couldn't be telephoned, door-stepped, or howled at.

Messages came via the room across the passage, the Communications Room. A civil servant worked in there and took messages which were sent in to us on notes. A double door (presumably for sound proofing) was used;

the Secretary to the Government or whichever Minister happened to be handy opened the door on our side and took the note when a red light appeared over the door. Once Jim Mitchell (a well-known practical joker) arranged for a note to be sent to me which read: 'Minister—a couple were arrested for drug offences this morning, and claimed they were your brother and sister-in-law. They are being held in custody and have asked that you be sent for to explain everything.' A moment's blood-chilling shock and then I saw the amused Mitchell's eyes across the table surveying my reaction! Between Jim's occasional pranks, Ruairi Quinn's cartoons and John Boland's uproarious Dublin yarns, there were some light moments amid the stress.

The method of working was, in theory, highly organised. Any proposal on legislation from any Minister was circulated to all other Ministers well in advance of its appearance on the Cabinet agenda. Any Minister who had observations communicated them to the sponsoring Minister, who tried to accommodate some or all of them. Finance frequently had strong objections, particularly if there were any spending proposals or implications for future spending in the document. So, the sponsoring Minister would then present a final version of the document to the Secretary to the Government, to get it put on a Cabinet agenda as soon as possible. In the final version, the Minister noted his colleagues' observations and how he had responded to them. And so the arguments started at Cabinet over whatever remaining objections there were—and these arguments were usually between the Finance Minister and the sponsoring Minister, with the Taoiseach controlling the discussion. Towards the end of our second year in Government, we tightened up the procedures, and before an item came to the agenda there were 'facilitating meetings' between the different Ministers, chaired by the Government Chief Whip, the calm and peace-making Sean Barrett: the object was to ensure the arrival of the item at full Cabinet with only the minimum areas of disagreement still to be ironed out. I found this procedure particularly helpful during the finalising of my

Green Paper *Partners in Education* when the principal point at issue was whether or not the new Local Education Councils would have a majority of elected representatives. Of course, the main problem was that Ministers for Finance rarely agreed to any spending proposal and fought the battles at full Cabinet, while the Taoiseach was always so concerned to allow such full freedom of speech that Cabinet meetings still took too long.

```
┌─────────────────────────────┐
│                             │
│      DECEMBER 1982          │
│                             │
│                             │
│                             │
│   THE FIRST YEAR            │
│                             │
│          TO                 │
│                             │
│      DECEMBER 1983          │
│                             │
└─────────────────────────────┘
```

The Coalition Government of Fine Gael and Labour takes office with Garret FitzGerald as Taoiseach and Dick Spring as Tanaiste —The announcement of school transport charges provokes a series of protests by all opposition parties and education interests—After special Cabinet meetings, the Government announces that the Haughey Government had illegally tapped the telephones of Geraldine Kennedy and Bruce Arnold and that Minister Ray MacSharry with the assistance of Minister Sean Doherty had taped conversations held with former Minister Martin O'Donoghue—At Easter, I make my first tour of all the Teachers' Conferences, to a mixed reception—By-Election in Donegal—The Government is defeated in the Dail on its proposal for the wording of the Constitutional Amendment on Abortion. It read: 'Nothing in this Constitution shall be invoked to invalidate or to deprive of force or effect any provision of the law on the ground that it prohibits abortion.'—The original Fianna Fail wording is passed. It read: 'The State acknowledges the right to life of the unborn, and with due regard to the equal right to life of the mother, guarantees in its laws to respect and as far as is practicable by its law to defend and vindicate that right.'— Fine Gael is deeply divided on the issue—Referendum: the

15

Amendment is carried 2–1 with a 50% poll—President Hillery decides to accept nomination for a second term of office as President of Ireland—A public disagreement erupts between the Taoiseach and the Tanaiste about the scale of cuts required for the 1984 Estimates—Fine Gael's first Ard Fheis during this Government's period of office —The Government decides on a pay increase for politicians and members of the Judiciary: a 'catching-up' on the level of the previous Public Service pay rounds in which they had not been included. Considerable public disapproval of this measure—Attended a UNESCO education conference in Paris—Fine Gael's vote plummets to 22.5% at the Dublin Central By-Election—Don Tidey, Chief Executive of Quinnsworth, is kidnapped—President Hillery is inaugurated for a second term of office—Frank Cluskey resigns from the Cabinet on the Dublin Gas issue—Joe Joyce's and Peter Murtagh's book, The Boss, is published—The Cabinet is re-shuffled to replace Frank Cluskey. Dick Spring is appointed to Energy, Liam Kavanagh to Environment, John Bruton to Trade, Commerce and Tourism and Ruairi Quinn is brought into the Cabinet as Minister for Labour—Don Tidey is rescued unharmed in a wood near Ballinamore, Co. Leitrim, but a soldier and a Garda are killed by kidnappers. Two of the kidnappers are arrested, four others escape.

Tuesday
14
December

I went into Leinster House at about 11.30 a.m. Couldn't bring myself to look at the newspapers in the library because the speculation about Cabinet appointments only made me sick and sort of nervy. All the corridors were being prowled by other nervous people and everybody was speculating madly; so I spent most of the time hiding in my office and only talking to people who came in (like George Birmingham who has a clever twinkle in his eye and a huge appetite for gossip). I wore my smart black suit, red blouse and specially made-up 'occasion face'. At about 1.45 I met Sean Barrett [Chief Whip] in the lift on my way back from getting a cup of tea; he muttered 'Garret's looking for you, stay around your office'. He looked so grim that I thought he was joking, but when I said something like 'Go on, Sean, come off it . . .' he wasn't amused. Anyway, I rang Derry [my husband] from the office to tell him what the scene was like, and to talk to someone!

Time went on, and at about 2.40 Sean put his head round the door and said 'Go on down, he's waiting for you'. Hoping I wouldn't meet George, I went into Garret's office where he was sitting behind the desk at the other end of the room in his shirt sleeves with bits of paper all over the place. He looked at me over his glasses and said, quite brusquely, 'You know what I'm giving you . . .'. I said well I didn't, how could I . . . and said too that I was very amazed to be getting anything. (In the back of my mind I had felt until that moment that he might be calling me in to tell me sadly that I couldn't be included in Cabinet.) So he said 'It's Education' and went on to say that he felt there was a great deal to be done in Education on the policy side, that the Universities had to be looked at, the whole curriculum looked at, and that he felt I was the best person to work on bringing out new ideas. Sitting on the edge of the chair across from him I said I'd do my very best and that I was most honoured to be given the job. He was obviously under considerable time pressure, so I left quickly.

Another long period of hiding in the office ensued, because I couldn't tell anyone at all until the official

announcement in the Dail, despite the accurate rumours
that were flying about. Garret was duly elected Taoiseach
about an hour later, and I was quite surprised and very
glad that there were civilised exchanges between Charlie
Haughey and Garret despite the bitterness and hype of
the election campaign. In the hiatus between Garret's
departure to Aras an Uachtarain and the resumption of
the Dail I rang Derry using our code 'Supper will be ready
at 6.30' which meant that I'd be in Cabinet, and so I added
'. . . and there'll be a lot of schoolchildren there'.
Anyway, I just about survived the whole scene until we
were all called in to Room 150 which is the Government
Whip's office near the Dail Chamber. There was rather an
uneasy feeling in the room as we all gathered, but we
gingerly congratulated each other. I think the most surprised person there was Austin Deasy who got Agriculture despite his public rows with Garret.

We all paraded into the Dail, behind Garret, round to
the centre of the lobbies and down the central steps, me
last (newest in Dail, last appointed) and Garret named us
all. I can only describe my feeling as numb, apprehensive,
delighted, proud.

Then we all got into big black Mercedes cars and roared
through Dublin with, to my astonishment, outriders holding up traffic. Despite my slightly dazed state, I thought
that was a bit peculiar and unnecessary, though I found
out later that it is the tradition for this occasion only. I was
also struck in the Dail by the very warm congratulations
from all the Fianna Fail people as well as most of the Fine
Gael people, including a warm handshake from C.J.H.
who said to me: 'I'm particularly delighted'. (Now why on
earth would he say that?) But I felt a bit bad that there had
to be people on our side with bitter disappointment inside
them.

Up in the Aras we stood around for what seemed ages
for photographs in the lovely big room, everyone gradually thawing out and beginning to relax. (Michael Noonan
was frankly thrilled and delighted with himself.) One by
one we took the little boxes with the Seals of Office from

President Hillery, who was in a very smiling humour, all benignly looked on by Garret. Then we adjourned into a rather dark room with a shining mahogany table for what was apparently a ritualistic first meeting, just discussing mechanics of Cabinet meetings. The enormity of the thing gradually started dawning on me, the vast world of education out there.

More roaring through the city, after a few very pleasant social moments with the President. I went straight to the Gresham Hotel where I knew Derry would be at the special 'thank you' party for Fine Gael organisers. I was given a very nice reception. We stayed there until 1 a.m. and came home, Derry driving me in our own car.

| Wednesday 15 December | Today the papers are full of the whole doings of yesterday, a bit of a sensation about me getting Education which is forecast as being a big job, but |

I suppose as the only woman there'd be bound to be a bit of attention.

At about 10 a.m. (having dealt for ages with family phone calls, friends ringing, telegrams and flowers, constituency delighted) the rather rickety black Mercedes arrived—I hate that car, it's ostentatious and noticeable—and we drove to Marlborough Street to the rather dour stone building which is the Department of Education. Peter Baldwin is my private secretary. He was hovering at the door and brought me up to the rather morgue-like office which I'm to have. (The sooner I get pictures on the walls and a few lamps the better.) The first person I met was the 'Runaí' [Secretary of the Department] Liam Lane, a most erect, correct and impressive man, and then the group of Assistant Secretaries. They seemed to me to be a group of rather elderly men, all with impenetrable Irish names. I wondered who was the more shocked, they or I.

After an exchange of pleasantries I left and went to Government Buildings where we had a more structured meeting about getting down to brass tacks, and Garret and Alan Dukes outlined the awful situation and how we had to take decisions to put flesh on the Fianna Fail estimates of last month, and do even more cutting because of the massive debt servicing which Charlie Haughey and Jack Lynch had piled up for us.

Nobody directed us where to sit when we arrived into the Cabinet room via the double doors, so it was sort of accidental. I sat down between Austin Deasy (who's at the end of the table) and Michael Noonan; Liam Kavanagh is on the other side of Michael. Austin pulls lugubrious faces and whispers a lot to me that the reams of figures which Alan and Garret pour out are all Greek to him — most of us are a bit glazed when they go on about EBR, PSP, GDP, at great and detailed length, but we certainly know enough to realise that the huge accumulation of debt since '77, but particularly in the last eighteen months, has left us in a desperate crisis. When looking around at them all I feel that we're an unlikely bunch to inspire a country the way Ireland's going to need inspiring.

Garret sits at the middle of the table with his back to the windows, and Dick Spring sits directly opposite, with Alan beside Dick on his right (appropriately enough). Peter Sutherland sits on Garret's right, with Sean Barrett beside him — positions fixed by tradition, I gather — and Dermot Nally [Secretary to the Government] very quiet-spoken and organised, totally expressionless except for the odd pleasant smile, sits on Garret's other side.

We get messages into the room by rather a cloak-and-dagger sort of method, but I suppose it's necessary: there's a red light over the door, which goes on with a click; usually Dermot Nally gets up to answer it, or if he's immersed in something with Garret, one of us will do it, and the civil servant who sits ensconced in the Communications Room across the corridor is waiting outside with whatever note or document he has. Austin already has said to me that he can see how one's prestige could be determined by how many messages one receives. John Bruton and Barry Desmond already seem to have an endless stream of them.

Wednesday
22
December

God, how little time there is to write anything in this book—and how much has happened since last week.

There was an impromptu and lovely Fine Gael party in Bray to celebrate my 'elevation'. They're all so jubilant and proud, I'm wondering what they'd think if they only knew what unpleasant things we have to cook up for them. I'm astonished at the flood of messages, letters, telegrams, flowers—so many women all round Ireland have written to wish me luck; God, it's a responsibility. I'm delighted for all the 'sisters' who have slogged and worked and encouraged, but I have a sinking feeling that I'm hardly ever going to see them for as long as this lasts, or anyone else either. I'm also beginning to realise that I'll be judged not only as a Minister but as a woman too.

Today we had Cabinet starting at 11 a.m. (after protestations that it would certainly start sharp at 10.30—but I prepared and pored over my papers with a cup of tea while I waited). We're beginning to get acquainted. Frank Cluskey is very funny, Barry Desmond is surprisingly deaf but has a lovely twinkle in his eye and is warm, Liam Kavanagh is solid and pleasant (despite a certain tension because of constituency rivalry). The subject matter of all these meetings has been the grappling with the Fianna Fail 1983 estimates announced on 18 November—but the stinky part is that there were cuts in money announced, but not the actual detail of how the cuts were to be made. I've already had awful hassle with Jim Mitchell over the £1¼ million Education subsidy to CIE, and it's bloody having to defend and fight when we're all so new to the game. Alan is dropping bombshells on us all, with memos flying around demanding further cuts for the Budget (I'm supposed to find a further £25 million; my officials are lugubrious about the consequences). He sits there, calm and quiet, never raising his voice, but demanding all this. John Bruton is forthright and impatient, Michael Noonan is quiet but determined, Peter Barry is hardly there at all. And while all this is going on, total immersion, Christmas is supposed to happen and I'm sick with worry trying to make lists, organise shopping, get presents that always seem to be missing no matter how well I prepared.

Anyway, with a heavy heart I finally cleared the school transport charges with the Cabinet so as to find the missing money, and will face the announcement of them tomorrow.

| Thursday |
| 23 |
| December |

This morning I met Frank Dunlop [Press Officer Department of Education] and Peter Prendergast [Government Press Secretary] along with the Runai and officials to discuss the best way to handle the school transport announcement. I like Frank. Bruce Arnold thinks he's first class. We decided it had to be done today. If I left it until after Christmas I'd be blamed for not warning people long enough in advance. I know what I'll be called—is there a female equivalent of Scrooge?

Then I met Liam Kavanagh and John Boland about giving over all youth affairs from Education to Labour; I don't like it. Garret wants me to give Sport to John Boland but I'll resist that, since I have to give Culture (Museums etc.) to Ted Nealon and I'd like to keep something pleasant in Education.

So at 3.45 p.m. I met the Education correspondents in Marlborough Street and broke the news to them, with all the explanatory background. Christina Murphy was sympathetic, I felt, John Walshe was excited but inscrutable, and for some reason I got quite hostile vibes from Pat Holmes of the *Irish Press*.

| Friday |
| 24 |
| December |

Rushed around the place with Derry, trying to put Christmas together. In the middle of it all, I did an interview with RTE radio (sitting at Garret's desk) on the school transport charges which haven't been absolutely huge news yet because of Christmas, but I reckon the fuse will be a slow burner and quite something when the explosion happens. So I'll try to get a lot of reading done on education over the Christmas. The three black briefcases are full of files and briefing notes compiled for me in Marlborough Street.

Monday
3
January

My daughter Rachel, her cousin Sarah and their friend Niamh are milling about the kitchen listening to young Mark Mortell on Bray Local Broadcasting (Pirate) Radio. I am feeling fairly exhausted after the thirty or so people that I fed after the funeral of an Aunt. Derry is, of course, a rock on these occasions, full of kindness and duty to his relations in his quiet way. We gave them soup, cheese, Christmas cake etc.

With some trepidation I have just refused an invitation from RTE to go on *Day by Day* tomorrow to do a whole hour taking phone calls from all over the country on Education. I explained to them that I was really not a 'wet week' in the Department of Education, so how could I possibly deal with all the questions from all over the country on the phone. They seem to accept that but how long will I get away with it!

Wednesday
5
January

The storm about the next series of cutbacks in Education is now breaking over my head. Big headlines in *The Irish Times* this morning. To my intense anger and amazement an *Irish Independent* reporter rang me at 2 o'clock in the morning about it — unbelievable! I was, however, as polite as I could bring myself to be.

Up very early this morning with the usual massive schedule: opening the Department of Education Inspectors' Conference at 9.30 a.m. (wonder what they think of me?), funeral in Bray, back to Cabinet meeting, long encounter with the INTO in the Department etc. I am pointing out at every opportunity that Fianna Fail made these cuts on 18 November last, when they announced their 1983 Estimates, and I had no option but to carry them through. Deaf ears are turned when I tell them that even more cuts are going to be needed — 'yes, but not us' is everyone's response.

I had a meeting yesterday with John Boland to give me pointers on Education policy ideas and it was not easy. I find him difficult though clever, but he was more forthcoming than I expected about Education, though full of dire warnings, and he told me I had got the 'dog' Ministry which was 'never good even in prosperous times' and would be 'purgatory' this time round. The large, wealthy, and articulate interest groups are formidable prospects.

Sunday **9** January

It has been a week of non-stop criticism in huge headlines in every paper, furious teachers, furious parents etc. You'd think the world was ending. I keep grimly calm, and smiling, smiling.

A *Today Tonight* TV appearance on Thursday went quite well (I am lucky to have a certain calm about all this. Perhaps I really am a sort of 'iron lady', as Tomas MacGiolla describes me.) Of course I made a mistake in not consulting the Government about Remedial Teachers' cuts—it seemed such a small amount of money [£100,000] I didn't realise the significance of it for schools. That's the problem with being inexperienced and having to make big decisions too quickly. I have retrieved that one, however, and got the Cabinet to let me substitute other savings.

The meetings this week with the INTO and the ASTI seem to go alright. My civil servants feel, I think, that I'm not totally incompetent. To get *their* measure is the problem. The Union representatives are well experienced and the meetings were really exploratory, sizing each other up. Mulvey and Quigley are political animals of a high order. They are so much quieter and milder in my office over a cuppa than when they're denouncing me in public.

Government meetings go on and on, the full extent of what we are facing is dawning gradually and everyone feels slightly desperate. It's becoming clear that Fianna Fail will oppose every cut, as if they had no knowledge at all of what faces the country. On Saturday I did another television programme for RTE. It was the early morning young people's programme but RTE had adults on it throwing brickbats. The interviewer was unfortunately a very young girl, but anyway I coped.

Then I toured the Aer Lingus Young Scientists Exhibition, and made a great fuss of them. It is, of course, a delightful show and very encouraging for any citizen let

24

alone the Minister for Education. Then dashed out to my
clinics in the Royal Hotel in Bray, which were packed out.
Supported by Seamus McEvoy, Mark Mortell and daughter Rachel. If I could only help all those poor people — well,
the ones that deserve help.

Politically, the huge price rises on Friday (as part of the
Budget process) and Alan going on radio today with dire
warnings may take the heat off me. But the TUI's strike
announcement without meeting me is a nuisance and a
worry.

Wednesday
12
January

Staggering through the complexities of dealing
with the crescendo of protest. An interesting but
harrowing session with Alan Dukes, myself, and
the officials, in Alan's quiet offices, on the further £25
million he wants. We got nowhere really, but Alan and I
had a very pleasant chat afterwards in his 'inner sanctum'
complete with a gin and tonic. He is nice and impressive.
But a row nearly broke out with Labour over the projected
deficit of £750 million that he mentioned on radio without
an agreement being reached. Anyhow it's all extremely
tense making. That particular row has been conducted out
of Cabinet mostly. Alan — like me — has to keep his head
up and temper down. Dick Spring has had to go to
hospital for more painful back treatment. All this gloom
and doom. The public reaction to the things we've already
done has been so violent that I cannot visualise anything
except riots or something at the prospect of further cuts in
Education. The hypocrisy of Fianna Fáil and the ferocity of
the Unions combine to stir the cauldron.

Tonight's Cabinet meeting ended in a three-hour session on security issues which are so secure that I can't
even write about them until the news actually breaks.
GUBU takes on a new meaning when the system we de-
pend on has been so threatened. Michael Noonan is calm,
incisive and quite strong as he deals with the revelations.

<table>
<tr><td>Friday
14
January</td><td>About midnight. We're just back from a Fine Gael constituency party in Dublin North Central hosted by the real charmer George Birmingham—</td></tr>
</table>

About midnight. We're just back from a Fine Gael constituency party in Dublin North Central hosted by the real charmer George Birmingham— intelligent, acerbic and delightfully humorous.

Frank Dunlop [Department of Education Press Officer] is still out sick and has been for quite a long time. I've badly missed the services of a skilled press officer during this crucial period, when all the powerful forces against me have full PR machines working overtime. The Government Information Services can't supply the deficiency; they're overworked already. I had lunch in the small Ministerial dining room today with Michael Noonan and Pat Cooney. I think Michael is really enjoying the power and the mystery of the Department of Justice and Pat is quite amazing, like a mischievous boy poking fun at me in a benevolent way. The little room we eat in is gloomy, dark, and grimy; it would put years on you, but if you eat all the time in the main members' room you can't get a second's peace from TDs at all.

Michael Begley from Kerry South has been cutting up rough about school transport but then he usually has some problem to complain about.

John Feeney of the *Evening Herald* is having a regular go at me and keeps mentioning this house, 'palatial Temple Rd.' which is rather strange considering he grew up in a house across the road. And the 'iron lady' tag floats around in the media. I must let that rip, it's after all what I have to feel like if I'm to get through the storm and come back strongly.

Alan Dukes made an uncharacteristic angry outburst to me about Fine Gael backbenchers' lack of support for the cuts. It was a measure of the stress he's under. There might be a danger of my becoming very identified with him; some comments ('the arch-conservatives Dukes and Hussey') making the connection already. I don't mind that; the job has to be done. Maybe he should speak out more strongly in public as he did in private.

The security issue which I mentioned before has to do with the phone tappings involving Bruce Arnold and Geraldine Kennedy, and the scandalous Ministerial office bugging. What a disgusting episode. It makes chilling reading and is a very difficult one for us to handle. I hope we do it right.

| Tuesday **18** January | Lunch between Cabinet sessions upstairs in a room above Garret's office—quite an enjoyable session, though I still don't feel terribly close to |

anybody in Cabinet despite the fact that they are all very agreeable. There has been some flak in the news about Barry Desmond washing his hands of the Abortion Referendum. Who could blame him, it's all developing into a frightful mess. Why should Labour have any truck with it?

| Wednesday **19** January | Cabinet last night went on and on and on until 2 a.m. on a very long, very difficult business. It involved a situation where we felt that Michael |

Noonan might indeed be in some personal danger when he went to face someone who had the reputation of carrying guns. It was all very dramatic, almost unreal.

| Saturday **22** January | Now at last it's all out in the open. Evidence about Sean Doherty tapping the telephones of Bruce Arnold and Geraldine Kennedy; Garda Commis- |

sioner and Deputy Commissioner retiring; MacSharry bugging O'Donoghue etc. Michael Noonan handled the matter calmly and superbly and thus covered himself with glory. The whole business has, however, an unreal ghastly air about it, being a sorry story of arrogance, malice, intimidation and a lot of crass stupidity. It is of course the *cause célèbre* all over every paper and every programme and Fianna Fail are in total disarray. Haughey trying to keep the thing at arms' length from himself.

Yesterday we got down to a twelve-hour meeting on the Budget: tense, difficult, impossible decisions facing us. Dick Spring was at least as lost as myself, I think, in the maze of figures; Barry Desmond was extremely impressive; also John Boland (when he speaks) is often blunt, clever, direct and humorous. Garret is brilliant of course but undisciplined and Alan is impeccable and persevering.

Monday
24
January

Today was 'Education day' at Cabinet and I survived nicely, rescuing through lengthy explanation and defence most of the situations which had given me dreadful worries and sleepless nights. I was supported by Garret who was, to give him his due, very horrified at the proposals which Finance were putting up. They must give me breathing space now to get the planning process under way. I explained again and again that further cuts on top of what I've already given will have to be very carefully and delicately done, and that we all need to be cautious in working them out.

Friday
28
January

I am writing this at 7.20 a.m. because it is quite impossible to find time to commit my thoughts to a diary between the continuing Budget crisis, the Fianna Fail crisis and the endless daily grind of work. There is just an exhausting round of movement, teachers marching, high level publicity against me, undercurrent of support in the editorials, but Fianna Fail leading the roars and ructions.

Saturday
29
January

Rumours emanating from Peter Sutherland and Michael Noonan that a Fine Gael 'volte—face' on the abortion thing is imminent; there is a growing 'anti' campaign but I feel we haven't too many options. I wonder, how I wonder, how we will stay in Government? God damn it, I would love to be a Minister for four years and really get something done, and do things for the right reasons and not the political reasons. I enjoy the huge challenge despite the awfulness of these Budget marathons.

I am getting fatter and fatter and I don't know what to do about it. Well I do, but I haven't the energy or the willpower to actually refuse meals, tea, sandwiches, etc. which keep us going like hell.

Tuesday
1
February

Exhaustedly sitting here. We had another marathon Cabinet session on Sunday which ended at 2 a.m. It was punctuated by a good lunch but no supper until they sent out a driver for chips an sausages at about 11.30 p.m. when a sub-committee started to work on the final figures. God, the tiredness! So we ate them out of bags, the only time in my life I ate chips and sausages washed down with gin.

The Fianna Fail show goes on and on, Haughey clinging on, dreadful divisions, total obsession by the media.

My special adviser, Dr John Harris, has started today. He will be a great comfort to me I can see. He is a calm, clear-minded expert who has the same kind of priorities as I have.

Saturday 5 February

Cabinet meetings have slowed down now but the bizarre Abortion Referendum debate looms next week and besides the Budget is a minefield. We have decided not to go ahead with the Fianna Fail wording; the legal advice is that the wording is not only crazy, but dangerous. To my great relief Pat Cooney is totally convinced that we are right, and he says it is unthinkable to go ahead because the evidence against is coercive.

At Cabinet I made a strong outburst about the way I had agreed to cuts and resented the lack of co-operation of others in different departments, and that I had acknowledged the crisis from day one and had carried the can for them etc. But I am worried about getting the 'Thatcher' image. This week the students marched, but not many turned up, and no one paid too much attention. I wonder how long it will take me to feel quite on top of the thing? I don't know, but I am learning fast anyway.

There was a very upsetting article by Anne Harris about me in *Image* and one is left wondering why she was so much against me? We had what seemed a most pleasant chat which I fitted in for her recently.

Monday 7 February

I have just discovered that there is a transcript in existence of conversations held between Derry and Bruce Arnold and his family and I find that alarming, intrusive and disgraceful. The thought of people typing out our words from a tape somewhere smacks of Orwell's *1984*.

Garret announced his Senate list today, and I was very

sad that there is only one woman, although she is very good: Brid Rogers of the SDLP. I had put forward a case to him that he certainly would have to have a strong representation of women and gave him several suggestions, but he explained to me today very sadly that because of constituency and political demands, try as he might, he couldn't get any more women on the list. Well, of course, that's all a question of priorities. And despite his very good intentions, even he doesn't put women high enough on his list. I had to say that to him. Labour didn't have any women, for all their talk.

Thursday 10 February

Here we are at the hind end of an eventful week which saw the Budget overshadowed by the appalling power struggle in Fianna Fail, which resulted in yet another victory for Haughey at 11.30 on Monday night. Disbelief and disquiet. I was quite depressed and low about it because really the economic situation will militate in his favour, plus Labour's fears of taking the right steps and Garret's unpredictability which might pull the plug. Anyway, the Budget also was approached in the shadow of the Referendum Debate which had to proceed in the Dail on Wednesday morning. Pat Cooney and myself made attempts to get a Party meeting called but Sean Barrett opposed that. The problem is the wording, particularly the possible putting in jeopardy of the mother's life which is the one I am most worried about. Anyway, Michael opened with a fine, low key speech on Wednesday and the roof didn't fall in. The Budget went calmly, no major rows, although Oliver J. Flanagan and a few others looked threatening.

Thursday 17 February

At the Young Fine Gael Conference in Galway there was a highly emotional, but really quite shallow debate on the Amendment. There was almost unanimous rejection of any form of Amendment and anguished pleas to Garret to abandon the whole idea. Garret was obviously deeply moved when he rose to reply. The clear-eyed emotion of young people always affects him and of course young people sense this regard for them which is why Young Fine Gael has become so strong. If only it was as simple as they think!

Liz Shannon [whose husband was American Ambassador to Ireland 1977–81] has arrived over and she was in the Dail today for my first session of Questions in the House, which I survived despite considerable nerves. Of course when I am worried about something like that I spend a lot of time in detailed preparation and so I don't give the impression of having any nerves. Liz said she was delighted to see me 'zapping all those men'! The huge unanswerable questions about Irish education in the next few years are mind-boggling — and the question that has to be faced is whether we can really get reforms underway and not just try to cope with expanding numbers which put so much financial pressure on us.

| Tuesday |
| **22** |
| February |

Sunday morning I was shattered by banner headlines about a new school bus crisis, obviously fed to the papers by someone in CIE. The school transport crisis deepened all day and became quite depressing. I know perfectly well that the original decision not to exempt junior cycle children from the Medical Card scheme for free travel was stupid; indeed maybe the whole thing was stupid and that is the worst feeling — that I may have fallen at the first fence.

So yesterday I had, among other things on that long day, a tense and difficult meeting with officials who I feel did not give me the full picture from day one of all the implications of different school transport categories, and how could I expect to be divinely inspired. But the Minister carries the can, and now we have to have a total re-think. God, I could scream.

| Friday |
| **25** |
| February |

Here I am lying on a bed in the Irish Ambassadorial residence in Bonn after a nightmare week in Ireland which is probably one of many to come. Really dreadful pressures; all day Wednesday was a total nightmare, with universal criticism, a long 'hate session' with the Parliamentary Party, ending up with a very sticky *Today Tonight*. That day I'll never forget, unless it gets lost in the worse things yet to come. Anyway, the relief of being out of it for 24 hours is considerable but I expect really terrible things to happen in the coming week on various fronts. This raises the awful underlying question: can I cope? Nuala Fennell is getting mauled as well, poor thing, mostly by women journalists.

Interestingly, last week Garret rang me as I was working one night late in the office, to get my agreement to the setting up of the New Ireland Forum. He was obviously most anxious about it and of course I gave my ready consent. He then went on to offer me the first bit of understanding or sympathy since I was appointed, saying: 'I never thought it would be like this when I appointed you—I thought it would be all policy . . .' Anyway, I suppose I'll have to tough it out.

The family are supportive and so are a lot of other people. Slightly dreading this evening's events, opening the Treasures of Ireland exhibition, which is a major cultural thing here, with the German President in attendance and a big speech to give.

Now I must wash and dress and put on the capable, bright, ministerial front again, charming and chatting and keeping up Ireland's reputation before all these Germans.

| Saturday |
| **26** |
| February |

Last evening and night went very well, very formal stuff. President Carstens was most pleasant, a tall, fit-looking, younger man than I expected, charming enough, knowledgeable about Ireland. A huge crowd of prominent Germans.

I had rehearsed the speech very well and delivered it slowly and with feeling, beginning in German. The whole early evening ceremony was interesting and what you might call a 'learning experience'. Found myself then rushed to a dinner with the Mayor of Cologne in a typical large Cologne pub where I made an impromptu speech which was received well enough. I hope to have a look at Beethoven's house. Certainly, the magnificent Irish treasures would make you proud of our historic past. But it's hard to get out of my head the worry about problems at home which threaten to engulf me.

I found the Ambassador, Robin Fogarty, not very cheering up. Perhaps he was having a bad night. He was inclined to worry greatly about life in general, and foreign affairs in particular. They don't seem very enamoured of Haughey in Foreign Affairs; of course they loved Garret and anyone else doesn't measure up. Or maybe they're just flattering us.

Thursday 3 March

Well I seem to have managed to survive the stress and keep it somewhat under control. Bad moments this week at Cabinet over the finding of £1,000,000 for the school transport concession which we are planning to make, but a 'tour de force' by Liam Lane at a bilateral meeting with Finance officials saved the day.

All in all it has been awful. I had to ring Derry for consolation on Tuesday. Endless hassled meetings with disgruntled groups and deputations which seem to go on all day. They make it increasingly difficult to get time to think out strategy. And all the time Fianna Fail are demanding more spending as if there was no tomorrow. And the constituency demands huge time, particularly on the road.

First meeting with my informal 12-person Fine Gael Education back-up group last night at home. They will be a great help to me, and some kind of conduit to the 'real' world of education as opposed to the official noises of the Unions, management bodies etc.

Sunday 6 March

Going to see Garret this afternoon after I speak to the teachers of travelling people. My meeting with Garret will be about the Abortion Amendment following the Cabinet session on Friday, when Michael apparently intends to put a detailed Amendment up, full of more nonsense on "the commencement of pregnancy", etc. I was quite adamant that we should have the absolute minimal amendment along the lines of "no law should be declared unconstitutional because it forbids abortion" and Garret feels the same. We are a minority of two, well maybe Alan will be with us.

Yesterday I spoke to the Modern Language Teachers

Association and had to tell them that I couldn't arrange oral examinations in '85. Needless to say they weren't pleased. They don't really want to know that Fianna Fail had made no preparations at all; I'm starting from scratch. I've had to tell the Secretary of the Department to tell me how we're going to do it, not why we can't do it.

Tuesday 8 March

Yesterday was marked mainly by an acrimonious (or fairly acrimonious) meeting with the heads of Universities. Tom Murphy of UCD was being clever and dominant and inclined to be avuncular with me but I was in a difficult position, unable as I am to say what money will be like in the future. So that puts up the blood pressure.

The Amendment is looming closer, the moment of decision coming. I told Garret my difficulties on Sunday; he has the same and says Alan Dukes agrees with us but he is not hopeful of many more. I intimated my willingness to resign or do whatever was necessary not to embarrass the Government, but I couldn't vote for it. He really is very sweet and very kind and the mind boggles at the pressures he must be under.

Sunday 13 March

Arklow and Bray clinics yesterday and finally a pleasant, small dinner with Bruce and Mavis Arnold.

Today I am speaking to an Alcoholics Anonymous Convention in Wicklow.

Now that the very worst of my Education pressures have receded, even temporarily, the breadth of the problem confronts me. I had all the Principal Officers and Assistant Secretaries in to my office on Friday for a drink—they seemed to appreciate it. That was after a difficult, not to say very awkward, interview to tell Frank Dunlop I was moving him out of the Press Office. He was *bouleversé* and I was a bit too—blast it. He has been so close to Haughey that many in Fine Gael don't trust him, and that has been putting me in a difficult situation. I liked him myself.

More difficult strains and stresses at home because of

my constant absences, which, even though one tries to control them, mount up and up again.

I get a worrying feeling that there is an impression growing up around the country that the Government is shaky. Garret should go on TV, and I wish he would, in a hurry.

Two Labour TDs are kicking up about voting for the Social Welfare Bill.

I watched the video of the television Amendment debate, and I can see the logical argument for going for the minimalist Amendment. The Pro-Amendment people say they have no intention of pushing for any other change in the laws afterwards but could you believe them? Anyway, I think I've got to the bottom line I'm afraid. God, I can't imagine what the pressures will be like on me. Roll on St Patrick's weekend in London; even though it's work, it's away.

| Thursday |
| **17** |
| March |

I am on the plane to London, having attended the St Patrick's Day Parade in Bray, where I got quite a good-humoured slagging on school transport.

Yesterday I talked to Monica Barnes about the Abortion Amendment. She is very feminist on the subject and is so uncompromising that she makes me feel a bit ashamed, but she did encourage me in the stand I may have to take. It's a slightly different situation for a backbencher and she fully accepts this.

| Sunday |
| **20** |
| March |

The Irish Centre dinner here was awful. Having been whisked from the airport to a really grotty hotel, we (Derry and I) got the Embassy to change us and they put us in the Carlton Towers, which we hadn't asked for and which was really ridiculously luxurious; talk about two extremes! The dinner, however, went on forever, full of people who all seemed to be strongly Fianna Fail and who were not the slightest bit keen on me and made it quite clear. However, they did listen politely to my speech. The Chairman made a few political jibes at Thatcher and a few at us. I tried my best to charm them all.

When I arrived at the Irish Centre in Kilburn for the dinner I was greeted by an anti-Amendment demonstration of young women from Northern Ireland. If they only knew the turmoil that I'm in about it! I stopped to have a quiet friendly chat with them; they were lively and nice.

The end of the evening was marked by a Republican demonstration of sorts too in the 'Glens of Antrim' pub.

I understand Brian Lenihan was here last year and wowed them all with the Fianna Fail republican line. We dutifully appeared at the Irish Embassy reception on Friday where I had good chats with Maeve Binchy, T.P. McKenna, Keith Kyle but I am not really into these receptions, standing around for hours.

A quite untrue report appeared in the *Sunday Press* saying that I arrogantly demanded to be moved to the Carlton Towers Hotel and had generally behaved appallingly in London. Who planted that? It's sickening, because people believe what they read and it upsets the party.

Monday
21
March

This morning I had a scheduled meeting which I had been dreading, with the Institute of Guidance Counsellors. I toughed it through and tried to be as forthcoming and explanatory as I could, and they were not unpleasant. They're another group of people who agree that cuts are necessary, as long as they don't affect them.

Wednesday
23
March

This was decision day. Cabinet in the morning. The Amendment finally decided on was one of Michael Noonan's, nearly like the Fianna Fail one. I fought and fought to no avail and told them I couldn't vote for it. Garret had disappointed me by vacillating, I nearly wept in Alan's office, and then we had a big marathon Parliamentary Party meeting where— mirabile dictu!—a big majority voted for the minimalist wording for which I had been fighting a lone battle and which the Cabinet was afraid to put before the Party. I was delighted, so was Garret. No one, but no one, of my

Cabinet colleagues even had the grace to tell me I was right. Ah well!

Home exhausted at 11 p.m.

| Thursday |
| 24 |
| March |

Instant hostile reaction to our Party decision by Fianna Fail, PLAC, SPUC, Oliver J. (who I think behaved disgustingly) and a few more. Good! I like being on the other side of that particular fence for a change.

Tense Dail situation. We all voted for the Second Stage with some exceptions which we knew about.

| Sunday |
| 27 |
| March |

Sitting at the fire late this Sunday night reflecting on the great difficulties we are in over this Amendment. Garret, understandably, has gone to Spain for an Easter break and there is silence so far from the Cabinet.

I spent a lot of today writing a speech about the Amendment for tomorrow night and had long conversations with Peter Sutherland on the phone. Peter is sick and angry and fed up, but then he always reacts very strongly to things.

Garret has shown a lack of leadership, and as for my Cabinet colleagues, I am unhappy about their unsure position. It is amazing too, to find in Cabinet some very deeply conservative attitudes when it comes to discussing the question of the family home. Garret and I frequently find ourselves 'at one' on these issues and Garret is genuinely dumbfounded when he hears colleagues expressing such conservative views.

| Friday |
| 1 |
| April |

Last Monday I travelled down to St Patrick's College in Kiltegan in the depths of Southern Wicklow to give my carefully prepared talk on the Amendment. The seminarians were very nice indeed despite my late arrival because the driver and myself got lost, and the speech got a lot of publicity, followed up by *Day by Day* with John Bowman—a long and satisfactory interview. I made sure the speech was circulated all round the Parliamentary Party and all round Wicklow and I would like very much if it could be followed up by my colleagues.

This week was also spent preparing major speeches for next week's Teachers' Conferences, which of course I'm dreading. The ASTI have made it clear they don't want John Harris as a guest and I have made it clear they can't have me without him. So we had to strategise on that issue.

I called a very big planning meeting with officials. Very informative and useful for a number of reasons but showing me quite clearly the huge variety of areas and demands — God help us! I wonder how many of these men, all doing their Civil Service thing, really like their jobs or really want to achieve something. I don't really know that yet and I have still to find it out.

I am impressed by Noel Lindsay, Bill Hyland, Sean O'Mahoney and also impressed by Finbar O'Callaghan, if slightly wary of him.

I have finally got rid of the black Mercedes and now we travel round in a more modest green Granada, but I wish it was a smaller one. Maybe we'll achieve that too. They protest that the car must be powerful for security reasons. There isn't a hope of a woman driver, because there's a long seniority list of people with a right to drive and they're all men. So that proposal is knocked on the head.

I've been working extremely hard trying to keep up a presence at home as much as possible so that the stress there won't become too great; despite all our knowledge before I took the job, we didn't know how bad it would be.

Paddy Heffernan rang me today to say that the ASTI climbed down and decided to invite John Harris. It's the least they could do, he's devoted to education.

Tuesday 5 April

(Really Wednesday at 1.55 a.m. Cork) At this dead hour of the night I am really exhausted and it is quite difficult to write this. But I have to record how very relieved I am at the ASTI reception for me tonight. In the very large ballroom, which was absolutely full of people, I was quite tense and anxious. Relaxed somewhat during the dinner, sitting between Margaret

Walsh, the current President, and Kieran Mulvey, who were both very friendly. Margaret is nearly a feminist, though not quite. Anyway, I delivered the extremely carefully prepared speech in a quite slow, deliberate manner, despite the difficulty of having to begin in Irish. It was received in silence and even got some applause. Though I say so myself I was quite proud of how I carried it off despite the nerves. In general you could say I had a warm welcome from most of the people and there was no hassle at all for John Harris. The INTO in the morning was alright too. They were warm and polite and I was pleased with that. Sometimes I stop to think and wonder at my nerve in venturing into this minefield at all!

So at this late hour I have just retired to bed after a long chat with John Harris, who is so supportive and helpful. He had to listen to my political philosophising at some length. I think it was a sort of unwinding process for me.

| Saturday |
| **9** |
| April |

Last Wednesday was my appearance at the third of the big Teachers' Conferences—the Teachers' Union of Ireland. They were the rudest, though not on a personal level. It was a huge dinner and despite all my work on the speech I wasn't happy that it was very good.

There was a highly dramatic period when the Vice-President of the Union, Larry Kavanagh, collapsed as he was delivering a very strong vitriolic attack on me and everything I have done. I was sitting beside him during this diatribe, trying to look impassive, puffing away at my cheroot. After some ministering to him he was helped away and the President of the Union, Tom Hunt, finished his speech for him, continuing the attack on me. I felt if anybody had a right to faint or collapse it was me, since I had to sit all week listening to teachers attacking me from every possible platform. However, I have smiled my way through and have survived.

So, I didn't like the TUI and they were not very polite after the dinner either.

Earlier on Wednesday I went to see the NIHE in Limerick and Dr Edward Walsh. Thomond College was not as impressive as the NIHE; they didn't have their act together half as well as Walsh.

The Conference of the Association of Primary Teaching Sisters was the last on my list for Thursday and compared to the others it was a pushover.

The present political *cause célèbre* is a continuing uproar about high taxes and tax evasion. Companies are threatening to withhold PAYE and PRSI, and Waterford Crystal are actually saying that they will do that.

Also this week it seems that Mary Harney is beginning to break ranks a little bit with Fianna Fail on the Abortion Amendment. The wonder is that she's the only one.

Monday
21
April

Back on the 16th after a week away. The Amendment Debate raged all last week going from one crisis to another, Oliver J. Flanagan being what I can only describe as hysterical, Tom O'Donnell being hostile, and Garret alarming me by a lack of decisiveness. Peter Sutherland seems to be totally disgusted by the whole thing and the Party of course is generally quite alarmed. There was an all-day Parliamentary Party meeting on Wednesday, which was quite good except for the sickening charade of some of the extreme conservatives. If I thought they were sincere—but only some are, including Godfrey Timmins who is very quiet. The battle lines are blurred by old enmities and jealousies within the party, that were there before my time.

Documents appear to have been leaked wholesale from either the Attorney General's Office or the Department of Justice.

I'm disgusted by Fianna Fail's antics.

My own pressures this week in Education are around the question of having a cut-off point for school transport charges on 6 May.

When I finish writing this I will get ready to go to Aughrim, Co. Wicklow, for the constituency's Annual General Meeting. For the first time I am dumbfounded and can't imagine what I am going to say to them on this whole question of the Amendment.

| Tuesday |
| 22 |
| April |

The Aughrim meeting was in fact very good. There was general support for Garret and myself. There was general odium of Oliver J. and his cohorts and indeed I found the whole thing quite cheering up. Didn't get home until after 1 a.m. Good old Wicklow!

This morning Cabinet at 9 a.m. mainly on the Finance Bill and we got through a great deal by 1 o'clock or so. Peter Sutherland for some reason seems to have cheered up too.

General headlines in all the papers about leaks and counterleaks. I am sure the population is totally confused.

More nasty fictitious stories in the *Evening Herald* written by John Feeney about me being in Marbella, where I wasn't, and about visiting the Hillerys, which I didn't. Why does Feeney get away with so much?

Worked very hard all afternoon, staggered home with huge amounts to read, at about 6 p.m. Then Derry and I went to the Department of Education's Dramatic Society Revue at the Eblana Theatre. I was delighted at the high standard and found it great fun with good strong spoofing of me all through it. The girl who played the role of myself was constantly decked out in a blouse with a bow tie at the neck. Afterwards I went backstage and had a good laugh with them all. It was pleasant to meet so many of the junior staff in such relaxed surroundings.

| Saturday |
| 23 |
| April |

Yesterday I had to deal with yet another escape from Trinity House Detention Centre. The young lads bottled up there are far more than a match for their benevolent custodians and have learned their tricks in what Peter Baldwin called 'the University of Life'. It is a continuing question mark for us all, those unhappy youngsters with such life and leadership all going into such futile channels.

| Tuesday |
| 26 |
| April |

I am just home (at 12.30 a.m.) after the Fine Gael emotional blood-letting at another Parliamentary Party meeting on the Amendment. Such incredible pressures; eight people standing firm on voting for the Fianna Fail wording, including Godfrey Timmins, my constituency colleague! Conscience crises all round. At the Fine Gael Ministers' meeting earlier I fought again for a vote to oppose the Fianna Fail wording after ours is defeated. But I did not prevail. The Parliamentary Party meeting was very fraught indeed, with Willie O'Brien (who is a dote) reducing us all to tears (it had become like an encounter group session) and the final decision was to abstain on the Fianna Fail wording. Monica Barnes and Alan Shatter are having serious problems about that. Garret has to survive these unmerciful pressures; mine seem small by comparison. And as well as all this we have a Donegal By-Election coming up—blast it to Hell!

This came after the full day in the Dail on the Amendment Committee and Final Stages, all very fraught and confused. Monica Barnes and Alan Shatter refused to abstain on the Fianna Fail wording. I asked Monica to do so for Garret's sake but she wouldn't. Anyway that bit is over. The rest is decidedly not. The other eight abstained on our wording—such a mess. In one way I could strangle Garret and in another way I feel sorry for him.

Friday 29 April It is 9 a.m. in this lovely old-fashioned home of Canon and Mrs Stewart in Donegal town, at the beginning of the By-Election campaign. I'm a paying guest here, a house specially chosen for its quietness.

Went to the funeral of the young murdered Garda in Ballyshannon today. His family in a dreadful state. Tears, tears falling like rain.

The close-mouthed Donegal people eyeing me very suspiciously at the doors, Liam Skelly doing his nut, and the canvassing is very desultory. Interestingly there wasn't too much hassle about Education (but enough). Despite all this, however, Donegal is a most beautiful county.

Saturday 30 April Mercifully early in bed 11 p.m. in this nice rectory. I spent the afternoon canvassing with Seanie Williamson in an outlying area called Ballydevitt. Seanie is the ancient, trusted Chairman of the

branch, a good old character. The weather made it agreeable.

We arrived, with Fonsie Nolan, another stalwart Fine
Gael worker, in one isolated, small, poor farmhouse
where an elderly, large man lived alone and was sitting at
the kitchen table complete with his cap, large brown coat
tied with a string at the waist. My companions said to him
'Well, Paddy, look who we've brought you. Who do you
think this is?' The man looked slowly at me, looked at
them and looked back at me, and announced 'Dolly
Parton'.

I had lunch with Garret in the hotel in Donegal town
and he mentioned *en passant* that Nuala Fennell had
seemed very cross when Alan Dukes made his famous
remark at the Parliamentary Party meeting on the 26th
about abstaining on the Amendment vote: 'To do it twice
is nice, but to do it once with gusto is better . . .' It was a
brilliant remark at the time and place and justifiably
caused great mirth and release of tension. Interesting that
Garret had noticed it so much as to mention it to me.

Thursday
5
May

Continuing By-Election campaign, where one
comes up and down from Donegal, dutifully
doing one's best for the candidate. Ministers, of
course, are expected to do twice as much as anybody else
and I suppose from a backbencher's point of view that is
perfectly reasonable. From the country's point of view,
however, it is questionable.

Presented awards at the Hotel School in Killybegs.
Received a deputation from the VEC complaining about
their allocation. Another deputation from Killybegs Vocational School. Fianna Fail kicking up murder in the Dail
about every possible matter. Looking for more millions to
be spent every day.

Among other things this week we went to Peter Barry's
dinner for the diplomatic corps, where I sat between the
Papal Nuncio, Dr Alibrandi, and the elderly Portuguese
Ambassador, neither of whom could be described as
scintillating companions. Alibrandi is impossible and the
quiet Portuguese must be a bit deaf.

The Amendment Debate which has now moved into the Senate is very difficult indeed for people like Katharine Bulbulia who is very upset about it. I tried to comfort her by assurances that campaigning against it afterwards is the best thing we can all do. God, it is, and was, and will be, such a mess!

Saturday 7 May

More pressures in the county of Donegal, doing my Education thing, my canvassing, my meetings, snatching quick conversations with Garret between tours and canvassing.

Thursday 12 May

This is the week of the Council of Europe Education Ministers' Conference. Twenty-one of them are here; this was all arranged two years ago.

I spent Tuesday, Wednesday and Thursday, in magnificent St. Patrick's Hall in Dublin Castle as 'Madame Présidente' of the conference, which was quite demanding. Three nights in a row of entertaining all these Ministers and very long days chairing the conference, worrying about keeping the Turkish Minister away from the Greek one.

One's mood is not helped by another poisonous piece in tonight's *Evening Herald* (John Feeney) about our very pleasant expedition to Russborough last night, where I took all the Ministers (except the Turk) in a bus, but it was described by John Feeney as 'a champagne bash around the County of Wicklow in black Mercedes'. We ate in the Loft Restaurant, modestly, and no champagne.

Garret gave a dinner for the Ministers on Tuesday night in Iveagh House where I had trouble making conversation with Alibrandi who, once more, was sitting beside me and was quite rude when I tried to begin a discussion about the Amendment—he absolutely froze me out with silence. So Garret and I spent the night talking to each other, which was really quite sad. He said he had learned a lot in the last few months about leadership and wondered if he himself had the qualities for leadership of the country as opposed to the Party. Amendment pressures getting to him?

44

Saturday **14** May

Listening to *Saturday View* there appears to be a general consensus that the country is becoming ungovernable and that it is in an appalling mess. Why doesn't someone point to Fianna Fail's role in that?

The Senate Debate on the Amendment goes on and Katharine Bulbulia broke ranks and why not? I wish I could have, but Cabinet responsibilities are another ball game.

Very bad By-Election result in Donegal. Spoke to Garret at some length on the phone. Naturally he is fed up about the bad result, but otherwise is in good spirits.

Margaret Thatcher is heading for a big win in the British Election. Is that a good or a bad thing?

Wednesday **18** May

Clonmel and Cashel school openings, deputations giving out hell, nuns exploiting the occasion to rant on and on about their special needs. Back to Portlaoise for the Irish Vocational Education Association dinner, which went very well, and I like those people. Jack McCann, the President, in particular is a complete dote and a much respected national figure. I thanked him again for his consistent reasonableness, ever since my first day in office when he came to Marlborough Street to wish me well. Finally home at 1 a.m.

Thursday **19** May

A massive public meeting at the Dominican Hall in Wicklow town about school transport on which pressure is inexorably building up with incidents around the country, Fianna Fail Private Member's Motion in the Dail etc. In the Dominican Hall they had marshalled the big guns from the ASTI, the TUI, the INTO, the Workers Party and Mary O'Rourke. However, I faced them all down and spoke calmly and refused to give in to the relentless pressure. A very sad feature of the evening, however, was the very late arrival of Liam Kavanagh, who modestly (my eye) refused to sit on the platform and when called upon by the Chairman to say a few words simply said 'Ah well, I'm only here as a person that lives in Wicklow and as a parent. So really I don't have anything to say' or words to that effect. I was shocked that a Cabinet colleague did not take the opportunity to come up on the platform and defend Cabinet decisions with me. Other Fine Gael people who were in the hall were astonished at Liam's behaviour and felt that he had let us all down badly. The very hostile reception in that hall certainly made me wonder what the next General Election campaign will be like.

| Saturday 21 May |

There are so many worries around at the moment, as well as the main ones for example: doubts about the Labour Party's resolve on Public Service pay, the comings and goings on the Amendment, the sudden closure of the pirate radio stations without legislation being ready, not to mention the enormous pressure from each of the TDs who want special cases made for their particular causes. Ah well . . . I made my own bed!

| Wednesday 1 June |

In Luxembourg attending a Conference of Ministers for Education and Labour, at which I spoke twice. At lunch I had Sir Keith Joseph beside me. He is quite a formidable old charmer and we got on famously. He said: 'You're close to Garret FitzGerald, I hear. A good sort of chap'. Liam Kavanagh is here too, fighting for the European Social Fund. Dick Burke represented the Brussels Commission at the Conference. He still strikes me as somewhat lofty and a little self absorbed, but then maybe I'm prejudiced because of past events, and in fact exchanged quite a lot of pleasantries with him during the day. I studiously avoided any harking back, but I can't look at him without remembering the blood, sweat and tears of the Dublin West By-Election which he caused by falling for the siren call of Haughey dangling Europe before him.

| Saturday 11 June |

This week saw Margaret Thatcher sweeping back to power in Britain. So now we know who we have to deal with! And Gerry Adams winning Gerry Fitt's seat in Belfast. Alas, Shirley Williams lost her seat. One 'soft focus' woman bowing out, for the moment anyway, and another definitely 'hard focus' woman on her way in.

Monday 13 June 1 a.m. Just back from a pleasant dinner with Garret and Joan, plus Mark FitzGerald and Dervla his fiancée; and the other guest was Peter Sutherland. The dinner was in the basement sitting room which the FitzGeralds live in. Garret was, understandably, preoccupied and we had a lot of talk about acquiring some kind of 'chef de cabinet' for him, and indeed the need for one for Alan Dukes too. At the end of the evening I don't think any of us were clear why we had been asked. Perhaps Garret just wanted to bounce these ideas off us, or maybe just for the oul' chat.

Monday 20 June The Cabinet assembled at 10.45 a.m. in Barretstown. Before lunch we had a long discussion on Northern Ireland and the implications of the Thatcher win, as well as the implications of the latest vote for Sinn Fein. After lunch we got down to the nitty gritty of the bad slippage on this year's Budget figures.

The large room where we meet for so many hours on end is very pleasant, bigger, more airy and with a rectangular table better suited to Cabinet meetings than the old-fashioned oval one in Merrion Street. At these meetings it is strange to be sitting indoors all day, grappling with discussions and difficulties, surrounded by long windows where one can see the rolling lawns and meadows, horses and trees, with an occasional shape moving in the undergrowth with a gun on his back— protecting us from the IRA or from the wrath of the population?

The discussions on the slippage were very intensive. I believe that the Cabinet is conscious of the great difficulties of further cutting in Education and we had a long discussion about the Public Service pay talks. I made strong and continued arguments against anything resembling a high pay deal, given the implications of that for cuts in other areas. However, it still looks as if there will have to be cuts again before the autumn. Frank Cluskey cut up rough a bit—he can be very blinkered.

After this very long, all-day session and quite a late dinner, I played poker with Peter Barry, Sean Barrett, John Boland, Frank Cluskey, Dick Spring and Pat Cooney, which was great fun and generally good for the spirits of all of us.

Thursday **23** June

A bad 'flu keeps me from going to Berlin for the big opening of the Treasures of Ireland exhibition.

At the Parliamentary Party meeting yesterday, John Kelly was very much opposed to Michael Noonan's proposal for automatic joint ownership of the family home. Amazing what deep fears this concept engenders! Alice Glenn was nearly hysterical about it. She is afraid it is the beginning of divorce. Unfortunately Monica Barnes damages her case by tense, emotional speeches, because she feels so deeply.

The Public Service pay deal talks broke down during the week, perhaps leading to a 'free for all'. Unanimous newspaper support for the Government on the issue, and inflation is down to single figures.

Saturday **25** June

I am getting anxious again about Garret, who is refusing to set a date for the Referendum; many of us are worried that we will be into a Presidential Election combined with it. Dick Spring certainly doesn't want to know about any date for the Referendum and, of course, that helps Garret to duck it. I think he hopes that if he doesn't think about it, it'll just go away.

Sunday **3** July

This was a week where I fought a losing battle on Public Service pay. We seem to be settling at 8%, six months pause, paid over fifteen months. I am not the only one going bananas; I think Peter Sutherland is too. Why on earth can't we behave like other European countries and have a bit of sense about pay?

The half-yearly Exchequer Returns showing that we need to cut another £100 million off spending this year.

What an extraordinary idea for a crowd which is busy adding millions upon millions to next year's pay bill!

I attended a large lunch for Henry Kissinger on Friday — he struck me as being very stolid and self-centred, but then I didn't talk to him so how could I know!

A bad first public reaction to our 8% offer, although it is fairly muted as yet.

To my great relief the Dail is rising next Friday and as a result we have all these midnight sittings, TDs dying to get out of the place which drives us all 'stir-crazy' because we're so 'whipped in' all the time. The air seems stale, nerves frayed.

Saturday **9** July

Dail finally rose and I spoke on Education in the Adjournment Debate to what I can only describe as a massively indifferent world. Some teasing by Maev Kennedy in *The Irish Times* describing me as 'jolly Gemma'.

This week I have tried to find the time and the energy to go into the Members' Bar late at night in order to fraternise and generally show willing, and indeed it works and turns out to be a very agreeable session. I wonder do any of these colleagues know how shy I am?

Wednesday **13** July

Long Cabinet meetings continuing today and got the school transport thing through.

Spoke to the Confederation of Irish Industry lunch at 1 p.m., which seemed to go alright. I wish I had more time to write these speeches myself. I sometimes have to rely on body language to convey goodwill.

Last night I opened the Derrynaflan Chalice Exhibition at the National Museum. The most astonishing and beautiful find; a good proud atmosphere despite the threats by the finders to sue the Government.

I met a deputation of the Inner City School Managers — they do indeed have a desperate financial problem, like the Government's. I'm trying to get a special fund for them and special extra teachers.

Went to the ear doctor because I thought I was going deaf — I couldn't hear what they were saying at Cabinet;

and the doctor, in quite an amused fashion, told me that I had absolutely no problem at all and should tell my colleagues to stop mumbling. So I did, and told them as well that it had cost me £45 to find that out. Barry Desmond and John Boland, who sit at the opposite end of the table from me, can speak very softly, but you'd want to be careful to hear what they say.

We are all gearing ourselves up for further Barretstown sessions next week, where the cutting has to start again, although I feel that Education is not under the microscope this time, at least not so much.

| Thursday |
| 16 |
| July |

These days are mostly concerned with long, all-day, heavy sessions in Marlborough Street working through files, each one requiring seemingly impossible decisions, on drunken teachers, unqualified teachers, choices between school repair projects, and a myriad of other tangles.

Extremely hot weather and we had to do a lot of preparation for our two-day marathon at Barretstown.

| Wednesday |
| 20 |
| July |

The two-day non-event in Barretstown is over. The main lesson that I learned was that Labour are very windy indeed, they're worried about their image and they're worried about their Administrative Council. Frank Cluskey was obdurate. Two days sitting at that table is very wearing, with Alan boring away doggedly; everybody afraid to push too hard because, I suppose, the bottom line is the break-up. So the upshot was a series of trimmings really to save money—no very hard decisions taken. There seems to be a general realisation that Education is a difficult and explosive area. Labour are inclined to enquire worriedly about fee-paying schools but Garret weighed in with a philosophical explanation. However, I made a series of more practical points, mostly that any attack on them would end up costing more because pupils would have to opt for free schools.

A couple of pleasant meals and a couple of short strolls in the fresh air—unfortunately too short.

The backdrop to all this is the looming Budget crisis next year and the Estimates sooner—no way out as far as I can see. At several points I felt I really would be better off if I had never thought about politics. The usual arguments and a fair amount of teasing about women; they may not understand, but at least they are hearing things they never heard seriously said before.

Some awful decisions were discussed and avoided, like halving Children's Allowances for the first child, removing the PRSI ceiling etc. If Garret was stronger, if we were on our own, if we found oil. And Garret seems to think I am going to magically produce an amazing new loan scheme to solve Third Level Education fees problems. Considerable talk about YEA [Youth Employment Agency] and AnCO; they won't like my pushing about that. Oh dear! where are we going? Behind all Labour's worry is the sure knowledge that Haughey will bring them up to the wire every week in the Dail with condemning motions on any cuts.

Saturday 23 July Sometimes I feel now that I am mastering the job at last but some unwise decisions are still hanging over me, like the VEC Scholarships two Cs business. I feel now that if only there was a fairly even sort of financial situation I could make a very good fist of being Minister for Education. The trouble is that in our present calamitous economic state it may be just one long fight with everyone. I really do feel that the only solution next year should be an all-round cut in wages for all the public sector, including doctors, teachers, Gardai, politicians, judges (the whole lot!), with a Family Income Supplement to help the worst off, otherwise how can there be a way out of this £500 million trap. We Ministers should show the way.

Friday 29 July During the week, some battles at Cabinet: about women, appointments to Boards (this is a constant factor), fighting Haughey's threat to chair the Womens' Rights Committee, and earlier weaning them away from any attempt to chop Childrens' Allowances. I find quite a hostile attitude from a lot of men to this kind of issue. Garret, however, softens them greatly. I get a lot of teasing and pointed remarks at coffee breaks and meals, but I continually fight my corner, I hope well, and keeping my sense of humour whenever I can.

| Monday
1
August | A very puzzling interview by Peter Barry on radio. The interview was extremely good and it was all about Northern Ireland and our relations |

with England etc. But then I was astonished to hear him agreeing to 'debate publicly' with Gerry Adams after the New Ireland Forum had reported. Sure enough, later in the day there was a retraction. I am sure Garret must nearly have had a seizure.

| Sunday
7
August | The big news all this past week was the possibility of a major oil find off Waterford. Atlantic Resources shares climbing up and up and news- |

papers speculating about the effect. I can't help thinking that surely it would ease pressures on us next year. I can't help hoping—all the pet things I want to do for the Education area.

During the week I also got involved again in the Amendment and I was on the RTE News. A poll shows public opinion swinging a little way from it but I am afraid it is not hopeful.

I attended the Aga Khan Cup at the RDS on Friday in the President's box. Everybody was very elegant and well-dressed but it went on far too long. I was fidgety and worrying about wasting time, I couldn't believe the hours and hours it took.

| Sunday
14
August | Last week saw me having a long session on the Education Estimates for 1984 with Sean O'Mahoney, the most talented and warm Assist- |

ant Secretary that I have to deal with. Finance has demanded that we take £68 million off our figures, which seems to be total nonsense considering both the rising numbers at all levels and pay deals that the Government has already entered into. So quite mischievously we did what we were told, and took off £68 million—eliminating school transport altogether, cutting out all equipment grants to everybody, and a host of other things which would be impossible to achieve. I would be known as the 'Mad Minister' as well.

This week I also got a lot of hate mail over the 'pro-life' Amendment. I wrote my 300 words against the Amendment for *The Irish Times*. The die is cast now and I am glad I am doing what's right, even though the flak is flying, and I hope Garret doesn't get pressurised into not issuing his statement.

I think that many of the Cabinet, and the TDs too, feel that Garret got us into this and that it's not their problem. Of course they were shaking with fright in 1981 when the abortion issue began to threaten our chances of Government and would have condemned him if he hadn't proceeded with an Amendment. If only there had been contact and trust between Fianna Fail and Fine Gael at that point to adopt a common noncommittal stance on the issue instead of a rush to the cliffs like the Gadarene swine. Anyway thank God I am finally able to do the right thing after all the messing, and I can campaign publicly against the PLAC Amendment.

Saturday **20** August

Getting myself geared up for the Amendment meetings. The campaign is really on full belt now with 'pro' and 'anti' in full swing. The 'anti' campaign, I'm glad to say, is better than expected. All sorts of Fine Gael fighting going on. Alan Dukes has come out of the closet to get rapped, along with me, by Kieran Crotty. Peter Sutherland, as usual, doing his nut in private. Good old Ireland!

Continuing rumours that Mary Harney might break ranks with Fianna Fail. That would be a sensation. She must be under a lot of pressure, poor girl.

Encouraging signs from the Wicklow Constituency organisation about the Amendment. My good supporters are strongly with me, but the letters denouncing me are flowing in, with hardly any at all in support. 'Twas ever thus. 'The worst are full of passionate intensity . . . .'

Sunday
4
September

This week has been dominated by the Amendment. Two Amendment speeches, on Wednesday at Young Fine Gael's meeting in Buswells Hotel and on Thursday in Wicklow town. The meetings were quieter than I expected and without controversy. I also did a radio programme with the pious, solemn Michael Woods on Thursday and my article appeared in *The Irish Times* on Friday.

The main depressing feature, apart from the hysteria of the argument, has been the damage to Garret.

At a rather tense Fine Gael Ministers' meeting on Thursday, Garret was seriously upset by rumours of an apparent impending defection to the 'Yes' vote by Paddy Cooney. Alan and I were heavily criticised for speaking out at a time when Kieran Crotty is trying to stop the pressures on rural Deputies to come out and say 'Yes'.

The Catholic Church, of course, is heavily involved — the Bishops' statement coming out strongly for a 'Yes' vote, although recognising 'the right of each person to vote according to conscience' and adding that 'it must not be suggested or implied that all of those who oppose the Amendment are in favour of abortion'. Monica Barnes is really emotional and strung up. More and more statements coming out on either side: about level pegging. The biggest shock was John Kelly TD coming out for a 'Yes' vote for an extraordinarily fudged reason: 'that the moral majority shouldn't be defeated on this one even though the whole thing is unnecessary anyway'. People are genuinely shocked by this statement and find it uncharacteristically confused. A lot of strong language flying about: John McManus of the Workers Party tried to attack me obliquely on Thursday in Wicklow but the audience wasn't having any of it. Dr George Henry of the Rotunda was there — he is being very brave and outstanding — and Mary McEntaggart [Dr Mary Henry] has been on a non-stop rampage about it and very effective. But the general prediction is for a 'Yes' vote on Wednesday, with a low poll.

We have widely differing predictions whether it will be 70%, 30% or as low as 55%–45%. (Bruce Arnold thinks the 'No' vote will win.) I'm so very glad I decided to get involved.

The full Cabinet meeting this week was full of awful intimations of more severe cuts—quite impossible to see where they are going to come from.

Garret has made his big Amendment statement and I think it's excellent. A little bit humble but that may be disarming.

Derry, I am glad to say, walked out of Mass when the priest started to read the Archbishop's letter—which was very brave because nobody else moved.

Peter Sutherland on the phone again; he is unhappy about the press reaction and the sermons in the churches today. I have a sinking feeling that the PLAC people may get a statement from the Pope before Wednesday. It seems far-fetched but it just might happen in this atmosphere.

Monday 5 September

I opened an AONTAS function this evening [Adult Education]. I had to give a fairly hard speech about money. However, I think and hope they respect me. Some fool man from Kilkenny told me I was a 'desirable woman'—can you imagine a woman saying something like that to a male Minister at an official function! There is a time and a place.

Tuesday 6 September

Walked at 7.30 a.m. and into Cabinet for four hours, with a long and important discussion on illegitimacy, the bottom line being whether in the case of intestacy an illegitimate child should have the same rights as those born within wedlock. Garret is quite mystified as to how anyone could want to end discrimination against illegitimate children and at the same time draw the line at property. If he is really surprised by such attitudes he is more naive than I think he is. Garret, Alan and myself find ourselves on the same side in these arguments.

Tomorrow is Amendment day. The latest opinion poll predicts a 70/30 'Yes' vote and others don't think that could possibly be right. I have met hardly anyone who says they are going to vote 'Yes' but I know they are all out there behind their doors waiting to pounce on us. No sign at all from the Pope!

Behind all these Cabinet meetings looms the so-called 'Estimates Campaign' which requires all of us to do the impossible — cut down to 94% of last year. I really can't think what on earth is going to happen. My main concern is that if we do any more to Education it may prejudice the future of this whole young generation.

<table>
<tr><td>Sunday
11
September</td><td>Well, of course, the main event this week was the Amendment vote. It was carried 2–1 with a 50% poll. North Wicklow voted 'No' I'm glad to say,</td></tr>
</table>

and so did five Dublin Constituencies with a massive 'No' vote in Dun Laoghaire. A sort of uneasy calm has settled with everyone claiming victory. I wasn't really surprised by the result and I wasn't too upset either. In the face of massive Church persuasion and SPUC and PLAC and Fianna Fail, only a third of the electorate actually voted 'Yes' when the huge abstention is taken into consideration.

Spent all Thursday (8 September) involved in John Bruton's whirlwind tour of Wicklow, which he did with his usual great energy. We saw Nixdorf, Cobbett's Biscuits, Solus, Noritake, Automatic Plastics, Tinahely, Shering Plough, Chambers of Commerce etc., etc. A most constructive and interesting day, not least in getting to know John Bruton better — a very committed, conservative, energetic person. He said in his main speech that I was 'the most courageous member of the Cabinet, including the Taoiseach' — my goodness! We had no hassle or problems about the Amendment, though I get the impression that John disapproved of the very heavy Church involvement at the end of the campaign.

John O'Connell, P.P. in Bray, was one of the brave priests who said that there were two sides to the story.

Wasn't at Cabinet on Friday and unfortunately missed the decision to throw out two Russian Embassy people. At least it gives the papers something different to write about.

The aftermath of the Amendment is hard to see. It does

56

seem, however, that Garret will have to sit firmly on the rump of the Party to retrieve anything; they must be brought into line or we're sunk.

Young Fine Gael are under heavy attack from Alice Glenn—who on earth does she think she is?

I'm getting more and more annoyed about Education cuts, while at the same time AnCO is announcing spanking new expensive courses every day. There is a daft conflict there.

Tuesday **13** September

All-day Cabinet. We spent the morning on Russian spies and a few other such items which we find altogether more amusing and interesting than the nitty gritty which came with a vengeance in the afternoon. We got down to sizing up the 1984 Estimates problem, and the timing, and immediately ran into problems of course.

Most worrying Cabinet since the beginning of the year. Alan put up a list of cuts and I simply turned them all down completely. The two main points were the Youth Employment Levy and the 8% rise in teachers' salaries. The thought of disimproving the pupil/teacher ratio at primary level by three units while at the same time paying teachers more, and with AnCO spending wildly on their own education projects is just sheer madness. So while I would be happy to join in the general national effort at cutting back, it must be in areas I could morally stand over. Anyway, two hours of facing each other across the table got us nowhere, except some respect for my position from the officials I hope.

Saturday **17** September

Liam Cosgrave Snr appears to be acting very coy about the Presidency. I am not looking forward to this forthcoming By-Election or the Presidential Election—if only the latter could be avoided.

Sunday **18** September

Out to the airport at 9.30 a.m. to meet President Hillery returning from Japan. Lots of ceremonial, various Ministers there and Garret too. Had quite an animated conversation with C.J. Haughey. He is undoubtedly humorous and charming in a sort of a roguish way, heaven help us!

Everybody is very shocked about poor George Colley's death in London and of course one looks at Haughey and one thinks about the pressures on Colley. I have often recalled, during these few days, my massive radio confrontation with George Colley in 1978 after he made his unfortunate remark about 'well-heeled, articulate women'.

Then we had a quick semi-Government meeting about the Presidency while we were at the Airport. Liam Cosgrave is apparently out, Mark Clinton too, Jack Lynch too. Somebody made a jocose reference to me running.

Despite my amusement originally at the idea, now I am quite taken by it—the first woman President, wouldn't that be something. An unlikely event!

I didn't enjoy today's All-Ireland Football Final between Galway and Dublin, though it was very interesting. They plonked me in a place which I didn't like, quite far away from my colleagues, between Archbishop Cunnane of Tuam and the Tipperary GAA County Chairman. The match was lively but very dirty with four sent off, and Dublin won. Well at least I've seen my first All-Ireland. The Bishop and the County Chairman were deeply embarrassed that I should have witnessed such dirty play. I assured them that it didn't bother me.

After a cup of tea in Croke Park we went out to the airport again for the very sad business of meeting George Colley's remains. Garret was quite upset. I spoke at some length to Jack and Maureen Lynch, who are such nice people. Dessie O'Malley and Jack Lynch had gone to London to travel back with the coffin and the family. It was all very sad and very bleak at the crowded airport. Seamus Brennan was quite upset too. They have lost a very decent man, even if he did involve himself in that bad Fianna Fail policy of 1977.

Monday 19 September	After a very long day touring the whole of Limerick East constituency I am exhausted.

Endless bouquets and 'off the cuff' speeches to massive numbers of children. I suppose I addressed

about 2,000 people today. The Limerick Fine Gael Constituency meeting tonight went extremely well. I am going
to have to really lay on the charm in the difficult times to
come. Tom O'Donnell wasn't there, which made it easier.
Michael Noonan seems to be extremely popular, while the
woman Mayor, Terry Kelly, was cool but agreeable. One
of the speakers at the Fine Gael gathering said loudly
'Minister, you're much smaller than I thought . . .' so I
retorted 'I'm bigger than Charlie Haughey' which went
down a treat.

| Thursday **22** September | Cabinet and Parliamentary Party meetings today. Feature of the Cabinet was Frank Cluskey and John Bruton sparking off each other—both are |

like very large little boys, though on the whole I would be
on John's side. Frank appears to feel that he has to jump
on everything John says. Their two areas of responsibility,
Energy and Industry, it seems to me, should be clearly
demarcated; there's overlap causing tension and more so
when you consider the ideological positions each starts
out from.

The Presidency question is entering another phase as
we approach deadline. President Hillery might be per-
suaded to run again, but he is such a complex and private
character no one knows what he really wants. I understand he meditates quite a bit and I suggested at Cabinet
that we could all benefit from a bit of that.

We discussed the Parliamentary Party meeting and
what strategy might be required. Sean Barrett and myself
both feel that Garret needs to show them really who's
boss. However, the outburst which was expected never
came at the Parliamentary Party meeting, which turned
out to be perfectly simple and ordinary and boring, I'm
glad to say.

| Saturday **24** September | The day started by going to F.S.L. Lyons' funeral service in Trinity Chapel. I wore my new black and white houndstooth suit with which I am not |

pleased, but then it's my shape that's the problem. It
was a most moving and solemn occasion. I was in the
pew with the President, Dr Hillery; Garret and Charlie

Haughey were the other two politicians present. Jennifer Lyons, the widow, was most impressive — attractive and very dignified; she apparently designed the whole funeral service in the solemn and lovely old Chapel. Poor F.S.L. Lyons, he was only fifty-nine, and was ill for such a short time. There was a very poignant meditation: 'I have only gone into the other room. . . . Call me by my familiar name. . . . We are still whatever we were to each other before. . . . All is well'. Garret as usual was very moved — I have never decided if it is attractive or worrying, the fact that he shows his emotions so openly.

Garret told me that he had an inconclusive meeting with Dr Hillery. We all hope that he will stay on in the Presidency.

| Sunday |
| 25 |
| September |

Today I went to the All-Ireland camogie finals at Croke Park — a much more civilised event than a hurling final. The women played in front of a tiny crowd, with great enthusiasm and skill and speed which isn't appreciated enough. They were delighted that I was there, and so was I.

| Saturday |
| 1 |
| October |

The end of an eventful, busy week. The significant thing was Cabinet on Friday. Garret arrived rather late; apparently there was a big problem about his broadcast last Sunday where he talked about £500 million in cuts, which apparently sent the Labour Party backbenchers bananas. Anyway, Dick and Garret had a good meeting and an agreement was reached that there would be no more statements 'off the cuff' about figures like that. That didn't leave all of us happy. I thought the whole point of such broadcasts was to prepare the people for the difficulties ahead. The media were on to it immediately. It was elevated into a huge 'rift', 'impending collapse of Coalition', etc.

Earlier in the week I attended the enormous Mass in the Pro-Cathedral for the opening of the primary school year. After a great deal of thought and discussion with Derry, I took a decision not to receive Communion, so it was a bit alarming to find myself on a prie-dieu in front of the thousand strong congregation; however, I didn't move when it came to the Communion and a bad few moments ensued while the whole Cathedral waited for something to happen. Finally somebody else went up, followed by all the crowd. That is a hurdle I have now crossed. There will be two such Masses next week and I am sure the situation will be equally public and awful. Peter Sutherland agrees with me that the word will spread quite quickly and probably has been signalled already to Archbishop Dermot Ryan—if not all the way to Rome! But as usual I feel much better for having done what I feel is right.

Thursday night we were lucky enough to have been at the opening of Tom Murphy's play, 'The Gigli Concert', at the Abbey. It was absolutely superb. Tom is his usual intense and emotional self; I was delighted for him.

A greatly relieved Government heard from the President yesterday that he will stay on.

Extraordinary headline in the *Sunday Independent* today: 'Government Wrangle over Hussey' over an article about my speech in Roscommon yesterday to the Primary School Managers' Association, where I mentioned some of the grim realities but actually used no figures. So I waited with some interest for the phone to ring, from either an angry Garret or an angry Dick, or someone, but no one did. More inventions.

The coolness, and feeling 'on top of the job' improves, despite the constant worry in the back of my mind that the Department might land me into another row through some oversight or failure to think out a problem.

I am very worried too about a recent Cabinet decision to bring the pay of politicians up to the level of the last Public Service wage agreement, plus rationalising mileage rates etc. It will cause major ructions, but the real worry, of course, is the effect it will have on the acceptance of huge cuts, despite the fact that TDs' salaries have fallen so very far behind and I can see that they shouldn't be asked to make sacrifices when everyone else is getting an increase. I feel that this decision, combined with the 8% for the Public Service (which I object to anyway on principle) will cause even more resistance to cuts.

Wednesday
5
October

Yesterday we had a long day in Strasbourg in the rarified, gobbledegook atmosphere of the Council of Europe, which seems to me to be a non-event and, as I have said before, a benefit for civil servants. Perhaps they're paid so badly that they need these perks. Between protocol, liveried flunkeys, limousines, beautiful meals and flowery speeches, the real world outside the glass walls seems very far away and it can be hard to remember that it's in terrible trouble.

The EEC is of course on a different level. It is very real and real for Ireland too. I had a meeting with the Irish delegation to the Council of Europe and had the experience of Oliver Flanagan kissing my hand and declaiming my brilliance and virtues. How can he be so two-faced? He detests me at home.

I am finally in bed at home tonight, having been through the whole first complete draft of our Action Plan, which was brought to me by John Harris at the airport. I am very pleased indeed with it and of course now I have to fight the considerable battle of getting it through Cabinet. This will be the first time any Minister for Education has ever signalled to the education world a four-year programme of priorities.

Friday
7
October

We took Liz Shannon out for a meal. She is absolutely delighted with her book *Up in the Park* and hopes that a film might be made of it. The book was slated in *The Irish Times* today. However, that doesn't seem to bother her too much; my own view is that she's capable of much better stuff.

I often reflect when I have time on the difference between the general outside impression of me and the reality. I think the general impression is that I am organised, somewhat unfeeling and quite assertive, whereas really I am very mixed up and worried, torn between Government hassles, education pressures and Fianna Fail's relentless pursuit, not to mention the great difficulty of keeping in touch with the family and making sure that everything is going alright there.

I continue to worry about the decision of the Cabinet to

go ahead with improving the TDs' pay and allowances, because of the great hostility it will cause and because it is very much out of line with my own views on reducing all Public Service pay, like other EEC countries had to do when they have had their crises. If only we hadn't Labour with us with all their terrible problems about the Workers Party, and if only Fianna Fail would think for a moment about behaving in a responsible way. I suppose that's too much to hope for.

I completed my series of school year Masses this week and mingled with hundreds and hundreds of people at various tea receptions afterwards, including bishops, priests, nuns and teachers. They seemed all to be very jolly and pleased with my presence there. Maybe they didn't notice the Communion thing. Bishop Dermot O'Mahony was being charismatic and charming and with a totally radiant smile—maybe he's a saint.

The *Late Late Show* has just ended with Bishop Eamonn Casey singing some verses of 'The West's Awake' to a very pained expression on Liz Shannon's face and also on Terry Prone's—that was funny.

Bruce Arnold has a theory regarding Liz's book about her time in the US Embassy here: that the State Department laundered it totally which is why it is so bland, and that having laundered it they then turned round and gave it the hard sell because it's charming and as *The Irish Times* editorial put it 'Sunlight in the Park'. It would have been a very good book indeed if she'd had a free hand to really 'tell it like it was'.

| Sunday 9 October | Liz says she's surprised that everybody here expected her to 'dish the dirt' as she put it 'when Irish journalists never have'. And we agreed that |

it was strange that journalists here let politicians away with extolling family life, condemning abortion, voting against contraception, when in many cases their own private lives are a travesty of all that.

The *Sunday Tribune* came close today to an exposé about a politician (unnamed) who has 'paid for two abortions, while playing a leading role in the Pro-Amendment campaign.' That's an amazing story but of course it will never be printed.

Peter Sutherland on the phone tonight for a long chat. He faces up to having to defend Ireland in Strasbourg on the case being brought against us on the divorce issue. Peter has a theory that Frank Cluskey is so experienced a negotiator that in fact he runs rings around us all.

| Tuesday |
| **11** |
| October |

A very interesting meeting with NUI Senator John A. Murphy who talked about universities and the third level challenge. It gives me a headache even to think about all the work I have to do on that. John A. is an original thinker.

Launched Rhoda O'Connor's *Education Ireland* magazine in the Douglas Hyde Gallery and had a good chat with Bill Watts, the Provost, in his lovely house, where he had invited me for a cup of tea beforehand. He is upset about the fines on Trinity because of the strike they settled earlier this year and I think perhaps that we are a bit unreasonable about it.

Our Action Programme is coming to a head; I'm having a series of meetings with all the chief protagonists, and going through it minutely. If it ever gets through Government it will be a big event, full of major departures, which the Secretary—to my amazement—has mostly agreed to despite initial reluctance.

| Wednesday |
| **12** |
| October |

Schull was pleasant. Went—for the opening of Community College—on the 7.30 a.m. train with John Harris. We worked, studied and planned all the way down there, then drove to Schull from Cork station and more work.

The new Community College is beautiful, and the ceremony was a very big deal with bishops all over the place. They presented me with a very nice Waterford glass bowl and the general atmosphere was most cheerful.

We came back by car and train again and got five more hours of work done, mostly on the Estimates and Curriculum and Examinations Board. It was a satisfying day and I ended up with a great deal more knowledge than when I set out.

Sunday 16 October 4 p.m. Just back from the final session of our long Estimates discussions which went over Friday, Saturday and Sunday. We have not made one really hard decision but we have talked around and about the subject, examined internal and external figures, watched interminable discussions between Garret and Alan. I am more and more impressed by John Bruton, both as a person and as a Minister; if only his social attitudes were not so conservative. Every time I mention the pay problem, it's knocked on the head — dismissed out of hand by Labour — but that doesn't stop me mentioning it.

Tuesday 18 October All-day Cabinet today, not on Estimates, despite the fact that I came ready with my figures and my preparations. Today we considered the emerging Insurance Bill to do with the PMPA crisis and precious little else. I had a go at the Labour Party about that *Sunday Independent* quote which said that one of them had described me as 'insensitive'. Everybody denied having anything to do with it, of course. I can see that we will never get the Estimates or the Budget done without the usual very late night meetings.

Sunday 23 October The Fine Gael Ard Fheis has just ended — the big, brash, annual 'love-in' one has come to expect.
    When the time came for my speech Peter Barry described me as 'our charming and pretty Minister for Education' which raised a number of hackles and caused some annoyance. So I thanked him when I spoke and described him 'as the silver-haired and handsome Peter Barry'. He didn't seem to be amused.
    Saturday was the big day at the Ard Fheis, which swelled in numbers and enthusiasm, culminating in Garret's speech. The new video of Fine Gael's history was shown and I am quite proud of the fact that Derry and I

seem to be almost the only husband and wife team in it. Interesting that neither myself nor John Boland got the almost 'de rigueur' standing ovation—I think everybody else got one.

The whole weekend was characterised by people stopping me nearly every three steps for a school, a teacher, to attend a function. It gets a bit nerve-racking. I work very hard on the smile and the agreeableness.

On Friday—before the Ard Fheis began—we finally came to the Education Estimates at Cabinet and I fought my corner hotly this time from a position of strength born of knowledge. Garret was unexpectedly acerbic with me but later he told me quietly at the Ard Fheis that he felt he had to do that. Anyway I am supposed to find £3 million by Tuesday, but it looks as if I will get my increased scholarship grant and special money for disadvantaged areas in the primary sector. If I can hold on tight to that position, we will be doing very well and Education can be spared a year of terrible hassle. The next important things are the Curriculum and Examinations Board and the Action Plan.

Today, the last morning of the Ard Fheis, the Women's Affairs Section was a bit ragged. Nuala Fennell wasn't as impressive as last year. (I remember I was a bit jealous of her last year and worried; this year I feel sorry for her. I hope she makes it alright, it is such a difficult position she finds herself in.)

John Bruton's speech was masterly today. I warm to him more and more. Once again he mentioned me strongly in his speech—is that why I warm to him? Derry and I wonder if he is signalling something to me about a post-Garret situation for leadership. Is that Machiavellian? He also contacts Derry a fair bit and he is certainly back in the running for leadership.

None of the so-called tensions in the party really surfaced at all this weekend. The real tensions nowadays are about the Budget, and the apparent impossibility of agreeing expenditure cuts on any scale at all, and the brinkmanship tactics of Frank Cluskey.

Monday
24
October

Opened the new buildings for the mentally handicapped at Marino Clinic in Bray. A very special occasion because the little handicapped children are so pitiful but at the same time inspiring and the carers are simply amazing.

Wednesday
2
November

Attending the UNESCO Education Conference in Paris. Staying at the Hotel Lutetia Concorde in Paris, which is a very big, old, expensive place (but half the price of the Hilton, which they were originally booking me into and which I refused). This hotel was apparently taken over by the Germans during the war and I'm somewhat chilled thinking about what may have gone on in this very room I'm in, on the sixth floor with its horrible little salon attached to it.

The UNESCO meeting is held in an enormous room full of the whole world of every colour. Speakers going on and on and on and I wonder if anyone is listening? The Jamaican, a woman Minister for Education, gave a speech strongly supporting the US invasion of Grenada; the Mongolian, a man, condemning it directly after her. So the whole thing became very political and not much to do about Education. Apparently our presence is required in terms of international status.

Friday
4
November

It was my turn to speak at UNESCO and somebody must have been listening because it seemed to go down alright. I don't think UNESCO is as bad as the Council of Europe and I am certainly glad all the money is going to the Third World. Still, it all costs such a great deal to have these meetings in the most expensive places.

Wednesday
9
November

After the Dail, Derry and I went to the dinner to mark the 75th anniversary of the founding of the National University. It was rather posh in the Berkeley Court. I had slaved over my speech because I got some dreadful dry gunge from the Department which was quite unusable. Anyhow, I am delighted that the speech was quite a triumph and all my own work! Spent a lot of time during the dinner in deep conversation with Ken Whitaker, who is such an extremely nice person, interesting and polished and witty too. Tadhg Ó'Ciardha of UCC spoke for far too long and was quite crude, to my surprise. Dr Whitaker doesn't approve of the FF position on the economy, to put it mildly.

I've been trying very hard to get a meeting with Garret to clear the Programme for Action in Education with him first before we go to Cabinet, but we have had some difficulty in finding a suitable time. To nobody's surprise, and certainly not mine, the Department of Finance has indicated total opposition.

The Curriculum and Examinations Board memorandum is also with Government now.

Sunday **13** November

Up very early and off to Berkeley Road Church near the Mater Hospital to stand in the freezing cold all morning until 1 p.m. canvassing for the Dublin Central By-Election. A lot of bad tempered people not wanting to communicate and who'd blame them? Some quite strong attacks on me which are dispiriting, but various other people came from Wicklow to help and that was very good.

We were given coffee in a little spotless Presbytery where five Carmelites live. Some gentle, humorous young men, shining with goodness, working and living with the poor.

Among the unpleasant people I met today on the canvass was a girl who teaches in Donegal, shouting sarcasms at me, which finished up with '. . . and congratulate Garret for his grovelling at Margaret Thatcher's feet', a young shop assistant roaring at me about the TDs' pay rise and a truculent Irish-speaking girl and her rude mother shouting at me for not speaking Irish. Who'd be in politics?

Monday **14** November

I met Garret on the Action Programme today with John Harris, although Garret seemed to be very exhausted and not feeling very well. He wallowed in statistics ('the age specific fertility rates in the latest French study') but enthusiastically approved the Programme and that was very satisfactory.

| Tuesday **15** November | We really got down to talking about Public Service pay when the other options were beginning to look extremely difficult. With a bit of luck we |

will continue to talk about pay/prices freeze, public and private sector.

Late drink in Sean Barrett's office with a group of the Cabinet afterwards. Pat Cooney swears he is going to call the new Naval Service vessel 'Seoidin' after me. He's pulling my leg of course. Anyway, I felt happier after tonight's discussion than I have felt for a long time and I hope we will be able to follow through. There was a very good atmosphere at the meeting and we all talked in a very friendly way afterwards for some time. I believe there is a strong common will to survive and do the right thing, however we manage it, in the face of this utterly unprincipled opposition. The meeting went on until 3.15 a.m.

| Friday **18** November | A long, long marathon Cabinet meeting. Started at 9.30 a.m. and was horrible for me. I lost the battle on the 20% third level fee increases and lost |

a further 4.6% on capital, as well as having to agree to try and get a .67% wage saving in the Department somehow. But then everybody was losing money, including Health — it's like pulling teeth out of our heads slowly or a psychological breaking-down process with exhaustion forcing agreement. Christ!

| Sunday **20** November | Out to Glasnevin for the last Sunday of the By-Election campaign. The polls show us doing very badly indeed despite Mary Banotti's obvious ex- |

cellence and the party's huge effort (though nothing like Dublin West last year — Fergus O'Brien is not a John Boland). Garret arrived in quite good humour and told me 'You have now confused Alan totally about how much you've actually given in the Estimates'. Garret, I'm glad to say, has strong sympathy for Education.

Monday 21 November

Long, long day ending with three hours in Alan's office with officials on the Capital Estimates. Noel Lindsay from my Department was there and was most impressive. After a long time and four cheroots I only gave what I set out to give: just over £3 million, their original demand was £13 million, and I came home more dead than alive.

Thursday 24 November

Appalling Dublin Central By-Election result— Fine Gael down to 22.5%. Five hours and freezing polling stations and grim. I supported Mary Banotti for a while today at the count, and brought Monica Barnes over to Kevin Street and we bought flowers for Mary.

Later I appeared on RTE's television programme on the results, and came near to walking off the set when Brian Farrell seemed to have worked himself up to a sweat, interrupting both myself and Barry Desmond; I was quite sharp with him, to his surprise and my own.

Sunday 27 November

Went to the Red Cross Ball last night in an official capacity—a lot of fuss being made because Prince Albert of Monaco was the guest of honour. I didn't enjoy the rather disorganised, not very pleasant, function. The Prince is a nice-looking, ordinary, quiet fellow.

In today's *Sunday Press* there is quite a decent photograph of me and the Prince, though I am looking rather fat and motherly.

Today I hosted a lunch for him at Iveagh House—my first such venture. We were allowed to invite some personal guests as well and so I invited one or two. It was all very civilized, only I found I had to work very hard beside the Prince. He is a young man who responds politely, even nearly warmly, to some things but overall is quite dull and lacks vivacity or much charm. Lord Killanin on my left was of course very easy indeed. All in all I suppose I worked for about two hours talking to the Prince and I was worn out afterwards.

Garret has gone off touring Europe to meet Prime Ministers of the EEC about the dangerous agriculture Super Levy. I'm much more relaxed when he is away; I wish he'd stay away for a little while!

| Thursday |
| 1 |
| December |

Yesterday at Cabinet we had a very long session with visiting experts, including one from Canada, on the whole Dublin Gas issue. It is becoming quite clear what the main areas of concern are and of course I got around to declaring my interest, which was dismissed by Frank Murray, Assistant Secretary to the Government, on grounds that that really has nothing to do with it (Derry has £50 worth of shares in it). We finally decided to go ahead with the Dublin Gas deal after a considerable discussion and with some worries about the attitudes of the Labour people, all strongly influenced by Frank Cluskey.

Garret is now in Paris on the Super Levy and yesterday he told me he had spoken to Margaret Thatcher in the middle of the night while she was flying over India. He had spoken to her about the whole question of whether or not there was ransom money being paid in England for Don Tidey, who has been kidnapped, and about whom there is not one word of good news and we're all sick with worry.

| Saturday |
| 3 |
| December |

Today I am still getting over the shock that the *Irish Independent* was carrying the whole of my Action Programme all over it. This is a massive leak of Cabinet documentation. What a very worrying development. The leak of course caused a huge stir. In terms of reaction the actual reporting and comment was good, but it certainly has thrown us all into a heap in the Department because of its appearance before we were ready. I spoke to a worried Garret and to Michael Noonan about a possible Garda inquiry into the leak.

Today was the Inauguration of the President and I presented myself in my neat black suit, purple blouse and black velvet pillbox hat and processed with my Cabinet

71

colleagues all looking smart in morning clothes, although
Frank Cluskey opted out altogether. The ceremony was
short and tasteful enough, in fact quite impressive. The
President spoke briefly and, it seemed to me, more easily
and more fluently than usual. I must say there was a
certain satisfaction in the fact that we were in charge of
such a ceremony and not Fianna Fáil. There was a good,
big reception afterwards and I sat down with Cardinal Ó
Fiaich for a moment, but I couldn't think of much to say to
him because there was so much that I would like to argue
with him about, and there he was in his splendid scarlet
silk and satin and it wasn't the place to argue. It is
satisfying to be a Government Minister on a day like this
because I am surrounded totally by men and at least I feel
that there is some woman carrying the flag!

Dublin Castle looked very well for the Inauguration and
it was all done smoothly, though I don't know if Maeve
Hillery really relishes the job very much; who'd blame
her?

Garret left today for a crucial Summit in Athens and by
some accident I was the only Minister who managed to
get to the Airport to see him off. He was in great good
humour. He loves the challenge at European level of all
that high-powered and complex discussion and when I
asked him yesterday if he was tired (after Paris, Bonn,
Rome, Copenhagen . . .) he said: 'It's a lot more enjoyable
than trying to run this country!' I know exactly what he
means.

Interesting: last week on an Estimates discussion I had
to fight for the restoration of the huge cut off the paltry
£135,000 which Nuala Fennell has for women's organisations. The big cut sort of slipped through, but with
Michael Noonan's help I stopped it—such a penny-
pinching exercise with such serious implications. On the
whole my role in fighting for women is not too unsuccessful. Nuala is very much in the wars and has managed to
alienate quite a lot of people, including Cabinet colleagues, so I spend a lot of time defending her and then
sometimes feel I am defending myself, because I seem to

be getting blamed for some of the things in her Department.

Sunday **4** December	I had a phone call very early this morning (without apologies or preliminaries) from Alan Dukes, worrying about a *Sunday Tribune* article on the

Budget. It is so inaccurate that I don't know why he is worrying, but he hadn't seen it apparently, just heard about it. Anyway, Shane Kenny of RTE might be trying to get me to go on *This Week* to speak about children's allowances, but I assured Alan I had no intention of doing it.

The Tidey kidnapping is dragging on and everybody is desperately concerned about it.

Monday **5** December	One of those days when I try to pack in as many things as I can. Left for Galway before 8 a.m. this morning, with John Harris, and worked in the car

all the way over. Visited the Digital organisation and addressed about 1100 workers in their canteen. There seems to be a very happy atmosphere there, and apparently no strikes; then visited three schools: a Vocational School, a Girls' Secondary School and a Boys' Diocesan College. I found the latter to be grim and wondered what awful things in the corporal punishment area must have happened there in the past. I had a cold feeling about it.

Got back to Dublin around 5 p.m. and went to another function involving prizes for the School's Management Game, and finally got home about 7.30 p.m.

I found George Birmingham was here closeted with Derry and he stayed until about 10 o'clock. George, like me and a lot of other people, thinks the politicians' 19% rise was wrong at this time, even though it was only to help TDs catch up with what everybody else had received, and wasn't giving them one single extra penny. Nevertheless it has been connected by the general public with any efforts we might make for pay restraint. I don't think the TDs would have revolted—if only the Cabinet had listened to me, but what can you do?

Friday
9
December

Frank Cluskey resigned yesterday. I met Michael Noonan early and he told me there were rumours. These continued all day and then I finally heard the announcement on the 9 o'clock News—a strange way to hear it indeed. His reason, as given, was the whole question of the Dublin Gas decision. That I don't believe; I consider it was only a part of it and I believe it did give Frank an excuse. Frank never liked being in Government or facing up to the grim reality.

I have been reading *The Boss*, the new book by Murtagh and Joyce just out yesterday, all about C.J. Haughey. It is the most positively chilling thing that I have read in a long time and makes Frank Cluskey's desertion of this Government all the more serious for the country. It seems unbelievable that Mr Haughey should still be Leader of the Opposition if that book is true and it is a sad commentary on Ireland. God bless us, at least Garret is very decent and straight.

There was a lot of speculation and alarm as a result of Frank's resignation—everybody going around with long faces. We have to keep our heads down, keep calm, keep working and let the Labour Party fall asunder in its own way. We should prepare for an election on our terms.

Saturday
10
December

Worked at clinics all afternoon. These were preceded by a quick dash to do Christmas shopping at Avoca Handweavers in Kilmacanogue and followed by dinner in Paddy Masterson's house which was most pleasant and included Margaret Downes and Helen Burke. It was an evening of political gossip, and laughs, plus some earnest education point-making by Paddy, who recently became Registrar of UCD and is of course very ambitious to become President of UCD when Tom Murphy retires.

Monday
12
December

Depressing to find over the weekend that some Cabinet member had apparently leaked the precise voting figures on the Dublin Gas question. Very depressing that this should happen after all the indignation expressed about leaks—it would make you sick.

Garret believes that Dick faces a possible re-shaping of the Administrative Council at their March conference, which may lead to a Labour conference decision to pull out of Government. This would not only split the Labour Party but might well finish the Government. Frank Cluskey has obviously set the wheels in motion for God knows what, and now we can only hope that Dick can stop it and control it.

Thursday 15 December 9 p.m. Just got home after the minor re-shuffle day in Leinster House. Cabinet started at 9.30 a.m. and there was a lot of buzz going on about the changes. Liam Kavanagh is in Environment, Dick Spring in Energy, Ruairi Quinn in Labour, and my own 'coup' is that I have managed to get George Birmingham made Junior Minister for Education and Labour, to begin to bring some reason into the clashing and overlapping of AnCO and the VECs.

We had a preliminary discussion about the awful decision on Irish Shipping which is before us; we also have had to make some sticky decisions on the Nicky Kelly civil action (whether the State should enter estoppal proceedings to stop it).

Friday 16 December Last day of the Dail before Christmas. Dramatic events unfolding by the minute because Don Tidey was rescued today amid gun battles in Leitrim which are still going on. A Garda and a soldier have been killed; their poor bodies lie in a no-man's land, surrounded by forces waiting to capture four gunmen. What a bloody awful scenario.

The Estimates have been masterfully handled by Peter Prendergast and they actually look tougher than they really are. There is a lot of flak flying about Education and the Union of Students is in a fury. I am glad to say that the Government is coming together and recovering quite well from Frank Cluskey's resignation. Dick Spring and Barry Desmond are being strong about Government unity, thank goodness. I can't fathom Dick very well. He is a bit flip and short with me. Perhaps he's not comfortable with me. I must work at it. He seems to be in constant pain from his back.

The Cabinet today decided on the fate of Irish Shipping. There really was no alternative to liquidation unless they could miraculously re-negotiate in Hong Kong. Ruairi Quinn was articulate and good on the subject—I believe he will be more constructive than Frank.

Sunday
18
December

Continuing searches, alarms, anger about the vicious Tidey kidnapping affair. Dominic McGlinchey surfacing too and a frightful bomb outside Harrods yesterday. A dreadful feeling that things are approaching an extremely serious pass. A lot of calls for proscription of Sinn Fein; Garret being extremely serious and good on television.

Sunday papers, particularly the *Sunday Independent* and the *Tribune*, criticised us heavily today about the Estimates and I must say I feel that those people who were so strongly pressing for the 8% pay rise have a lot to answer for.

Tomorrow I will go to the two funerals of the IRA victims, so my plan to further the Curriculum and Examinations Board at Cabinet will be delayed.

Tuesday
20
December

The two funerals, that of Private Kelly in Moate, Co. Westmeath, and that of Garda Sheehan in Carrickmacross, were desperately sad. Most of the Cabinet were there. A very sad scene in Moate—and very ceremonial afterwards when we all walked down the long grey street behind the gun carriage. A cold, dark day, the widow in a terrible state and four little children. A feeling of drama and tension in the air connected with the ongoing search for the killers in Leitrim. Then we dashed across country to Carrickmacross, trying to keep up with Garret's driver, all over the back roads of the north Midlands. We arrived slightly late in Carrick; it didn't matter as it turned out, but I hate being late for anything. Anyway, that was another sad, sad occasion. He was very young, poor fellow. What must his mother feel?

Then when I finally got home, Peter Prendergast asked

me to go on the *Today Tonight* special on the whole sorry
business; so I did and was quiet, solemn and fiercely anti-
IRA. The programme, I think, was good. The Government
is considered very sound on these issues, at least.

Today, after all that, we took my Curriculum and
Examinations Board memo in Cabinet, at which I was
most unsuccessful—and that left me feeling fed-up and
angry. Perhaps angry at myself and John Harris. The
Cabinet were obdurate about appointments and staffing,
even without John Boland, and I found it very long and
very tiring. The Cabinet also decided against any sudden
new anti-IRA legislation even in the face of the most
recent provocation.

Wednesday 21 December

The huge search operation continues in Leitrim in
this awful December weather, with no results.
Constant rumours and constant whispers, sporadic ugly incidents in other places—Enniscorthy, Mayo,
Kildare. Morale among Gardai and Army in Leitrim must
be sinking fast as they muck through the rough country,
mists, rain, bad light. Reports of hostility to the Army
and Gardai in Ballinamore surprise no one. Sometimes I
think that half of the country is disastrous. Maybe that's a
Dublin outlook! But there certainly is some strange thinking West of the Shannon.

Tuesday 27 December

The four days of Christmas have been, as usual, a
haze of work, walking, family matters, kindness,
Christmas feeling, entertaining, pot-walloping
and occasionally worrying about the various issues coming up in Education: the Curriculum and Examinations
Board, the terrible problem of its personnel, and in
particular its Chairperson. The Action Programme is a
marathon coming up. John Harris says not to worry, we
will arrange it and we will get through it. And we will.

Thursday 29 December

Spent an hour this morning on *Day by Day*—the
phone-in that I didn't do a year ago. I took a long
time yesterday preparing for it, and then of
course there were other people, Des O'Malley, Catherine

McGuinness, Ivor Kenny (plus Desmond Fennell from Galway). Dessie O'Malley was chortling about *The Boss* before the programme and seemed in good form, but then turned out to be quite dull during the show. I had all the figures ready on a whole range of issues and managed alright. Before I went down to the programme I rang Garret to make a date with him to discuss the looming problem of third level numbers and the resultant capital investment problem. Alan rang me later to see me tomorrow about it. I am coming to a point of despair once more about all these things.

I went round to the basement in Palmerston Road to see a tousled, sleepy-faced, shirt-sleeved Garret, and we had a good, lively talk for 35 minutes on the third level investment problem. He sees it quite clearly and suggests that I try to get somewhere with Alan on the most urgent problems but, more importantly, he also promises support. I left when Derry came to discuss strategy committees and later Derry and I walked in the park.

Garret doesn't believe that Dick will pull out of Government, even if the new Administrative Council of that daft party want to do so, and he believes the others wouldn't pull out of Government either. I think that Garret is over-optimistic about other people's actions; I remember last year he believed that Fianna Fail dissidents might actually leave Fianna Fail and come to us.

Friday 30 December

Went down to the Department in Marlborough Street and had a long, long meeting about the third level problem, with Paddy Maloney, Noel Lindsay (who continues to impress) and John Harris, plus the Secretary, who on principle of course I address as 'Secretary' always.

At 6 p.m. I proceeded up to Alan's office where I got agreement on the first stage of the three Dublin RTCs in exchange for postponing other decisions on capital investment pending the General Capital Programme. Alan is a very cool customer.

This is the last but one day of 1983, the year when I

started on the job I longed for and never really thought would come so soon. The whole vexed question of why I got it (close to Garret? ability? Derry's input into Fine Gael's struggles? the only woman really suitable?) hasn't been answered but it has always been in my mind this year and I fear in a lot of other minds too. I know that I haven't been outstandingly able, but I know that I haven't been anything approaching a failure either. There may perhaps have been a failure to make friends and 'partisans' among the Fine Gael Parliamentary Party—something which I have always found difficult and which I must undertake. I have no clear idea of what my image is. I seem to perform well on television and radio—articulately and pleasantly, and being myself. Perhaps I haven't much personality.

If, at the end of this year, this page is going to be about self-analysis, let's continue. I have limited powers of retention of long lists of figures. This is alarming when Garret shoots sudden questions at me about percentages and statistics and 'age specific fertility rates'. I deal more with basics, with logic and with argument. I'm inclined to get flustered, though I try to conceal it at Cabinet. Is there anything on the plus side? Maybe that's a bit dangerous but here goes. I suppose I am intelligent, a fairly good public speaker, an honest if perhaps too reticent feminist, fairly tough and resilient under pressure, good at chatting to whoever it might be, 'King or commoner', a stable and happy family person, well-organised in the constituency, I would be pleasant looking if it wasn't for my weight problem! And I work very hard.

All this self-analysis is caused by the fact that Garret has given me no indication whatsoever of how he thinks I am doing, so it is hard to know what to change or where the weaknesses really are.

The end of 1983. What a year it has been—quite extraordinary and extremely significant personally and politically. The big question must be if the Government will have the nerve and the support to stick to what it needs to do because of the longer term benefits for the country. I don't know the answer to that one—who does?

On re-reading Cecil Woodham Smith's *Queen Victoria* I discovered that her daughter destroyed all or most of Victoria's carefully written journals, more than a hundred of them. What an awful blow for history—I don't suppose mine come into that category!

THE SECOND YEAR

TO

DECEMBER 1984

Launching of the Curriculum and Examinations Board—Publication of the Action Programme for Education 1984–87—Anne Lovett of Granard, aged fifteen, dies while giving birth in a field to a baby who also dies—The Catholic Bishops address the televised public session of the New Ireland Forum—The Government protests at the visit of Prince Philip to a military barracks in Co. Armagh—News of an attempt to bug the home of Seamus Mallon of the SDLP—Dominic McGlinchy is arrested and extradited to Northern Ireland—I obtain funding for students attending RTCs from European Commissioner Ivor Richard at a special meeting in Brussels—The National Planning Board, chaired by Louden Ryan, gives its report to the Government—The New Ireland Forum concludes its discussions and publishes its report; Mr Haughey immediately distances himself from it—I issue a document on the age of entry to school and the duration of the post-primary cycle—President Reagan visits Ireland for four days in June—Elections to the European Parliament: Fine Gael wins six seats, Fianna Fail eight, and one Independent. Only 47% of the electorate vote. On the same day the Referendum to extend voting rights to non-Irish citizens is passed overwhelmingly—Geraldine Ferraro is selected as Walter Mondale's

81

running mate in the US Presidential election—Peter Suther-land's appointment as Ireland's next European Commissioner is announced—Nicky Kelly is released from Portlaoise prison on humanitarian grounds—Garda Frank Hand is shot dead at Drumree, Co. Meath, during a Post Office raid—The Govern-ment launches its plan Building on Reality *which, among other things, plans to impose stringent controls on Public Service pay—At a press conference in London after a meeting with Garret FitzGerald, Mrs Thatcher dismisses all the options in the New Ireland Forum Report—The appointment is announced of John Rogers as the new Attorney General to succeed Peter Sutherland.*

| Tuesday |
| 3 |
| January |

Very well attended first Cabinet of 1984, with quite a good atmosphere since everybody seems to have had a bit of a rest 'over the Christmas'. Ruairi Quinn is certainly a great improvement on Frank Cluskey—he is concise and constructive. We got quite a lot of decisions made, before I went to Marlborough Street where I spent three hours getting a lot of the strands together on the Curriculum and Examinations Board and the Action Programme. I feel a mounting anxiety about them and also about the expenditure cuts Alan may come up with for the Budget. John Boland (to whom I am trying to be very pleasant) rang me with the alarming news that Noel Lindsay (who is a Principal Officer in my Department) has re-applied to work for the World Bank for an extended period—I'll have to try to change his mind.

| Thursday |
| 5 |
| January |

I sat down with John Boland for a considerable length of time today to try to sort out the Curriculum and Examinations Board staffing. I know he has a very difficult job to do but I find him a strange and abrupt person to deal with. Anyway, after a marathon session, I hope we have been able to arrange it alright. John Harris was with me but I think he is somewhat inhibited in John Boland's presence.

| Sunday |
| 8 |
| January |

Delighted!—the Curriculum and Examinations Board was finally agreed. But my energy seems to be draining away and I don't like the fact that I am so tired at night and I have no time in the mornings. I suppose one of the reasons that I spend a lot of time being tired is that I worry so much about the latest lists of suggested cuts which Alan sent. Hardly any of them would yield money this year but would cause endless damage, trouble and disruption in the education system (for instance disimproving the Primary pupil/teacher ratio by three units). All Alan's comments so far on the Action Programme are totally negative, but then he is doing the job that a Minister for Finance is expected to do in terms of curbing any expectations of spending, and frightening the life out of us with suggestions of cuts.

Today I also had the pleasure of being able to ring some

of the Curriculum and Examinations Board appointees and they are all absolutely delighted.

Having had so much to do with John Boland in recent times over the Curriculum and Examinations Board, I can see that he is certainly some kind of genius. He can be extremely amusing but I can see why the Department might prefer not to have him back in Education.

My next hurdle is to get the Action Plan through the Cabinet nearly intact. And I can't rely on Garret to give me too much help, because he must be absolutely impartial as between me and Alan (in fact he has often said that his duty is to incline towards Finance).

There are slight nervous flutterings these days as the 1984 Budget approaches. Garret was on radio again today —much better and more firm.

Barry Desmond—the 'Elder Lemon'—went on radio and TV and in his very avuncular and amusing way pooh-poohed the suggestion that contraceptives were going to be sold in supermarkets, as a result of the Family Planning Bill. He is really very funny; he wears us all out at Cabinet with long agonised dissertations on health cuts, all the time with a roguish glint in the eye.

I have been wondering how many of my Cabinet colleagues would like to be Taoiseach: Alan Dukes, John Bruton, Michael Noonan, John Boland, Jim Mitchell, Peter Barry—Uncle Tom Cobley and all! I certainly don't have the hunger to go for it or for the cultivation of every TD, every constituency, public image, Cabinet cultivation etc. Peter Barry and John Bruton are already established, Michael must be the dark horse.

Monday	Today we concentrated on putting the Curric-
9	ulum and Examinations Board together and I had
January	lunch with Ed Walsh. He seems to me to be a

most impressive, courageous gentleman, with oodles of charm and utterly determined.

Long session then with the National Youth Council in Garret's Conference Room. I think they are a bit of a nuisance and I also think that Garret overdoes the fussing over them. However, despite feeling a bit ill in my tummy,

I was able to perform well and rushed home to cook supper for Andrew who is going to boarding school tonight in not very good humour.

Then I went over to St Patrick's College in Drumcondra to launch Tom Kelleghan's book on *Equality in Education*. That Teacher Training College is a very impressive institution, Tom K. is very good, and Sam Clyne, the Rev. President, is my kind of cleric.

Tuesday **10** January	There were more leaks again tonight in the paper about the Curriculum and Examinations Board, which threw me into a fuss and a temper. This

morning the Trade Union member turned us down and we failed to get immediate sanction from Donal Nevin to let my suggested substitute, Joan O'Connell, serve on it — all because the ASTI are grumbling loudly about their representation not being high enough. I really feel quite angry that they should talk about making trouble when we are doing such a fundamentally revolutionary thing in bringing them in to Education policy-making for the first time. They're looking a gift horse in the mouth.

In Cabinet today we had a rueful discussion on the contraceptive issue which has surfaced again. There is a general weary feeling that enough damage was done to Fine Gael and the country on the Abortion Amendment, and that the scars haven't yet healed. The Budget doesn't seem to be presenting quite the agonising dilemmas that it might have.

The *Irish Press* phoned just now to say that the ASTI are calling a special meeting because they haven't enough people on the Curriculum and Examinations Board.

Friday **13** January	I am angry, tired and frustrated. The Curriculum and Examinations Board is under threat from the ASTI and after a week of meetings, studies, con-

cessions, there was a total mess-up at Cabinet today, and I felt that Garret was less than supportive. Alan produced yet another list of cuts, with Education providing most of them, and the final insult was Garret ringing me tonight about the ASTI and the Board, having been charmed by the clever Kieran Mulvey. I refused to budge and said I was dealing with it. The upshot was an arrangement to meet in Garret's office next Tuesday with Alan, to iron it all out. I'll believe it when I see it.

Saturday
14
January

Cabinet all day. Inconclusive, little enough in the way of tensions, but worrying implications. Nothing at all in this Budget for the taxpayer, and too much new VAT, the deficit standing at £1090 million. Ruairi, as well as being much easier than Frank, also has talent as a cartoonist and passes around clever drawings with captions which are very apt. We glanced briefly at cuts and passed on.

Sunday
15
January

Am I hearing right? Ó Fiaich is saying extraordinary things on RTE's *This Week* about Sinn Fein, extolling their work for housing and refusing to denounce them or membership of their party. He twists and turns and won't answer the straight question: 'Given that every Sinn Fein candidate must support the armed struggle according to the rules laid down by the most recent Sinn Fein Ard Fheis, do you not condemn membership, or voting for them, as immoral?' The Cardinal won't do it and his silence speaks volumes. Now he is condemning the British Government, in particular 'this one'.

One asks oneself where's the country now? It has a weak enough Government because of the Labour pressures within it and the relentless Fianna Fail pressure against taking any of the right steps. We have an insecure, but thoroughly honest and intellectually brilliant leader; a divided Opposition, with a distrusted and destructive leader; an economic/demographic crisis which is unique in Europe; an inability to show strength on Public Service pay, (a colossal misjudgement to award that 19% to politicians in October). We need to get the Government's act together and to give the impression that we are firmly and calmly in control. The generally favourable economic indicators have given the people the idea of an easy Budget, which of course we cannot produce.

Behind all this the brooding Northern trouble, which

deepens in complexity and danger as Sinn Fein get stronger and the IRA/INLA make fools of the Army and Gardai. Crime of a troublesome and violent kind escalates, connected with the drug scene and the economic crisis. What the country needs is a firm, enlightened Government which will try to help the poor and the weak, involve the young and restrain the strong.

The summary of the state of the country makes me think that I have to hang on in there and, despite all the difficulties, do whatever I can to get things sorted out right.

Tuesday
17
January

Marathon Cabinet meeting yesterday which went on until 2 a.m. this morning, and another four-hour session today, but the whole thing is markedly less tense than heretofore. A great deal of work in balancing and totting but the real awfulness is gone, along with Frank Cluskey. However, the crescendo is mounting about the Curriculum and Examinations Board — an extraordinary statement from the JMB [Joint Managerial Body] condemning the Board members and me and ending 'we live in the morning after optimism'. I was very taken aback and hurt and annoyed, but I rallied strongly later and can even feel a bit calm about it now. I can't understand the destructiveness of all the interest groups which are being invited right into decision-making on a legal, permanent basis.

Ruairi keeps on pushing for a whole lot of ideological things, like non-denominational education on which I fully agree with him — but which would be difficult to put in: a) for financial reasons and b) for Constitutional reasons. People already know that we're positive and helpful on multi-denominational primary schools.

A shock this evening about Fords of Cork closing down.

I am delighted today because I got £2 million extra for special primary school building projects, as a Budget 'sweetener' for the building industry. Some of the worst cases can be helped now.

Wednesday
18
January

Hallelujah! Today the Action Programme sailed through Cabinet without a problem. Only had token resistance from Alan, who saw the writing on the wall and bowed to the collective will of all the colleagues, who think it's a good thing.

I had gone to Cabinet weighed down with briefcases, documents, briefing notes, tons of paper, and in the final analysis it wasn't needed. However, since I am such a believer in fullscale preparations and acutely aware of my own less than perfect arguing technique, I need the assurance of all that stuff. So I am absolutely delighted, although I know that not everyone will welcome it when it comes out. However, I can deal with that. Thank God I can cope with most things now despite moments of stress, angst etc.

At last we have finished the whole Budget and it's over to Alan now to bring it through.

There is terrible upset around about the closure of Fords of Cork, and Cork deputies are in a total whirl, naturally.

Friday
20
January

This morning we set off early for Belfast with two officials of the Department, leaving John Harris behind to pull a lot of things together for next Monday. The weather is snowy and cold.

At the Border my driver, Tom O'Flynn, handed over his gun to the Gardai as usual and an RUC car collected us and friendly Minister, Nicholas Scott [Northern Ireland Parliamentary Under-Secretary for Education] was waiting for me. We had a solid chat about possible cooperation areas. Nick Scott seems the archetypal Tory from Chelsea, 'awfully jolly', not very serious, with an elegant, cool English second wife. But I am sure there is more to him than that. He mentioned the Dowra affair when we had a drink after looking at the Osbornes in the Ulster Museum. He was at pains to convey great goodwill. I was very careful to be non-committal, exuding good vibes at him. All in all that visit was a step in the right direction and will contribute in its own small way to progress, if there is ever going to be any solution to this on-going disaster.

Belfast, or the little I was allowed to see of it, looked calm, busy, peaceful on a cold winter's day.

| Saturday |
| 21 |
| January |

Ed Walsh's proposed speech for Monday's big day is a gem. He mentions the curriculum as also having to do with 'the appreciation of the fragile beauty of an Irish village street, the enjoyment of food well cooked, the mental and physical joy of being in love . . . .' I think that's great altogether, and at the same time I wonder if I will regret his appointment when he has us all driven mad, as I am gloomily warned by the Department that he will.

| Sunday |
| 22 |
| January |

I enjoy writing this diary; it's a sort of therapy, and indeed writing generally, though I wish I was more descriptive, analytical and anecdotal—the stuff of good diaries. I must consciously try to change that.

Reverberations following the Government statement last Monday on Sinn Fein, in which we strongly condemned them. I wonder were we wise—should we have done it more subtly? I gave a long interview to Gerry Barry about that matter and nothing appeared. Maybe he didn't find anything to write about because I was so straight, boring and careful.

Having been through so much over the past several months I am beginning to see how you can run a huge Department, and how you can get and use expert advice like I have from John Harris. I don't think at this stage I'd be afraid of anything. I am going to work hard on the implementation of the Programme and the beginnings of curriculum reform, and hope that I will be seen and respected as a good Minister for Education.

| Monday |
| 23 |
| January |

We launched the Curriculum and Examinations Board at a big press conference and it all went very well indeed, with excellent media coverage and very good feeling. The whole thing, of course, was slightly nerve-racking. I wonder will that diverse collection of people really get down to work. I see it as a strong beginning for reform, and I think it is generally seen that way, but it has to be more than just a beginning. I was pleased anyway, and despite rumblings from so many different quarters it is now in place.

Today at Cabinet we got the shocking news that the Budget has been changed; apparently there were indications to Dick from Labour backbenchers that the food subsidies reduction wouldn't be accepted in the Dail, and the whole thing was re-vamped. General depression among Fine Gael Ministers; Michael Noonan sees it as the beginning of the end. I'm in a fit at the thought of the weakness it shows about future pay deals—we had compensated for the food subsidies most carefully by increases in Social Welfare. I made my point about pay again—will anyone listen and how far will I go down the road with them?

After that long and busy day I battled my way down to Aughrim through the snowy roads to find that the Fine Gael meeting was cut short; so got home relatively early at about midnight.

There is a pre-Budget air about the place but no discernible tension. I can't help suspecting the Labour Party of dirty work, even the most innocent explanation amounts to that—Garret must know that he has sown dragon's teeth or at least one tooth.

Wednesday
25
January

12.30 midnight. Home in bed at last after the Budget and the long, long voting session on it. Everything went smoothly. Fianna Fail seem subdued enough. Rumours abound again about another hassle there. My big trouble today is the ructions which Public Service Junior Minister, Joe Bermingham, is kicking up about the transfer of Primary School Buildings from the Office of Public Works to my Department. If Garret lets me down on that I will kick up murder. I spoke to him and to Dick about it and they are trying to see what they can do. Infuriating. Politics today look unattractive—the Coalition is proving not to be a great thing for the country, but the Fianna Fail alternative is worse. Oh! I dislike so many of those people and I am sure the feeling is returned with interest. Funny thing, I like most of the women in the

Dail, particularly people like Avril Doyle and Nora Owen—they're full of guts.

Fianna Fail TD Ber Cowan has died at the age of only 52. I didn't know him at all but he was a decent, quiet man by all accounts.

Thursday 26 January

Budget reaction has been generally low key and there is all sorts of wheeling and dealing going on to try to find something to give Joe Birmingham instead of Primary School Buildings. Michael Noonan is being very funny about it.

They finally sorted out the Joe Bermingham thing but not without a great deal of trouble. My next hurdle now is the big launching of the Action Programme on Monday next. I am trying to forestall and foresee any questions that might arise, so I put the senior officials through a big session of firing every possible question at them, and watching them squirm while they try to think up answers, and reminding them that I'm the one who will be in the hot seat. I hope it won't be a damp squib after all my work.

I reluctantly conceded the National Gallery and the Museum to Ted Nealon, Junior Minister (Arts and Culture) in the Taoiseach's Department; having managed to get Primary School Buildings from Joe Bermingham, I couldn't very well fight to keep the Museum in the face of Garret's wishes. I regret this because now that I have the Board set up and the Action Programme under way, I could have looked very hard at the Museum to give it a businesslike and new dynamic approach. However, what's done is done.

I'll have to target my next area: trying to deal with the selection procedure for VEC appointments. There are very queer things happening there. Politics shouldn't come into teacher appointments at all; it's quite wrong.

Sunday 29 January

I am in a fury about a very prominent *Sunday Tribune* piece about me 'topping the list' of Ministers sending out Christmas cards at taxpayers' expense, saying that I sent out 1,300. It's sickening, considering that I put in £100 of my own money for any personal ones. I will have to get that damn thing answered.

I am also sick and tired of the continuing talk in the papers about Labour 'wresting humane conditions' from the 'hard-faced, right-wing Fine Gael' and putting Fine Gael in the wrong corner altogether. Twisting and turning through all the options, it is impossible to see a way out. It is so dispiriting to be part of a group which has so much courage and honesty in the centre, and that courage and honesty are so severely tested all the time.

I had a huge, long clinic yesterday of people mostly coming from schools all over the country, finding their way to Bray, vying for attention with all the genuine constituents who get quite aggrieved as a result.

Monday **30** January

Finally in bed at 11.30 p.m. after the extremely long, involved and complicated launching of the Action Programme which went on for hours and which I really believe went well. It has had, of course, its usual mixed reaction because I don't think any of the big groups in the Education world would be generous enough to say 'well done'.

Wednesday **1** February

Tonight I was on a major *Today Tonight* programme with Mary O'Rourke. I prepared most carefully for it during the day, looking at everything inside out and upside down and as a result I had a very smooth ride indeed. Mary was strangely quiet and mild and the whole thing really went my way. Having done all that work for it I am rather tired now. It has been a full week. Everybody is pleased with me and the Action Plan was received better than I expected. I was quite surprised at Mary O'Rourke not having done her homework efficiently, and anybody who saw the programme has been congratulating me this morning.

Thursday **2** February

Now I have started a new healthy life and am going for early morning walks in an attempt to deal with my weight/stress problem. I can think as well as walk, in between trying to get the dog (Socks) not to attack animals twice as big as himself.

Went through mountains of files, letters and problems today and I had another Irish class in the Department, though I don't think I am making progress. However, it can't do me any harm.

I spoke in St Patrick's Drumcondra, ran into a mild 'demo' by students about the withdrawal of their Medical Cards and I had a good chat with them. They were all decked out in bloodstained bandages. I gave them a copy of Barry Desmond's speech—they were really quite reasonable people.

I feel better already on the new health regime and it is only day 2!

Garret actually congratulated me today on last night's television programme—is this a record?

A point to note: today Alan said very firmly to us all that there will be no Public Service pay increase this year. That will cause ructions, both in Cabinet and with the Unions, and I'll stand by him, which won't surprise anyone.

| Saturday |
| 4 |
| February |

Attended Ireland v England International Rugby match in the Committee Box and had a particularly good and friendly chat with Nicholas Scott afterwards at the tea, to which Derry came too. I always feel I must be particularly charming to Scott to compensate for all the public unpleasantness which goes on.

Huge ructions today about Prince Philip's visit to the UDR barracks in Armagh. Peter Sutherland says it is Philip himself who is the problem. It appears he is very hung-up still about poor old Mountbatten and the savage murders in Sligo four and a half years ago.

I am basking in the unexpected congratulations of one and all about the Action Programme, while dreading the *Sunday Tribune* profile tomorrow. It is a good feeling to think that I might be considered competent at last.

| Sunday |
| 5 |
| February |

The *Sunday Tribune* profile was as bad as I had expected, portraying me as arrogant, middle-class, pushy, out of touch, fumbling and unpopular, so I'm trying very hard not to be upset.

I did a brief spot on the *This Week* programme on the

Action Programme and I think it went well, although RTE for some reason didn't say at the beginning that it was going to be on. The political row goes on and on about Prince Philip's visit, Haughey weighing in on the radio in a very Republican way indeed.

| Tuesday |
| **7** |
| February |

I am just home now from what was probably the most difficult television programme I have ever done. It was all about the poor young teenage girl, Anne Lovett, who died eight days ago in a field in Granard, giving birth to a baby. It's so heart-rending that it's difficult to think about it. Nuala Fennell unfortunately rushed out with calls for a public enquiry and talked about 'squinting windows'. The Cabinet felt that I should go on the programme. Brian Farrell was strongly accusatory, but I think I coped alright. Nuala will undoubtedly be annoyed. It is all so difficult and so delicate.

I have the Department investigating what kind of counselling and pastoral care there was in that school, and particularly the history of Anne Lovett. I am gradually discovering that there is an awful lot more to that family background than we have known about; what happened was the most appalling tragedy and it is hard to see how it could have been avoided. The poor child was unfortunate from day one of her life, but what a really awful end.

Had a long talk with Rachel and Ruth arising from it and emphasised the need for total trust in us their parents. And will get some serious work done in widening the scope of sex education.

| Friday |
| **10** |
| February |

Many of us are talking about the performance of the bishops at the New Ireland Forum. Bishop Cahal Daly performed extremely well and they seem to have presented a conservative face very attractively.

On the Lovett case, the doctor did see Anne in November, and prescribed for shingles. Barry Desmond rather rashly wanted to make a statement and we were all against that. I am expecting the Department to give me a good report next Monday. The whole thing reeks of a combination of neglect, lack of perception (at best) and then a conspiracy of silence. But who was to know that her mother or someone wasn't in charge of the situation? It all goes back, alas, to the vulnerability of young people.

Nuala has infuriated Barry Desmond by a further statement in the Dail yesterday. I didn't think she had done it too badly at all—her job is impossible anyway.

My stock has perhaps begun to rise within the party. I am beginning to think it must be very low generally and of course I don't have any close friends in the party except people like Katharine Bulbulia and she isn't in Dublin often enough.

If Garret wasn't Taoiseach tomorrow, or if we had an election which we won, and if we had a new Government under Peter Barry, or Alan, or John Bruton or Michael Noonan, would I be re-appointed? Yes, I think under John or Michael, perhaps under Alan, but very doubtful under Peter. Nora Owen should certainly be a Junior Minister in my view, as should Avril, if there was any justice.

Sunday **12** February

While I work I am watching the video recording of the bishops' Session at the New Ireland Forum. It is fascinating. Mary Robinson is so impressive—scandalous really that she never made her way to Dail or Cabinet. I wonder will the obvious goodwill of everyone (with a question mark over Haughey) result in something which will be a turning point in the Northern Ireland context. What a wonderful end to Garret's political life if that would be the case.

Wednesday **15** February

Had a little chat with Martin O'Donoghue, who says that Charlie Haughey is under threat again—which might be wishful thinking. His own perspicacity is not famous but he is undoubtedly agreeable and pleasant.

Tonight I had the Fine Gael Education back-up group to the house, a group of very pleasant people. Naturally they are worried about where Education is going, and we have to thrash out a great deal about the third level part of the Action Programme.

One of my deputations today was very tricky indeed. It was about a nasty lock-out situation in Finnore, Co. Clare, concerning a deeply unpopular teacher, a picket, an alternative school and a generally complicated and seemingly intractable problem. Careful preparation, lashings of charm and clever help from Finbar O'Callaghan, Assistant Secretary, brought us to agreement which I hope will carry through. Madeleine Taylor-Quinn expressed herself as delighted with me. No kindness from her constituency colleague, Donal Carey. Brendan Daly of Fianna Fail showed subtlety and good spirit which I wouldn't have suspected him of.

| Sunday
19
February | A lot of very strange news today about the attempted bugging of Seamus Mallon. Everybody |

bemused and confused by it. Garret issued a 700-word statement which we felt was typically Garret. Anyhow, it now seems (late tonight) that the INLA or someone else was responsible. Peter Sutherland was very surprised that the Security Committee was unaware of it, and Peter Prendergast — Svengali himself — calming everything down.

Certainly it was a bizarre incident, all connected with the closing stages of the Forum, which by all accounts are very tense and very difficult, with Ray MacSharry being impossible. All will, I hope, be revealed at Cabinet tomorrow.

| Sunday
26
February | This has been such a very hassled week that there has been no diary writing. I have been out late |

every night of the week: Rotary Clubs, Endeavour Awards, Oireachtas Press Dance, Fine Gael Ministers' meetings, Dail meetings, Constituency meetings.

Uproar in the Dail this week about the bugging of Seamus Mallon. Unhappiness in Cabinet about Garret's handling of it and very straight talking.

I am pleased with my health progress. Did lots of clinics as well. Really too much activity altogether and I suppose it is not going to get better for a while.

The Oireachtas Press Gallery 'do' was last night in Killiney, and I had a little chat with Mr Haughey, who is of course erudite and charming when one meets him face to face socially. Garret was in bubbling good humour and made a pleasant and amusing speech with a little seriousness about the Forum. Haughey's speech was clever and amusing also and Tom Fitzpatrick, Ceann Comhairle, was not up to their standard.

I sat beside Raymond Smith of the *Irish Independent*. He made quite a lot of speeches to me about how he blames women for the unemployment of 'young girls'. I couldn't believe some of the stuff he came out with and had a fierce argument with him.

Found Stephen O'Byrnes of the *Irish Independent* to be a nice, intelligent man. It was quite an amusing evening and Mary Harney, who seemed to be in great good humour, was telling Garret in conversation (with just the three of us) that he was far too nice and should be more aggresive in the Dáil.

Anyway, I am now in the Sunday throes of cooking a big meal for tonight for general family members all over the place.

At Cabinet on Friday Garret gave out hell to us about an article by Geraldine Kennedy on the Cabinet in the *Sunday Press*. Jim Mitchell and John Boland condemned the disloyalty of people speaking to her at all. He seemed to be particularly hurt that we hadn't criticised his chairmanship to his face—but of course everybody has, for ages, but he never listens, and anyway he's hardly going to change his personality.

Last night I had one of the long-awaited pleasant dinners with Maurice Manning, David Maloney, Nora Owen, Tom Enright and Fintan Coogan. They are a very nice bunch indeed (several of them should be Junior Ministers). It was a good and friendly night, and I appreciated their generosity in drawing me into the group.

Sunday
4
March

Opened the splendid Arklow Musical Festival and the speech was well received. A nun is behind that astonishing success story. It went on for hours.

Monday
5
March

I spent a full day in Donegal with the Protestant community, surrounded by stern, quiet Presbyterian Ministers in long black gowns and their very quiet, settled-looking ladies. I think John Harris liked it more than I did—Methodist upbringing shows. Visited a beautiful spot called 'An Grianan' and architect Liam McCormick's beautiful little round church underneath it. It is a grim reminder of our troubles that when you go through the North it is really bad—the barbed wire, sandbags, young soldiers and machine guns—what a tragedy.

Thursday
8
March

A two-hour meeting in my office with the Conference of Major Religious Superiors—a very high-powered group—led by a quiet and nice Bishop Flynn and an aggressive and eloquent Brother Jerome Kelly of the Presentation Order, who was pushing me hard for a 'clear statement of values', which really meant that they were very deeply suspicious of me and of the whole Action Programme. They were making remarks about their 'confidence' in me but suggesting that they had a fear that 'somebody else' in Cabinet might be Minister for Education. I got Sean O'Mahoney to do most of the talking from our side because I didn't trust myself not to come out with something a bit angry, which would upset the apple cart. Sean O'Mahoney is a very clever man.

Friday
9
March

Home at midnight after speaking at the 'Dean's List' dinner at UCD School of Business Administration where I was the guest of honour. Derry came with me. Don Carroll of Carroll's cigarettes (somewhere to the right of Genghis Khan it seems to me) replied to my speech with a series of perfectly tenable-sounding remarks which, however, don't take into account the realities of politics. It was an overwhelmingly male evening. I told them they should mobilise past graduates for fundraising and lobbying.

We have had more problems with difficult or misjudged speeches from Nuala Fennell—at least they seem misjudged from inside the Cabinet room—and I believe a lot of the problem stems from a lack of definition of her job. She and I hosted a reception for Dr Thekla Beere on Thursday. Thekla is 83, looks 70, is bright, physically fit and quite inspiring. It's extraordinary that she remains the only woman who was ever Secretary of a Government Department.

This week I feel that as a Government we are sort of muddling along, not going well but not going badly. Garret is unpredictable, and of course it is a very bad thing that I worry every day on the Order of Business that he'll have forgotten something or blurt out something and sometimes it happens. Haughey looks across at him with an expression of slight disdain, or at least he tries to convey that. But Garret still has the 'good' image and the thing is that everybody knows it is true.

Next week is St Patrick's week and the Government appears mostly to be going to the States. I am being sent off to London.

Wednesday
14
March

Since I last wrote this diary, the *Sunday Independent* published a transcript of a Peter Prendergast and Geraldine Kennedy telephone conversation which apparently was tapped in 1982. A great furore broke out and Fianna Fail didn't push it as hard as I thought they might, but it is quite bad for Geraldine.

On Sunday we also had the Fine Gael Leinster Euro Convention in Goff's in Kildare, a splendid arena. The feature was a superb speech and performance by Henry Mountcharles—theatrical, strong, charming and attractive—who was then only defeated by six votes by Deirdre Bolger. He nearly swung it.

Our TD and Forum member, Nora Owen, told me the other day she is worried about the Forum, and Garret giving in too much to Fianna Fail, to get them to agree to sign it. I wonder if I could do something about that?

Saturday **17** March

Dominic McGlinchey of the INLA was captured today and extradited fairly promptly to the North.

Sunday **18** March

Last night the Irish Club affair in the posh Grosvenor House hotel here in London was extremely dull—really stiff and the speech went down like a lead balloon, despite lots of congratulations afterwards. Perhaps the raison d'être of the Club here has gone. Michael Mates MP was agreeable and, in the context of the Unionists feeling let down, didn't seem over-concerned. It was a pity not to feel one was doing something more constructive for the 'oul sod' than that dinner!

Before coming home we had dinner with Derry's cousin, Deirdre McSharry, who is a warm, friendly, family person, quite different from her public image.

Wednesday **21** March

Garret reported to us all at Cabinet about his travels last week, the very carefully rehearsed Super Levy EEC walk-out yesterday in Brussels, the Dominic McGlinchey extradition—Haughey very ratty about that in the Dail.

Apart from all the usual whizzing around Department, Dail, Parliamentary Questions, functions in the constituency, there was also a book launching and opening Tree Week for An Taisce. Then I joined Derry at the Spanish Embassy for a formal dinner with Dick Spring, Ruairi Quinn, Peter Sutherland, Sean Donlon, Michael Lillis—all very pleasant. The food was ruined by being stone cold but Luis de Jordana, the Ambassador, is charming, as is his very attractive wife, Mari Luz. Looking around the table I felt that all of us Irish politicians there had so much time and energy invested, and so much hope for the future of the country and in the context of that particular gathering, the future for Northern Ireland, that surely we have to make some ripples in history?

Monday **26** March

The work schedule is once again piling up to where it is totally ruining all family life. I suppose it culminated in having to go to four functions during the day yesterday—Sunday—none of which I was enjoying either. So I have sat down again to try and sort it out. How can one say 'no' when each group feels that its own particular function is the only one in the world?

As I write this now I am in bed in a Brussels hotel, having come over with two of my senior officials Paddy Maloney and Turlough O'Connor. Tomorrow I must wake up very early and do a lot of 'reading myself in' for this important meeting with Commissioner Ivor Richard on our new RTC funding schemes. I suppose our Education concerns are relatively small compared with the on-going hassle of the Agricultural Super Levy and the threatened breakdown of everything to do with that.

It is extraordinary how fortunes ebb and flow and people blow hot and cold according to the latest media slant, which itself is manipulated by strong PR people in all the different interest groups. I think this would be a very good Government if (a) Garret could be more tightly organized (b) if the talent in Government Departments was better (or there were more special advisers like John Harris), (c) if Labour had more guts, (d) if there were fifteen Ministers who were all chosen for talent/political savvy and no geographical and token people. Would that include or exclude me?

| Saturday |
| **31** |
| March |

A very successful meeting with Commissioner Ivor Richard. I've been in search of increased funding for the RTCs and I think that we may well manage to get an enormous injection of money (about £37 million). The result of this would be that all the RTC students would have their fees waived and would get grants depending on how far they live from the College. What I can't understand is why no Education Minister came over and did this before now?

Great! the agriculture Super Levy deal has been finalised at 4.67% and Irish priority in the future—condemned, of course, by Fianna Fail (whose Ard Fheis is on this weekend) and farmers.

A very interesting thing we are doing now in Education is our draft position paper on the Age of Entry, which I checked through today with John Harris. It is full of controversial but very good ideas and could be a big breakthrough. If only we could get rid of the unfairness of some schools having five post-primary years while others have six—and get a really good wide transition year in place, as well as persuading parents that there's no need to send little ones to school at four years of age. There's a lot to be done before we get to that point but it's great to be tackling these issues.

| Monday 2 April | A good day in Tallaght—most informative. Visiting primary schools in the morning and opening a fine sports hall in the afternoon. |

The thing about Tallaght is that the Department of Education has provided very decent school facilities for the people; some of the little children are victims of terrible inadequacies on the part of their parents and the teachers are trying to cope with that.

| Monday 9 April | Dail day and touring schools and doing a big school opening in Grange Community College, near Baldoyle. |

The most memorable part was visiting a hospital/school for the mildly to severely handicapped, mental and physical. The sight of some of the mindless, deformed bodies on the mats on the floor or floating in the pool catches at one's heart—why do we ever imagine any of our own troubles are serious? The staff and the volunteers were all cheerful, matter of fact, magnificent people and I am glad that we have jealously guarded and improved the Budget for Special Education.

| Sunday 15 April | This weekend the Labour Party Conference is on. They really have a bad case of schizophrenia. |

What would they do if they were actually in the uncomfortable position of being in a minority Government with no one else to blame?

I am sitting here preparing for the Government's discussions of the medium-term Capital Investment Programme. It is a great big worry because of the huge amount required for third level.

The conundrum of the UCD Engineering School is mind-boggling. They are looking for £40 million to build it to modern standards and they say that kind of money will be needed whether or not we build a new one. There is no question of finding that kind of money and it will have to be very much reduced.

| Tuesday |
| **17** |
| April |

Louden Ryan presented the National Planning Board's conclusions to Government this morning. It sent most of us into a state of shock because Table B predicted that, in spite of all the strong measures, unemployment would stand at 250,000 in 1987. The presentation of this Report and our comments on it took up most of the day and everybody gradually calmed down.

I went up to Slane Castle for the inaugural meeting of the Meath Fine Gael Women's Group. Found that there were some factions and tensions within the group. Lord Henry Mountcharles was there and he asked me to have a drink with Bono of U2 and his companions at the end of the evening, so I sat with them downstairs and had a good chat with them. They are certainly most impressive young fellows. They were all very interested in Education and had lots to say about it. To my amazement John Bruton eulogised me again ('courageous, dignified, wide-ranging').

Peter Barry presented us with a report on the state of affairs in Northern Ireland, reflecting the Foreign Affairs thesis that the Provos will, if nothing happens to stop them, get more than 50% of the Nationalist vote in the May '85 Local Elections, and painting a scenario of a gradual slide down to the doomsday situation. It was all quite shocking. The only (rather dim) light is the feeling that Mrs Thatcher is finally beginning to grasp this reality also and is making certain moves in the right direction. This is all very difficult, delicate and important.

The Forum drags on. Today we were given the Draft Report. It is good and should be an important step on the road.

Sunday
22
April

Last night we went to Slane Castle as guests of Henry Mountcharles for dinner. I find on closer acquaintance that Henry is very naive indeed about politics. What a pity because it would be very good if he could come down to earth. The castle is certainly astounding and he has managed it remarkably, though I think the main hall looks a bit like a hotel. He has, of course, some very fine paintings and he gave us a very nice dinner upstairs in a small baronial-type room.

Thursday
26
April

This is the Thursday of Teachers' Unions Conference week, my second such marathon. I set off at 6.15 a.m. from home on Tuesday, through the sleeping, sunny countryside, to Galway, changing into blue linen at the Galway Ryan and then on to Leisureland for the INTO session. An audience of about 1,000 and the atmosphere was not tense—why should it be, I am doing my damndest for the Primary sector. The President's speech wasn't too bad and mine was received politely enough; I suppose that's all I can expect. The long Irish bit, which I rehearsed and re-rehearsed, taped and God knows what else, went off smoothly. I even enjoyed it.

The weather is scorching in Galway.

Lunch with the INTO, then a quick walk to freshen up and get some air. Back to the hotel, dodging various pickets; sat down and re-prepared the speech for the ASTI.

Then I did several radio and television interviews before going to the ASTI dinner which—as usual with these things—was much pleasanter than expected. My speech was well-received, the only difficulty being an unexpected rabble-rousing tirade by an incoming INTO President, John Joe Connolly, a real Dublin roarer.

Yesterday, before I went to the Teachers' Union of Ireland dinner, I went to the launching of Bruce Arnold's book: *What Kind of Country?* Another very nice chat with Jack Lynch, who as usual made a point of coming over to talk to me. Garret spoke well and sincerely but a friend remarked that 'no one with so much self-doubt should be leader'.

The TUI dinner, again not as bad as expected, not too much barracking. The Vice-President's speech wasn't as insulting as last year's. I had warned my officials that if it passed a certain level of rudeness I would certainly get up and walk out but I judged it not to be necessary. The support from his audience was not too warm and many of the guests sat in silence, not applauding his tirade.

I suppose all in all you might say the week was a draw between the teachers and myself. Their 28% salary demand hasn't done them any good.

I think all my interviews on radio and television sounded reasonable, reasonably good-humoured and reasonably concerned.

Friday
11
May

The most significant development this week has been the historic discussion at Cabinet about Garret's response to the British overtures which were made on 1 March. A Memorandum came before us to approve of opening negotiations on the 'joint authority' model. Some were totally opposed to this on the grounds that it might mean abandoning the unitary state and confederalism and might involve our security forces north of the border. However, agreement was reached on the Memorandum. Everyone felt pent up and anxious about it. The fundamental feeling was that we had to do something; that this arrangement would be the very most we could hope to achieve; and that we must strike while Thatcher is in a responsive mood. My own strong view is that on this matter Garret deserves the support which he has wanted for such a long time.

Incidentally, I got VAT removed from sanitary towels.

Saturday
12
May

I'm glad to see that Senator Eoin Ryan has come out with yet another statement taking a different position to that of Haughey on the Forum and on any forthcoming British/Irish discussions. There are denials also by 'a Government spokesman' that there are any discussions on joint authority with the British. There is so much high level and tortuous media manipulation, diplomatic double-talk and all sorts of things going on,

105

that one must assume that Garret, Peter Prendergast, Michael Lillis and Dick Spring know what they are at and are following a very carefully thought-out course.

| Sunday |
| 20 |
| May |

Garret was looking grey and worn out at Cabinet on Thursday and also on Friday. A week of worry about the economy, about the leadership. Education worries on a broad front, TDs pressing me on a number of insoluble problems.

| Monday |
| 21 |
| May |

Managed a complete day until 7 p.m. in the office—a hard slog of paperwork and catching up on developments, policy reforms, files. Of course it all made me come home full of frets and worries about the intractable problems, but the unusual—and too rare—pleasant evening at home cleared the mind. They tell me I'm the first Minister to give so much time to the Department, which is queer because I worry about not giving it enough.

| Tuesday |
| 29 |
| May |

An air of desperation and gloom has come over me again, although I admit it only to Derry and myself. It comes from a deepening worry about Garret, who seems to exist in a whirl of over-demanding activity, sometimes leading to mistakes, or damaging 'obiter dicta'. I work so hard and put up with so much, that more and more frequently I ask myself what it is all for. How can we achieve if the Government itself isn't organised and purposeful?

Yesterday, Monday, I did one of the things which gives a feeling of rare pleasure—the Dalkey Multi-denominational School opening in brilliant sunshine. A lovely feeling of a real breakthrough, smashing children and nice speeches. I am proud to have encouraged that initiative from day one, and for once I got a little credit for it. Those people have put so much into that school!

Had to spend all day Saturday in Abbeyleix with the quite pleasant Charlie McDonald, canvassing the people of Laois for the By-Election.

Supper later at home with Brian and Sue, then a dash back to Co. Laois. After-Mass speeches in Borris-in-

Ossory, Knockaroo and Killismeestie—I think I was alright, at least they all stopped, were polite, and listened. Charlie McDonald was well organised with his microphone etc.

I had a day in Dunlavin and Donard in Co. Wicklow on Friday. Prize-givings in both places and I hope that they were all pleased and encouraged—at least they said so.

An extraordinary incident in the Dail on Thursday, which was Education Estimates day. John Wilson of Fianna Fail, roared across the House that 'sectarian advice' is being brought into the Department of Education,—a very direct and obvious reference to John Harris, who was actually sitting in the House. That led to a big row which involved me demanding apologies from Wilson. On Tuesday afternoon more roaring and bombast and no explanation. I was furious.

Wednesday **30** May

20th Wedding Anniversary. I find it hard to think of myself as anyone who's 20 years married. Derry and I must be two of the luckiest people ever. All our endeavours have succeeded, our children are normal and happy, we are happily married to each other and we have our health. All that should be cause for thanksgiving to whatever deity one believes in—and what do politics really matter?

Sunday **3** June

Home from the State Banquet for Ronald Reagan in Dublin Castle, which I suppose must be described as an historic occasion. Elegance and some excitement, tinged with a slight reserve and ruefulness on account of the mixed feelings in Ireland about it all. It was done extremely well and I think I looked okay, if only I didn't feel so plump! Garret made a very good speech, suitably light but touching the right note. Ronald Reagan and Nancy looked exactly as they do on television. He is erect, wrinkled, but ruddy, lively-faced. She is very small and thin, pretty and elegant, but with that fixed vacant expression which is so peculiar. When I was introduced to them in the VIP reception line the President launched into quite a discussion: 'So pleased to meet you,

Mrs Hussey. I've heard a lot about your Education reforms
and understand you are particularly working on the
Curriculum; of course you know at home we are quite
worried about our Education system' etc. The fact that he
was sufficiently well briefed and remembered to say all
that took me somewhat by surprise. Nancy just shook my
hand glacially. All in all, despite the bloody security
everywhere—which was obtrusive and annoying—it was
good. There were some quite big demonstrations in
Dublin against Reagan but no violence, thank goodness. I
feel the Gardai over-reacted.

| Monday |
| 4 |
| June |

Reagan addressed the Joint Session of the Dail
and Senate today which was rather marred by the
shouting of my male colleagues at the Workers
Party and Tony Gregory when they stood up and spoke
(which they shouldn't have) just as Reagan was beginning. His speech was long and international mostly,
strong on anti-nuclear stuff, weak on Central America, but
it was undoubtedly an important speech. Nancy sat in the
Distinguished Visitors' Gallery, all in Kelly green, Reagan's eyes searching for her before he spoke, warm
glances exchanged.

The whole Reagan weekend has been odd. A mixture of
television success, worries about demonstrations, Garret
performing extraordinarily well, security gone mad, sen-
timentality and commercialism in Ballyporeen which was
a bit embarrassing.

| Friday |
| 8 |
| June |

A searing hot day and a long sweaty drive to
Athlone where I called into our Examination
Branch, having to meet a very stiff deputation
who were suspicious about my Curriculum and Examinations Board, fearing for their future. Then on to Galway to
address the Catholic Primary School Managers Association. The speech went well. Dinner with my Flavin
cousins in Galway; Jim, who is on the UCG staff, in his
quiet way objected to the Reagan conferring in UCG and
didn't go to the ceremony.

Very sad to hear today that a school bus crashed in Leitrim. A little seven-year-old boy was killed and others injured. I have just rung Peter Baldwin about it to get information and to send messages of sympathy to the family. The poor unfortunate parents must be shattered.

Saturday **16** June	A long day on Thursday visiting polling stations which were all deathly quiet, with a low poll, standing outside St Fergal's on the Florence Road.

Very tired yesterday when we had a long Cabinet meeting which was very disjointed because tally results kept coming in from all over the country and upsetting things, particularly when it became apparent that Labour was doing badly and Fine Gael was doing well. Michael Noonan's jubilation about the Limerick vote was ill-concealed. Peter Sutherland in a fit of activity, giving out murder 'sotto voce', passing notes; he veers between rage, frustration and laughter. So it was a Cabinet much like any other.

Today I did the radio *Saturday View* post-mortem, all quite low-key. It went quite well I think.

The amazing facts of the Euro Election results are sinking in and I am delighted that Fine Gael seems to have held its own, even doing slightly better than that. Quite, quite astonishing and all very nail-biting of course because the count begins on Monday. Mary Banotti is in there with a great chance. Two in Munster looking definite.

Derry is in a welter of facts and figures and everyone is trying to conjure up those extra seats out of fairly complete tallies. However, it is immensely encouraging that the Fine Gael organisation seems to have worked well on the whole. The Labour people are in a fit; I feel it might exacerbate our difficulties. Alan sees that too. Where will it all end? 50% of the electorate stayed home, which is not really surprising.

Thursday **21** June	I am in bed here in the Lissard House Hotel in Skibbereen, a lovely old place, having been at the Irish Vocational Education Association Confer-

ence last night.

Sad, sad President, Jack McCann, who is dying on his feet, was there, obviously for the last time. My speech (reworked, shortened, mangled up) went well. It was made less contentious for the sake of poor Jack. As we exchanged gifts with each other, he kissed me twice and his gaunt, yellow, grey face was cold and wet with sweat. Poor, poor man. He is a fine person.

Dinner, served in the school hall, was therefore quite difficult, sitting as I was between Jack and the quiet Monsignor Daly.

The European Elections were a triumph for Fine Gael in Dublin and Munster. Fianna Fail did well in Leinster and Connacht/Ulster. Mary Banotti's win was lovely. Labour lost all seats—deservedly—they did no work. But life is now tense and Cabinet difficult, with Dick, it seems to me, thrown slightly off balance and very voluble, rumours in the air and Garret trying to calm things.

| Monday |
| 25 |
| June |

Today I launched the Department's Equality Seminar at 9.30 in the morning, to a disappointingly small audience, and then I launched our exciting Discussion Paper on the 'Ages for Learning' at a press conference. All sorts of contentious issues have to be raised in it and I hope we will make good decisions on them.

Garret is off in Fontainebleu at the EEC Summit doing what he loves to do most, while at home he finds it impossible to do or get anyone else to do what he likes least—like governing the country. An opinion poll yesterday showed Garret behind Haughey in everything except honesty, and most people fed up with both of them. John Kelly has made another speech about the need for Fine Gael and Fianna Fail to declare a truce and 'come together on a programme of progress and reform'.

| Saturday |
| 30 |
| June |

Continued speculation about the EEC Commissionership. My name has actually been mentioned, purely and simply because Wicklow might be winnable in a By-Election, no other reason, alas!

The Adjournment Debate on the Taoiseach's Estimate was marked by another attack on Haughey—but Garret is right to do it, even if it would be better if someone else did. No one pays much attention when I do it.

But John Kelly made a blistering attack on 'this pocket Mussolini—this Duce', his manipulation of the Forum etc. John has the most amazing gift of colourful language, always the apt word.

All the time I worry what we are doing to recapture the switched-off and turned-off young working class urban population, who neither understand nor care about our international financial problems and who look blankly and balefully at you on doorsteps when you try to explain it. They ask how they are to get a job, how they're to live if they have a job, why they're paying such huge tax, why 'others'—dole drawers, self-employed farmers—'get away with murder'.

Barry Desmond is really getting quite deaf. He is smaller, more odd-looking and is really quite a character. Undoubtedly clever, hard-working and quite formidable.

| Sunday |
| **8** |
| July |

This week we had Wednesday and Friday Parliamentary Party meetings in the scorching weather in Malahide. A long litany of complaints mainly centering on indecisiveness and lack of leadership. Alan explained the appalling financial difficulties ahead and that shocked and upset a lot of them. Did they think it was any different?—where have they been?

Friday afternoon's session was on social legislation. Oliver J. made one of his usual shocking outbursts, condemning all us 'liberals', as misguided and malicious, and out to ruin the party.

At about 10 p.m. on Thursday I was sitting in my office when the door opened and Garret came in and said he 'needed to talk to someone' about Nuala Fennell and a row he had just had with her because of her remarks about the Judge who said controversial things in dismissing the Eileen Flynn appeal. Anyway, we talked about it at some length and I think he was glad of the chat. He said I had calmed him anyway. Nuala may be hasty, but Garret never thought out her job—if I'd got her job I would have left it in a puff of smoke ages ago. Anyway, judging by her calm demeanour the next day, he must have sorted it out.

| Tuesday **10** July | Long Cabinet session. Some tensions, with Garret working very hard at keeping us together. Dick getting very uptight about the White Paper on |

industrial policy, John Bruton tense but controlled; it all seems to be going to survive.

| Saturday **14** July | Yesterday I spent a half-day at Jack McCann's funeral in Daingan in Offaly. Poor old Jack. He was a lovely man and he's a bad loss. Naturally |

there were thousands of people at it and the IVEA laid on a lunch. Unfortunately, I couldn't stay for it because I had to get back to deal with a whole bundle of items and to go on the 6.30 p.m. News to answer Brother Declan Duffy's diatribe at lunchtime.

In the US Walter Mondale has picked Geraldine Ferraro as Vice-Presidential candidate. To use a cliché, that's an historical breakthrough and she seems a really together lady. I must send her a telegram. I would vote Democrat anyway, but more so now. I wonder would this have any hope of changing their chances—Reagan is so far ahead he may not be caught.

The dining hall in Trinity College got very badly damaged by fire last night. What a great shame.

| Tuesday **17** July | Had a great long chat on the phone with Garret on Saturday. He rang about 6.30 p.m. Among other things he told me he had decided on Peter |

Sutherland for Commissioner—to my great delight. I told him that I wanted to pick Justin Keating as Chairman of the NCEA [National Council for Education Awards] and he was pleased about that because of not being able to give Justin the Commissionership. He also told me not to be worrying about taking a holiday in September and that I should go ahead and do it. He is concerned about third level and about Maynooth. He is right to be worried about the third level because Finance consider third level student participation to be 'discretionary'. He was in good form and told me he was very pleased indeed with my handling of my job ('very skillful'). As regards 'others' he doesn't seem to be pleased with, I told him that I didn't want to hear about the others—not that he was going to tell me anyway.

Thursday 19 July

There was an earthquake at 7.56 this morning— quite dramatic really.

Saturday 21 July

My press conference on Monday to announce the new European Social Fund for the RTCs, which I won in Brussels, was quite well reported. They should be dancing on the streets—what a hope!

We've had two heavy sessions in Garret's office on the Education Estimates, the first on Monday for three hours. Garret and Bill Hyland, the chief statistician from my office, wallowed deep in confusing statistics about third level. Anyway, at the end of it all and a lot of worry and nail-biting, we agreed a figure which Paddy Maloney, my top third level official, thinks we will survive. But it is only round one, and God knows what we will have to go through before it's all over.

All-day Cabinet yesterday. We made some progress alright. Poor Barry Desmond was in the firing line but he is very skillful at defending himself. Anyway, Garret had taken any reference to Education off the list, which doesn't solve anything really because Finance and ourselves can't decide on the base line figure. I notice a very co-operative spirit from Dick Spring—is there a shift there?

I spoke to Peter Sutherland about the Commissionership and how delighted I am about it. He seems pleased himself. Austin Deasy worries that Peter will not be 'political' enough.

A lot of pressures caused by the Government's decision to halve food subsidies. Last night I was at a FG North

Wicklow Executive in Bray and made a strong speech on the realities of foreign debt servicing and told them about the food subsidies. I was taken aback by the fury of the reactions of some of the relatively well-off people. Some Fine Gael people, I'm sorry to say, have the attitude: 'Why don't we go mad for four years, and get re-elected'. But the majority are sound and co-operative.

Garret has gone off on his holidays today at last. He really deserves that.

Saturday
4
August

Appalling flak going on about the food subsidies. The hysteria from Michael D. Higgins, Joe Higgins of the Labour left, John Carroll, the housewives, you name it, as well as Fianna Fail's Michael O'Kennedy being extremely rude on radio. The media are totally gone off mad; the whole attack is pointed straight at the Labour Party. Dick Spring was on radio yesterday evening. He was extremely strong in support of the Government and determined-sounding about the country. I am listening now to *Saturday View*. John Boland is on and he is very calm and good, as is Justin Keating.

Justin came to see me during the week canvassing for the Commissioner job. We decided at Cabinet not to make any decision until 6th September because Pat Cooney is away.

I am hoping that Garret won't find himself under any unsustainable pressures by then. He is so very painstaking about ensuring that everyone gets a fair deal. The country doesn't really deserve him. Maybe he will be proved right in the end.

Thursday
9
August

As the week went on it became clear that it was the most appalling mistake for Garret not to have gone on the media last Thursday night on the food subsidies thing. I spoke to the returned Peter Prendergast tonight. He says that Joe Jennings wanted Garret to go on television, and that John Boland never asked Garret, and since John Boland was put in charge of media relations Garret felt he had to be guided by him. Anyway, the flak flew all the time this week, with the Labour Ministers getting most of it from their own people.

On Tuesday an old friend, Tom White, — now Archbishop and Pro-Nuncio in Ethiopia — came to lunch in my office. He is very liberal, very interesting, but depressed about the terrible political/social situation out there, caught between Russian support and starving millions. Somewhat to my surprise, he told me he had had a chat with Garret, who eulogised me — Goodness!

Saturday **11** August

Here we are at 8.30 p.m. in the middle of Lough Derg, in one of the Emerald Star boats, with Andrew and some of his friends. Lough Derg is looking magnificent in the setting sun tonight — swans abound.

The day started in Dublin with Denis Johnston's funeral. Following a very beautiful service in St Patrick's Cathedral, he was buried in the Cathedral Close. Shelah Richards, his former wife, decided not to sit with the family — which, I suppose, had to be, but seemed rather strange. Dick Spring and myself were the only Government representatives.

Terribly bad news has come about a young Garda murdered by armed robbers early yesterday.

Monday **13** August

There was a very nasty incident in Belfast last night. The RUC tried to 'lift' Martin Galvin of NORAID and in the ensuing melee a man was killed by a plastic bullet. Peter Barry issued a statement looking for an enquiry. I don't know if I approved of that but what can you do?

This morning I left Garrykennedy, collected by Tom the driver, and went to the funeral of Detective Garda Hand. It was a sultry day, an enormous funeral and of course a desperately sad affair. Garret came back from France for it and Dick postponed his holiday too. Michael Noonan's break has been totally interrupted as well. I think a lot of my colleagues were upset by some blaming of the

Government in the media. Afterwards we went for soup and sandwiches to Pat Cooney's solid old house on the Shannon outside Athlone, with Liam Kavanagh, Barry Desmond and Peter Sutherland.

Got back to the boat here in Mountshannon at about 6 p.m.

This short week is quite idyllic on the Shannon and on the lakes, with warm, not quite sunny weather, beautiful still water and lots and lots of lovely space. However, it seems to be a prelude to a stormy time in Government, as we set about preparing our new National Plan, which is looming in my mind as a big hurdle to be crossed in terms of attacks on my Education budget. Just when things were beginning to look under control, moving well, a new spirit about in the Education world, coping totally with previous cutbacks and I think there is generally respect for what I am trying to do. I'll have to fend off any really damaging policy decisions but I feel that Garret will understand their implications.

I'll have to offer as much as I possibly can, of course, to be co-operative and helpful. If only they'd come to terms with the real issue which is pay.

There are still a lot of recriminations — low-key — about last week's food subsidy debacle. John Boland seems to be the villain for mishandling the communications, but in reality we are all to blame. However, Peter Prendergast, who always sees an angle, says that one good thing is that 'they're not talking about the actual prices at all, they're talking about how it was handled or mishandled'.

Garret looked very tired today. He says the weather is bad in France. He spent last night working on the Plan — on which he pins his hopes of settling us down and governing for the allotted span.

It seems that the Gardai have made a big breakthrough in the matter of the Hand murder. They have found the money and the weapons. They have the men or some of them and it appears to be the IRA. There are on-going ructions in the North, the RUC under fire generally, Peter Barry's statement doesn't appear to have been that wrong

116

after all. Jim Prior has come out in criticism of the RUC, but I'm annoyed with all the double-talk about Martin Galvin, who deliberately went to Belfast to flaunt his fundraising for the IRA in the United States to outfit the kind of crew who killed Garda Hand last week. My hope is that Thatcher realizes she'd better get something happening in the London/Dublin post-Forum talks before the IRA takes over the show.

| Friday 17 August | Last night we moored again at Kilgarvan, which we found to be the most beautiful place on the whole trip, peaceful, beautifully open to the lake, |

lots of fishing opportunities. I suppose it would be very exposed in bad weather.

Derry and I walked a fair bit and then went to Byrne's little restaurant for a very pleasant meal. The area is gentle, rolling, lots of nice hidden houses and combine harvesters working away late into the dusk.

Now I am sitting on the deck here at Kilgarvan, the sun shining a little weakly, but it is warm. Derry has gone walking to Ballinderry. The sun is glinting off the water, the tall reeds shimmering among them, someone in the distance seems to be shooting—but maybe it is a bird frightener for a crop? The sky is blue and white and there is a fresh breeze. All in all, this is a perfect day so far.

The three youngsters seem to be enjoying themselves hugely and I very much hope it has been a success for Andrew, which was the object of the exercise.

| Wednesday 22 August | News from the US is that Geraldine Ferraro is in terrible trouble over her husband's finances; it's awful how she is being hounded and the husband |

seems less than supportive, to put it mildly. Reagan looks like romping home handily.

2 a.m. Two potentially difficult meetings today went alright—I may be able to deal with the school transport problem in Valleymount and as for the Joint Managerial Body's position on examination fees, I hope we can go towards them on that.

Lunch with George Birmingham, who's always worried about the political situation, about the Plan, about the Parliamentary Party and the state of disaffection. Since I agree with him about the problems and about their causes, without having the answers, I don't think it was all that much help to him.

| Friday **31** August | Cabinet yesterday and today. Today's was a 'special' on Northern Ireland with the next stage of the discussions pending. It all seems a big |

gamble, very worrying and very delicate and needs a lot of teasing out all the way through. Articles 2 and 3 [of the Constitution] in the balance. I don't believe we could get enough from the British in the Agreement to fight a referendum on these Articles, if we decided to take it on.

I distributed my Wicklow Newsletter this week, pushing it into a million doors, back aching. It got a very good reception on the whole, but apparently half of the Fine Gael organisation in Wicklow is fighting me and the rest fighting with each other.

There are considerable ructions still going on about the Government generally, Mervyn Taylor is roaring and shouting, as is Frank Prendergast. Austin Deasy and John Bruton made strong speeches simultaneously, which were immediately condemned by the Workers Party and the unhappy Labour lads. Fianna Fail have gone very quiet these days and why wouldn't they? I wonder if Garret has any idea of how impossible it is going to be to get agreement on the kind of cuts we want during the Cabinet marathon starting on 7 September?

| Wednesday **5** September | A huge clinic in Bray on Monday, which was absolute bedlam, and I have a health problem which is going to mean hospitalization for a day |

on Friday, and all sorts of preparations during the week before it. I never had health problems before I started this job.

Meanwhile, our new National Plan meetings loom up like icebergs around *The Titanic*. Garret is most anxious to get agreement on a Plan so that Dick will stick by it and we can move on for another three years, together.

Wicklow Fine Gael needs a great big shot in the arm, so I have to work on that and I had meetings every night this week.

| Thursday |
| 6 |
| September |

The day was long and difficult, tension high, Garret low, Alan with even more desperate news about this year's borrowing shortfall and the added strain of the Commissionership to be decided. Dick became very stubborn about the new Attorney General to replace Peter Sutherland and I exploded, which Dick didn't like at all. That made Garret even more fed-up.

We had rather a tense Fine Gael Ministers' Meeting at 6 p.m. so that we could discuss the relations with Labour and the implications of the new National Plan. Peter Sutherland is getting a bit uptight about the messing that's going on about the Commissionership, and who's to blame him? I am his staunch ally anyway.

Garret, despite his crushing worries found time to be kind to me about my health — not that I have told him the gruesome details. These difficult days of working our way through very long Estimates and discussions are really a great strain. Derry and I are supposed to go to Crete on Monday week — what a strange outlook, I can't see past tomorrow morning, these tests, and then the next few days.

I think that the problem that Dick has is that if we can't put something in there for his people, not only would he lose a vote in the Dail but he would also lose his leadership in the next Election. My view is that no matter what happens, an Election would result in the eventual coming in of the IMF and the people — especially the poor people — would be much worse off than they are at present or than they would be because of anything we would do to them; and Fine Gael, Coalition and all, will be held responsible — and will be responsible — for not being able to govern and control when we got a mandate.

But that's only half the truth, because the total immorality of Fianna Fail's behaviour in the face of the country's problem is what is really behind the difficulties we face. I look at them, or meet them in the corridors, and can't understand how they've shut their minds and their consciences to the state of the country. Surely some of them must at least question what they're at?

Most of today was spent on the economic scenario, which is as grim as ever, but it could be dealt with if there was very decisive and united handling of it or if there was a decent response from Fianna Fail. Underlying all this is a fear in the back of my mind that stupid or hasty Education decisions could be made.

So I spent three hours in stuffy old Marlborough Street, closeted with the top officials discussing our figures. John Bruton rang me from the States at the office, to get a run-down on the scene and to ask me if he should come home. I told him the set-up but I couldn't advise him about coming home—I told him too that he wouldn't be a particularly calming influence, which he ruefully accepted.

Friday 7 September

I had my major medical tests this morning in St Vincent's Hospital (kind nuns whisking me in and out secretly) which were not the slightest bit pleasant, so I won't dwell on them. Anyway, Glory Hallelujah!! all clear, all clear. The worry was always there.

Then I dashed in and spent the rest of the day at the Cabinet meeting, high tension caused by the Commissionership/Attorney General crux. Peter Sutherland up to ninety. I got very angry and told my Fine Gael colleagues that I couldn't wear any reneging on Peter. The whole thing is not looking good at all and makes me dislike Dick at the moment. I feel that Garret is too understanding and sympathetic to him. Behind and underneath it all Garret desperately wants to stay in Government and who can blame him? If we collapse, apart from the damage to the country, the person most damaged will be Garret, his plans for Northern Ireland in tatters and his leadership gone.

Tuesday
11
September

This morning I was delighted to accept the Curriculum and Examinations Board's first document, which they have got out in double quick time. Then I went to Liam O'Flaherty's funeral mass.

Over to the Council Chamber at 3.30, where Fine Gael Ministers had a desultory enough chat about our National Plan. Then we had another go at sorting out Garret about the Commissionership and succeeded, because much later in the day it was finally decided and Dick accepted the decision.

Then the Cabinet had an interminable, or it seemed interminable, discussion about CIE. It only took an hour and a half but it seemed forever. In a way it was high comedy but it's difficult sometimes to look at things that way. Austin gave me a note at 9 o'clock saying 'What are they talking about? cutting CIE? giving more to CIE? abolishing CIE?' and then at 10.30 p.m. he wrote another note to me saying 'I'm more confused than ever'. This somehow got passed around and several of us were reduced to slightly hysterical laughter, which was perhaps a release of tension after all the difficulties of recent days.

Saturday
15
September

Today I went on *Saturday View* again. It was rather a dull and bitty programme, but I think I kept my end up and the Government's end up. Then a one and a half hour meeting with Garret in Palmerston Road, to which I brought Sean O'Mahoney and John Harris and we had a considerable discussion on Education Estimates. I had a short, private talk afterwards with Garret about the Higher Education Authority chairmanship and the wider difficulties we face. He was quite cheerful, why I can't imagine! Then three hours back down in Marlborough Street with Peter Baldwin, discussing loose ends and problems, so I hope everything is being left fairly well under control—I leave on Monday for a fortnight's holiday in Crete.

There is an air of great worry about, Fianna Fail obviously scenting severe problems for us and licking their chops. Garret will be a hero if he gets us through this because the problems appear at times to be quite, quite insurmountable: land tax, rates, food subsidies, 1985 borrowing crisis, Labour being promised 'consultation' before the Plan, and Fine Gael backbenchers up in arms.

| Thursday **20** September | On holiday in Crete. What kind of holiday is it when I am worried all the time about what's going on back home? At the moment I am in a |

total rage because I have been on the phone to John Harris and he tells me that the Cabinet is now considering all Alan's list of Education cuts, despite everything I have done and said. I can't understand why this has happened after my long talk with Garret.

I am now waiting to be rung by Garret, who is entertaining the Prime Minister of Spain at home.

Alarms and excursions and Greek telephone systems breaking down, and inaudible distant shouts from Peter Baldwin, and then Garret; but it all seems to be okay and I am weak with relief.

Dinner tonight with some people we met in the hotel was interrupted by these calls and I couldn't concentrate at all on polite conversation. It really was quite funny trying to take a call in the back kitchen of the hotel, with staff banging pots and pans, and Garret obviously quite relaxed and ready to have a good chat, not realising my situation on the other end. He told me that the Parliamentary Party meeting had gone very well and then he wanted to have a chat all about the cultural side of Crete! The only worry I have now is the big increase in school transport charges and the apparent decision by Cabinet to tell schools about the six-year senior cycle only from next year. I'll have to control education spending like the Iron Lady (if only the education world knew what I've saved them from, they'd be down on their knees).

The final date for launching the Plan has been fixed for October 1st—I wonder will it be shifted again?

<table>
<tr><td>Saturday
6
October</td></tr>
</table>

It's the weekend of the Fine Gael Ard Fheis.

It has been an amazing week, which saw the Government rising like a phoenix from the ashes, on the booster of the famous Plan *Building on Reality*.

Our departure from Crete was delayed by twenty-four hours—the aircraft broke down at Heraklion airport; we finally arrived in Dublin at about 1.45 p.m. on Tuesday. I was met by Liam Lane, the Secretary of the Department, John Harris and Peter Baldwin, then zoomed into town trying to read the Plan quickly in the car, and went straight to a formal and slightly theatrical affair in Iveagh House where the Government solemnly faced leaders of industry, Unions, farmers, semi-States etc. and produced the Plan. Luckily, I was wearing respectable navy (but no stockings and white shoes). Anyhow, the Plan seems to have the right mix of realism and new ideas, and generally good news for Education, with a good increase in capital and without any severe cuts on the current side. Then I went down to Marlborough Street and had a press conference; the nerve of me! The only worry was whether or not the increases in school transport charges were what the Government had actually agreed. A good reception all round and quite a relief that it's over. Of course, it won't stop all the loud demands for more money particularly from FF.

So the Cabinet early on Wednesday morning met in high good humour. Peter Sutherland told me that while I was away the strains and tensions had been very bad, with some extraordinary behaviour, and some quite bad scenes, and I am thanking my stars that I wasn't there.

Worked and re-worked my Ard Fheis speech, rehearsed it, transferred it to cards and the result of all that was a good speech, well delivered, and—to my amazement—a standing ovation from the smallish Friday night crowd. They seem to have forgotten the whole low period of school transport charges.

Sat beside Garret for a while. He was very pleased with me and said 'You've done more in two years than three

Ministers for Education put together'. Will he ever realise that people need the odd words of praise like that?

Then we had the, by now, regular Ard Fheis Wicklow Fine Gael party at home and most of the faithful came. All very exhausting indeed and we didn't get to bed until 3 a.m. or so; and then back down to the Ard Fheis this morning. I feel much more confident this year, though I still worry about being a bit of a loner.

Something that's on my mind at the moment is whether the excellent Noel Lindsay, who has gone back to the World Bank, will apply for the job of Secretary of the Department which will become vacant shortly. I had enquiries made in New York and I gather he will be applying, though not without some hesitation.

Garret has relaxed considerably, now that the Plan is behind him. He has slipped very far down in the opinion polls and is no longer everybody's favourite good person but generally considered now, I think, as a good-hearted, brainy, very well-intentioned man, who can't be totally relied on and who lacks steel. I wonder can he be rehabilitated in public opinion or can he rehabilitate himself? There's a lot of talk about Peter Barry and a lot of speculation about Garret possibly stepping down. It has been suggested that Garret should be made special Minister for the North of Ireland and step down from being Taoiseach. While that's not a bad idea, I think the best thing would be if he can come back strongly and assert himself, lead us successfully to 1987, then step down a few months before an election, taking the North of Ireland job and putting . . . who . . ? in as Taoiseach.

Sunday 7 October

Garret's Ard Fheis speech went down well. He is not an orator but it was solid enough and received, of course, with the usual ecstasy by the capacity crowd which turned up. His real triumph was the Open Forum this morning, where he excelled himself in an answer to Mrs Bonar of SPUC on the topic of sex education. Generally he has had a very good Ard Fheis.

Saturday
13
October

The bad news has come from the United States that Noel Lindsay has been offered wonderful things by the World Bank and won't be coming back for the Secretary interviews.

Looking around at the farewell party for Liam Lane (retiring Secretary of the Department), I felt depressed as I wondered how we could possibly achieve what we want to achieve. The Secretary's speech was stiff, old-fashioned, without much humour, but quite touching and it had a certain old-world charm when he spoke about his roots in rural Cork, just beside Shanagarry. He has been an upright, solid and loyal civil servant.

On Thursday at Trinity College, where I went to speak to Fine Gael's Freshers' Week meeting, I was barracked by students (but no one actually threw anything). Then dashed up to Belfast to speak to the Irish Association on the position of women in Ireland. The RUC protection was as tight as ever. I invited our RUC escort to stop somewhere on the road to have a chat and a drink. They brought us to the Culloden Hotel in stockbroker territory outside Belfast. It was interesting to hear a bit about their life. Two solid youngish men, caught in a dangerous and dispiriting job, they were depressing about the possibility of progress.

Today, Saturday, Liam Lane came to see me to tell me that my new Department Secretary will be Declan Brennan from the Department of the Public Service, who, according to Liam Lane, will be first-class. Since the Noel Lindsay disappointment I am sort of fatalistic about it and I trust that the person this high-powered new committee has picked will be good.

But the big shock and worry of the week was a bomb in the Brighton hotel used by Mrs Thatcher and the Tory Party at their Conference. Horrible scenes, Mrs Thatcher rising majestically to the occasion, the IRA claiming responsibility (Gerry Adams condoning it), Norman Tebbit and his wife injured quite badly, and an other MP and two MPs' wives killed. The whole thing is very shivery, middle-of-the-night stuff. Garret, while deeply sympathising, is insisting that he and Mrs Thatcher won't be put off doing what they intend to do. The grim reality is that you can't stop people doing that kind of thing if they really want to, unless we all live locked up in a cage or an armoured car. Even with all the security in the North, they still have bombs and murders everywhere. The aim of the IRA is the breakdown of normal politics, hence the attempt to destroy any rapport between two democratic Governments; they don't consider any of us to have done right by the North and consider that we have no rights there.

| Tuesday |
| **16** |
| October |

I went on a horrible live television programme from twelve to one o'clock on Sunday. RTE had a panel which included Michael Farrell, who seemed heavily sympathetic to the Provos, Giollaiosa O'Liadha, USI [Union of Students in Ireland] president, and a British National Union of Mineworkers heavy—they all launched into a concerted attack on Thatcher, McGregor, the British police. Brid Rogers, who was also on the panel, was voluble on the North but on nothing else, so I was in a somewhat difficult position—it was all awful because it was hardly my responsibility to defend Thatcher, but RTE had a very unbalanced panel. So someone had to do it.

Rather difficult to break the news of the new Secretary to all the Assistant Secretaries in the Department. Some of them were particularly resentful and bitter and I was quite surprised at an outburst from one of the senior officials. Is this new appointments system causing a lot more problems than it is solving? It certainly has upset things in Education just when I'm getting things under control and need their enthusiasm.

| Saturday |
| **20** |
| October |

Dinner last night, which was specially set up to arrange an 'informal' contact between the Provost of Trinity, Bill Watts, and myself. He wanted to talk to me about Trinity's particular problems.

Cabinet met several times on Thursday and I got agreement, though not without difficulty, to appoint Liam Lane as Chairman of the Higher Education Authority.

In the Dail this week Garret closed the debate on the new National Plan but I wasn't pleased with his speech. Most of it was good stuff but it seemed to me that there was an excessive amount of sermonising in it and also that it was somewhat self-righteous.

He had a triumph during the week at something he does extraordinarily well—dealing on an 'ad lib' off-the-cuff basis with a great crowd of students in UCD and also impressing people greatly at the Dublin Chamber of Commerce, all on the same day.

| Thursday |
| 25 |
| October |

Imperial Hotel, Tralee—the end of the first night of my Kerry marathon. In fact, it is 2 a.m. on 26 October.

After a week of tiring days and nights, this is my first taste of the Kerry North constituency. Tom drove us down fast and we had a quick drink at the Shannon Bar in Tarbert, where the local drinkers did double-takes at the sight of me.

Since the week has involved work every night without break and an average 15-hour work schedule, I can't imagine what it must be like to have a normal job!

Met J.B. Keane during the evening—unfortunately the decibel level of the band made it impossible to talk to him. As Senator Jimmy Deenihan pulled me and tugged me around the room, shaking what seemed thousands of hands, I was struck by the plainness of the men, their lack of polish and grooming, and the extraordinary difference of the women, who were well turned-out and smart. I suppose I got out reasonably early at about 1.30 a.m.

| Friday |
| 26 |
| October |

Early morning:
I am now reading my very thick Kerry file early in bed and dreading the endless 'words in my ear', some friendly, some hostile eyes, hassle, which is always lightened by pleasant things, like the smiles of young-sters, friendship offered without any expectation of gain, well-motivated teachers and a lot of very decent people.
After midnight:
A tour of fifteen visits, Castleisland, Tralee, Listowel,

Tarbert etc., etc., bright sun, a myriad of young faces, damp hands, warm words, flowers, gifts and underneath it all, a deep worry 'what are all these children going to do?' The anxious Jimmy Deenihan (and Dick Spring accompanying us for the morning, placing himself squarely in the middle of every photograph). Everywhere there are beautiful buildings going up or completed or about to start. Where on earth does all the money come from? — but I know, alas I know.

Teachers are mostly very polite, but they do make a lot of talk about staffing, remedial teachers. . . . The latter is what I really worry about. The huge numbers in the infants' classes; little ones from bad homes have small chance in that situation. The deeper social implications of so many tiny ones with serious problems.

By dint of my rather severe insistence we kept almost perfectly to time on the huge schedule. A particularly lovely welcome was the last — a tiny National School at Coolard in a flat rural setting, an old, old building, bunting out, lovely children with paper flags and a present of a little engraved dish and, of course, a major building problem.

Tarbert Comprehensive was by far the most impressive; the least pleasant were Tralee CBS. (a cold, politically-minded Christian Brother) and Listowel Vocational School (a long-winded principal and, it seemed, cynical youngsters). The old snob divisions between Vocational and Secondary are firmly evident. If I was a dictator they would be all mixed up together.

A short rest before a stiff dinner with the Officer Board of the Fine Gael organisation here, the outstanding person being Bernie Gannon, a young, intelligent, humorous woman, who organised the whole thing.

The final function was a so-called informal gathering of Education interests in this hotel — utterly exhausting, moving around chatting with a million different people with their own strong points of view, but I kept my smiling, greeting, listening, interested air to the end.

128

I think I've certainly done my bit for Jimmy Deenihan and Kerry North and feel that perhaps I took on too much!

| Thursday
1
November | Indira Gandhi was killed yesterday by Sikh fanatics among her body guard. After the Brighton bomb and so many violent things like the attempt |

on the Pope, attempt on Reagan—the world is getting more violent and darker. What a sad end for a woman with such a colourful, determined and promising career.

The Ethiopian famine is touching everyone. There is a huge response to appeals for help, but the fundamental world imbalance and impossible political wrangling on the ground there make it so sad, and so difficult to see the way out. Our problems here seem so trivial in comparison but they crowd in so.

| Saturday
3
November | A visit to the Wexford Festival, which is always such an inspiring and amazing thing to come to. We are lucky to be able to get here and last night |

we had a very interesting dinner with the redoubtable Dr Tom Walsh, who has achieved so enormously and with whom I get on extremely well. He has made an extraordinary contribution to the musical appreciation of so many people.

| Friday
9
November | The contraceptives debate has exploded too. Our Parliamentary Party debate on it was interesting; the consensus was that there should be an age |

limit of eighteen years but surprise, surprise, Alice Glenn and Oliver J. dissented. I think the whole thing is daft. We're spitting into the wind talking about age limits and refusing to look squarely at the need for sex education. Anyway, a crisis is blowing up which will rock us all over again.

I think there is a feeling that things are starting to happen well in Education.

John Boland came to Aughrim this evening to give a speech on our National Plan, but he struck me as being tense, and I'm afraid the whole constituency found him quite unimpressive. Maybe if I killed myself being charming to him, he would blossom for me!

| Saturday **17** November | A very long day yesterday in Cork, whizzing around, starting with breakfast at 7.45 a.m. with Fine Gael people and then visiting school after |

school, from establishment ones like CBC to pathetic travellers' children in a small Convent school. All went well, except for constant worries about poverty and bad buildings and single-sex immovable bastions of prejudice.

Home finally, via Fermoy, where I had another stop, more tea and scones, more dilapidated buildings worrying me.

| Sunday **18** November | This week the journalist John Feeney was killed in a night plane crash over England. What a terrible end for him. John Feeney was someone I certainly |

didn't like, but what a really dreadful way to die—and the shivery intimation of mortality.

Garret is to meet Margaret Thatcher tomorrow, amid very gloomy views of the situation, and fears that there is going to be no progress.

| Monday **19** November | Went to the funeral of John Feeney. It was all very strange; so many people disliked the poor man but the grotesque and tragic manner of his dying |

was so awful and he was so young, that it caught at the heart and made everyone turn out to show that an occasional straying from righteousness was a mere triviality. He was buried in Curtlestown Cemetery in Enniskerry, a steep, beautifully situated spot on the hillside near his home, leaving a wife and five sons. God help them.

| Tuesday **20** November | Arrived in Paris yesterday (for the OECD Conference) with senior officials, including the new Secretary of the Department, Declan Brennan. |

On arrival, we went to an international teachers' reception which was very boring, and then to dinner at the invitation of Kieran Mulvey and Gerry Quigley. We went to a slightly disorganised but quite jolly, cheap place, which was very pleasant and they all seemed to be pleased that I went along and had a bit of fun with them. George Birmingham is here with me and we were a bit depressed by the communiqué we got via the Embassy from Garret's meeting with Thatcher — it seemed to have nothing at all in it, a very bland statement, but then I suppose that is probably a good sign rather than a bad sign.

| Sunday |
| **25** |
| November |

Political chaos and depression about last week's unrolling of events after the Anglo-Irish Summit. Poor Garret is totally on the floor, having given a wrong impression of being weak, confused and fumbling. This came immediately after Thatcher had dismissed all the Forum options in her imperious manner at her Press Conference, saying 'Out, Out, Out' to any option.

I arrived back from Paris to find Fine Gael discussing the storm and all during the week it got worse. Hard feelings against Garret on this side and particularly against Thatcher. It's alarming and upsetting and depressing in the extreme, and right into the Provos' basket. Haughey rounded on Garret in the Dail like a vicious mongrel dog. It is difficult to defend Garret's handling of it, although he is certainly right not to rant and rave and there is no point in putting us on a collision course. Part of the background seems to be an alarming communications problem between the two press conferences in London and the lack of a direct line from the Irish Embassy to RTE. Anyhow, it is all quite appalling.

Petra Kelly, of the German Green Party, spoke at the Women's Political Association seminar this weekend. She is a brilliant, stormy petrel. If half the things she says about the environment are true, we are all in terrible trouble. I foolishly agreed to sit on the platform and so everyone rounded on me when Petra had psyched them all up about the state of the world.

| Tuesday |
| **27** |
| November |

Here we are in Brussels at the Conference on Equality of Opportunity in Education, which I have set up, and I have some Department people with me. I'm delighted to have got this on the Euro-agenda.

131

Today, I addressed the opening of the Conference, gave a press conference, had lunch with the Commission and Council officials, met the Teachers' Unions, the Parents' Associations and attended the reception. I suppose it's not surprising that I'm a bit tired. I don't know if this will achieve anything. Sometimes I feel it is not for anything much.

George Birmingham is being Cassandra-like again about the disastrous state we're in. He's afraid about the Family Planning Bill coming up. If we're all that weak, we should finish it and be damned!

Reverberations are going on and on about the miners' strike in the UK. It has some very ugly sides to it and has dragged on for a very long time.

| Thursday **29** November | A special Cabinet meeting called by Peter Barry, to get our opinions as to whether or not Thatcher should be allowed to use a special kind of secu- |

rity, heat-sealed, military helicopter when she is coming to the EEC Summit next week. She is under such threat from the IRA that I was surprised that there were any reservations at all. I felt strongly that it would be appalling to risk upsetting her and upsetting the Summit, and anyway after Brighton and God knows what else, who'd blame her for the security worries. Garret has gone whizzing around Europe to get Summit agreement on a range of things.

Interest rates have to go up 2% — there'll be bloody murder over that.

Jim Mitchell, Michael Noonan and myself had a serious chat after the Cabinet meeting. We are all very worried about the down spiral we're on, liquidations, the Northern Ireland debacle, the interest rates and Garret's image so severely shaken.

| Sunday **2** December | Peter Sutherland rang to talk to Derry and me about Garret's problem; he feels that he needs support and lifting. But we have tried so often, so |

many have tried so often, and apparently the prognosis of

the Summit is not good and will worry him even more. Will we get out of this tailspin?

| Saturday |
| **8** |
| December |

I have had some sharp words with Alan about a really peculiar letter he wrote to me following a request of mine to transfer money within the Education Capital Estimate. It was a sort of scolding, sarcastic diatribe, which ended up saying 'yes'. I was very cross with him and he was, I feel, taken aback. Anyway, he sent some brilliant smiles in my direction subsequently! Poor fellow, the dimensions of his job are such that I don't like to add to his troubles, but I wish he would be careful with his letters. I told him I was a supporter and fan of his and he shouldn't lose his supporters by such stupidity.

Thursday was another endless day, mostly spent between Cabinet and the Senate, where the discussion was on the Oireachtas Joint Committee's Report on Sexism in Education. I was glad to be able to report that we are taking a lot of initiatives in that area for the first time ever, despite reservations and incomprehension on the part of officials. Cabinet didn't seem to be achieving much, Garret seemed totally exhausted and at the end of his tether. There's a lot of newspaper speculation about his leadership; my name was even mentioned, which always amuses me.

Went to the very elaborate celebrations of the ASTI 75th Anniversary in the Mansion House. I was surprised not to be invited on the platform and was left standing on the floor all through, but I suppose that's typical ASTI. They can't bring themselves to be warm and polite to any Minister for Education.

Education is now under control and going forward steadily, except for the impending problem of settling ten or so disputes about the different kinds of Secondary School types! A part of my eighty-hour week is spent looking at the developing ideas over a lot of fronts.

Monday
10
December

Fine Gael function in Bray tonight was good, but the air of gloom, foreboding and despair about the Government and the country is bloody awful hard to take. I am at my wit's end. Shafts of light, like Peter Sutherland's excellent portfolio in Europe, Garret's Summit victory, get lost so quickly in the welter of despondency.

Friday
14
December

Have just had a reprieve from having to get a helicopter to go to Achill. The Air Corps says (8.30 a.m.) that the weather is quite bad and they won't fly. Glory Hallelujah!

I am so tired with things going on every night on top of every day. We are in the middle of the Adjournment Debate, the idea being to attack Fianna Fail on all fronts. The new Attorney General is young John Rogers, a saturnine, tall fellow, whose appointment has caused some uproar. Peter Sutherland has changed his opposition to the appointment and says it is all fine.

Appalling behaviour by Oliver Flanagan at the Parliamentary Party meeting. He said 'we all hold our noses when we think of the Labour Party'. I jumped up and demanded a withdrawal, so he changed it to 'I hold my nose . . . . ' and then Maurice Manning objected when Oliver started to attack John Rogers, so he subsided, said he would do it elsewhere and did it in the Dail later.

Sunday
16
December

The Achill trip, would you believe, happened after all. The Air Corps decided to 'have a go', so I dashed to the Phoenix Park and up we went. Peter Baldwin came too. Across Ireland, through the driving rain, in a six-seater military helicopter with a cool pilot called Gus, the rolling fields of the midlands looking peaceful and empty and the majestic hills and water of Clew Bay. It wasn't very frightening really and the only complaint was the cold. Then we swooped down in sudden sunshine to meet the waiting crowds in the beautifully placed new Vocational School, where it all went merrily and I seem to have been a big hit. Even my chunk 'as Gaeilge' went down well, and as I descended from the skies I felt like a combination of the Virgin Mary and Margaret Thatcher, with a dash of the Queen thrown in for good measure. So immediately after my speech, because of bad weather looming, we zoomed off skywards again, bearing flowers and a Christmas cake and lots of goodwill. The swooping up and up was a lovely feeling and then the weather became appalling, sleet and rain and cold, and we battled our way through desperate visibility across Ireland because I had to be into the Dail for the final Adjournment Debate vote at 4 o'clock, which was the reason I had to take the helicopter trip in the first place. So we made it to Leinster House just in time to see Charlie Haughey walking out of the Dail with all his cohorts, in disgust at some remark of Garret's, so in the end there was no vote.

People are fiercely battering us on the John Rogers Attorney General appointment.

The Government is really on the floor. Garret is terribly damaged, with no sign of a break. 1985 will be murder, if we survive the public pay deal crisis, family planning, divorce. We must, or the Fianna Fail landslide will swallow us all up forever.

Sunday
30
December

Yesterday I wrote a long letter to Garret and delivered it by hand. I set out a whole range of ideas for improving communications between himself, Cabinet, and backbenchers, and offered to help organise all this. It was a long four pages and followed up a meeting that Derry had with him yesterday morning. Derry said that Garret acknowledges that his leadership is definitely under fire but feels that there isn't anyone else to take over, and given the circumstances the national interest requires him to stay on and put the thing right.

THE THIRD YEAR

TO

DECEMBER 1985

A new Archbishop of Dublin—Eileen Flynn, a New Ross secondary teacher, fails in her appeal against dismissal on the grounds of living with a married man—The Crown Prince of Japan and Princess Michiko visit Ireland—In Education I announce the 'Ages for Learning' decisions which give the go-ahead for all schools to provide a six-year post-primary cycle and a transition year after the junior cycle—I establish the National Parents' Council to give parents a voice in education policy-making—Local elections; severe disimprovement for Fine Gael in Wicklow as elsewhere—An Air India jumbo jet crashes 250 miles off the Kerry coast killing 329 people—Moving statues are reported from several places all over Ireland during July and August—The Social Welfare (Amendment) (No. 2) Bill 1984 is passed by the Dail without opposition. It provides for the implementation of the EEC equality directive on Social Welfare, giving 46,000 women improved entitlements and meaning disimprovements for some families where double payments for spouses were being made. The Minister (Barry Desmond) announces during the debate his range of alleviating measures to help these families and gives details of the cost of the implementation to the Exchequer (£18 million)—Bob Geldof's Live Aid raises over £45 million for famine relief in Africa, including £8 million from Ireland—The Government announces a Public Service pay freeze for twelve months: the teachers' Unions threaten to strike in Wicklow and North Dublin because the Ministers for Education and for Public Service represent those constituencies—I make a speech in Bray questioning the morality of high Public Service pay claims which would require severe cuts in services to fund them—Charles Haughey is rescued as his yacht sinks off Mizen Head—The Curriculum and Examinations Board announces the new junior cycle examination which would replace the Intermediate and Group Certificate examinations—A general one-day strike is held by the Public Service, following the first one-day teachers' strike—I publish the Green Paper Partners in Education. *This sets out proposals for unifying the post-primary school structures by establishing new Local Education Councils. It also proposes a much greater autonomy for Regional Technical Colleges—Anglo-Irish Agreement signed at Hillsborough, Co. Down by the British and Irish Governments—The Dail approves the Anglo-Irish Agreement, opposed by Fianna Fail—Double murder of two women in rural Wicklow—20,000 teachers hold a mass rally in Croke Park in pursuit of their pay claims—Foundation of a new political party, the Progressive Democrats.*

Saturday
12
January

Just had a two day Cabinet meeting which was quite good. (We've almost abandoned Barretstown on the grounds that public opinion misunderstands and disapproves). A preliminary look at all the Budget aspects; not as good as we'd like but a lot better than the awfulness of previous years. Garret has returned after Christmas full of new resolutions and ideas, but how can he overcome his worst problem, which is his unerring capacity to take on too much? The big question mark now is whether we can haul back from the all-time low of where we're at in public opinion. We met until 9 p.m. on Thursday and until only 4.30 p.m. yesterday, since Garret, Jim Mitchell and myself had to attend the inspiring opening of the Young Scientists Exhibition. The winner was a lovely young fellow who had invented a 'musical typewriter', inspired by his father who is a blind composer. The humour, maturity, balance and sheer good fun of all the young people, along with their high spirits, is a great shot in the arm.

Sunday
13
January

More political outbursts in today's papers—'Fine Gael Cabinet divided on Family Planning', Peter Barry quoted as being against it, Pat Cooney producing outbursts on neutrality, Dick Spring contradicting him publicly—all great gas, dammit, just when we've made resolutions about solidarity, decisiveness etc. I feel Garret must be decisive on the contraception thing and the Divorce Referendum. His personal credibility will be ruined if he doesn't take a firm stand, even if we're defeated in the Dail or at a Referendum. I certainly can't vote for anything to do with the words 'bona fide' on family planning and will be in rather an awkward spot, to put it mildly.

There's a lot of pressure about on the question of Public Service pay since the Arbitrator has given 6%, which is very awkward indeed. I'm not looking forward to the 100% resumption of activity next week, with Wicklow and speeches and Cabinet and deputations and no home life.

138

Friday 18 January

A week of meetings, naturally on the Budget, where the crunch issue is Public Service pay. The Arbitrator's award of 6% is small enough to make it very difficult for us to refuse it—but it would break the guidelines.

We met until 11 p.m. last night. The day was not so fraught because we were discussing easy things, like reductions in VAT and income tax and all those permutations and combinations.

Sunday 20 January

Yesterday, I spent the afternoon at home here with officials, to prepare for Monday's press conference, and today I'm all dressed up to go to Archbishop McNamara's Installation ceremonies in the Pro-Cathedral. We are all wondering mildly whether he'll attack the Government in his homily, and there is some talk of a 'plan B' to boycott the reception and issue a statement if he does.

Before I go out this morning, I'm making a steak and kidney pie, peeling potatoes and sprouts and generally rushing around the kitchen because of various family people coming to supper tonight.

Tuesday 22 January

Well, the Episcopal Installation ceremony on Sunday was long, cold, but well done. Such an amazing number of mitred gentlemen, huge show of Church power. McNamara small and grim looking, a dry homily, full of references to being a 'fearless good Shepherd' and 'standing up to the wolves', but nothing to be offended at. It was just as well I went, Ministers weren't thick on the ground. I really am terribly turned off by these huge shows of strength by the Church. Such an all male phalanx. Then we all went up to the impressive Clonliffe College for tea and buns, among milling mobs of people. I was introduced briefly to the Archbishop, who was cool but friendly.

Today's papers were surprisingly full of yesterday's Education press conference, which also figured on the RTE News last night. *The Irish Times* front-page headline announcing my 'confrontation' with the new Archbishop

on sex education—what a strange story, quite unnecessary, but I wasn't sorry really; it counteracts the hymn-
singing image in the Pro-Cathedral on Sunday. If a recent
relatively mild statement of mine on sex education is going
to cause those kind of headlines, what will happen when
we really get going!

The Irish Vocational Education Association is kicking up
a big fuss about my school amalgamation and building
decisions and I went on radio to calm that down. All in all,
it's amazing how cool I am these days.

I attended Shelah Richards' funeral service at St. Anne's
in Dawson St. It seems such a short time since Denis
Johnston's death. It was a most moving ceremony and a
little bit bizarre—extremely emotional when the actor Des
Cave sang the Nora song from 'The Plough and the Stars',
unaccompanied, standing right beside the coffin, a very
theatrical moment beautifully done.

Out to the Royal Hospital, Kilmainham, for the UN
Decade for Women reception hosted by Nuala Fennell. I
invited a lot of Wicklow people but not too many came
because of the snow. The Royal Hospital is magnificent
altogether and why wouldn't it be, when Fianna Fail spent
£19 million on it? We should use it all the time after that
investment. I can't believe it was right to spend so much,
but still, it's a glorious place.

Saturday 26 January

I've had a week of considerable publicity, most of
it positive, except of course that one would prefer
that the IVEA and the TUI wouldn't keep on
giving out murder about the closure or amalgamation of
some VEC schools; they don't like giving one inch.

An all-day meeting on Thursday was wrapping up the
Budget 'sweeteners'. John Bruton and Labour at odds
again over the National Development Corporation. I gave
out hell at the beginning of Cabinet about it, Garret was
conciliatory; it's really too awful that there should be
another huge public row after all our resolutions to
present a united, decisive front. However, apart from that
it was a good week.

There is a very bad scene developing in Arklow. Noritake will close on Tuesday with the loss of one hundred and thirty jobs. The poor Arklow people will go totally mad and something will have to be done, which I keep on saying to the IDA all the time, to no avail. They tell me it's impossible to interest industry in Arklow—no amenities, lack of executive housing, bad Union record.

| Saturday |
| 2 |
| February |

An eventful week, which included our fairly popular Budget, the most popular for years, very well presented by Cabinet; a lunch with the embattled Director General of UNESCO (a long-winded, quiet spoken but fairly determined Senegalese); a frightfully long Credit Union dinner in Portlaoise; a visit and luncheon at the College of Surgeons, followed by my polite refusal to address their Charter dinner on February 9th, having discovered from Una O'Higgins-O'Malley that they 'discourage' female guests.

The most fundamental event of the week was the Cabinet's consideration of a memo on British suggestions for structures in Northern Ireland which would involve us. This came with Margaret Thatcher's own imprimatur and in my view was quite stunning. So we considered our response, toughening up and extending the document. Thatcher has been very struck by the reaction here and in Northern Ireland to her ill-judged display last November. If Garret could only make a breakthrough there it would give him enormous satisfaction, and be very fundamental for the future of the country.

| Sunday |
| 3 |
| February |

Today, Garret was supposed to be on the radio programme *This Week* talking authoritatively about the Budget and answering all the criticisms, but instead when he got there they decided to do the whole thing on Northern Ireland because of John Hume's idea of talking to the IRA, so that part of the Budget strategy just disappeared totally. I wonder if he has over-reacted to John Hume's proposed meeting?

To my astonishment there was an amazing compliment

to me in the *Sunday Press*: John Kelly TD said that I was 'head and shoulders above' Ministers he had known. . . . Heavens, I was quite amazed.

A row is blowing up about my refusal to go to the Surgeons' Charter Day dinner because of the 'male only' guest rule. Victor Lane of The College of Surgeons rang me at home, very upset and quite angry about a *Sunday Independent* piece on it, wanting me to withdraw it or correct it, but how could I since it was true?

Wednesday 6 February

Yes, the College of Surgeons thing got quite big and quite controversial, but I stuck to my guns and tried to be reasonable and conciliatory but firm at the same time. There's simply no excuse for their rules on women.

Two busy days and long Cabinet sessions. There is a rumbling about a major Dublin Corporation strike. We have to concede a little to them on the date of the implementation of the Arbitrator's special award and that just might give peace.

Finally got agreement on the UCD Governing Body appointments: Ronan Fanning, the student president, an administrative staff representative, and Sr Eileen Doyle (two women, two men). It isn't the ideal, I would have liked my own list entirely, but I will be very firm about the Higher Education Authority when these appointments come up.

Ib Jorgensen has resigned from the National College of Art and Design Board because of student picketing of his shop. That's rather a peculiar thing to do.

Thursday 7 February

The contraception legislation has been published and the Church/State wrangle is in full spate.

We went to the Oireachtas Press Gallery party this evening. I spent a lot of time talking to Joan FitzGerald, who's into theology in a big way. The contraception issue is obviously a big test for the Government and particularly for Garret. Then he has to go on and grasp a few more nettles firmly.

142

| Thursday |
| **14** |
| February |

The contraceptive crescendo mounts—the bishops in full cry, TDs cringing, the country in a mist of sexual anxiety, and Garret firm but strained. Parliamentary Party meeting, dramatic emotional call for charity and love from Deputy Joe Doyle, usually a conservative, who said that when he meets his God he hopes it will be a God of love and not a God as represented by the hate-filled letters he is getting and the harassment. Oliver J. Flanagan emitting fire and fury, directed against all of us 'liberals', Alice Glenn confused but I think on this one honest. Tom O'Donnell gives the impression of being a disappointed man. The rest of us are hoping it will be alright. Fianna Fail, as usual, are behaving dishonestly and totally politically. Isn't it extraordinary that they have no TDs who have 'consciences'. As I write even more bishops are shouting and condemning; it's beginning to look as if they've overdone it, although in the heel of the hunt it all depends on how many feet go through the 'Ta' lobby in the Dail. Brendan Griffin is shaky, Frank Prendergast is shaky, Sean Tracey . . . Oh . . . Oh!

| Saturday |
| **16** |
| February |

My main worry this week has been the struggle over the £30 million we're supposed to save on pay this year—a figure lightly thrown around in pre-Budget discussions, never appearing to anyone to mean £30 million cuts. So I was very angry over that at Cabinet when it was demanded of me to find £6.3 million.

It was decided to include the figure in the Estimates and have a 'star chamber' of three Ministers to identify the savings. I've discovered that when I worry myself sick, things often don't turn out to be as bad as I expect; I can only hope it will be that way this year.

| Wednesday |
| **20** |
| February |

Today we defeated the bishops and Fianna Fail and Oliver J. Flanagan! The vote was won 83/80; we kept our honour and it is a significant day for Irish politics, Irish political maturity and idealism, Garret style. A sweet victory.

Des O'Malley made an historic speech announcing that he stood by the Republic and wouldn't be 'one of the lads'.

Combined with the special Bill to seize the £1¾ million IRA money yesterday, the Government has had some positive days. All of us 'liberals' are jubilant but dignified.

Thatcher made all sorts of avowals of solidarity with Garret when addressing the US Congress and Garret feels there are significant things going on there. Reagan is obviously interested in us, and let's hope, let's hope. Great work being done by diplomats behind the scenes.

| Saturday
23
February | I appeared on a platform with Bishop Brendan Comiskey in front of huge numbers of parents in Wexford last night. I came in for any brickbats |

going; he just smiled and twinkled.

No Cabinet crises this week. There are, however, worries about the Radio Bill to licence new commercial radio stations around the country.

And I flew around the place: Arklow, Bray, Greystones and Wexford, doing my constituency and ministerial duty. Where would I be without a driver?—probably dead in a ditch from falling asleep. Tom Flynn particularly is a great friend. I suppose it would be terrible not to have a good rapport with drivers, we're thrown together for such long periods.

| Thursday
28
February | I am just back from a West Wicklow FG Annual General Meeting in Donoughmore, to hear that nine RUC men were murdered in a bomb attack |

in Newry tonight, a reprisal for the killing of three armed Provos last week. It is a horrible escalation, really horrible.

This has been the week of yet another Fianna Fail bloodbath when Dessie O'Malley was expelled and left in a welter of accusations against Haughey. The media seem to be totally against Fianna Fail just now, but how long will that last?

Today we wrangled all day with poor Jim Mitchell over the Radio Bill. Labour are messing him up completely.

I'm getting far too bogged down with documents and my weight has gone totally out of control. I am feeling fat and unfit and mad with myself. Thinking time on real issues in Education is at a premium.

Receiving my seal of office as Minister for Education from President Hillery while the Taoiseach, Garret FitzGerald, looks on

With my colleagues in government, December 1982

Ruairi Quinn's talent as a cartoonist was frequently exercised during Cabinet meetings. These are from among my small collection

Sunday Tribune

Visiting schools was a frequent and often inspiring aspect of my work as Minister for Education

Three women ministers: Susan Ryan, the Australian Minister for Education (*centre*), with Nuala Fennell, Minister of State for Women's Affairs, and myself

Working for women. With Ailbhe Smyth of UCD (*left*) and Sylvia Meehan of the Employment Equality Agency at publication of report on the position of women academics in third level education in Ireland

In discussion with Tom Hunt, Jim Dorney and Máirín Ganley of the Teachers' Union of Ireland

With Peter Barry, Minister for Foreign Affairs, Mr M'Bow, Director General of UNESCO, and the late Seán MacBride

The Programme for Action in Education was launched in January 1984. Three of its architects were (*from left*) Finbarr Ó Ceallacháin, John Harris and Liam Ó Laidhin

With Dr Edward Walsh, Chairman of the Curriculum and Examinations Board, at the presentation of three discussion papers

Irish Times

In my own constituency near Bray on land donated by Dr Tony Ryan for a sculpture park

With my women colleagues in Fine Gael: *Back row*, L to R: Myra Barry, Monica Barnes, Nuala Fennell, Avril Doyle, Mary Flaherty; *Front row*, L to R: Nora Owen, Alice Glenn, and Madeleine Taylor-Quinn

Sunday Tribune

In Bray during the 1987 General Election campaign with the
Taoiseach and the local Fine Gael organiser, Aidan O'Donoghue

Irish Times

With Peter Prendergast, Government Press Secretary, at the
beginning of the Coalition government in 1982

| Saturday |
| 2 |
| March |

I'm over here in Mayo. Paid a whirlwind visit to the Knock Shrine and couldn't resist the temptation of going for a drive up and down the new Knock airport runway. All this on my way to a successful session at the Fine Gael Western Conference, which involved a speech from me and then an almost two-hour question and answer session, which I enjoyed greatly. Stimulating, I learned a lot from students, teachers, lecturers.

Also fitted in a visit to Lissadell, which I thought was a horrible, grim house, not a bit as I had imagined from Yeats' poem—the graves and the lake are beautiful, though.

| Tuesday |
| 5 |
| March |

Today I accompanied Prince Akihito of Japan and His Crown Princess when they visited Mount Anville, my old Alma Mater in Dundrum. He was extremely quiet, rather dour, and seemed to have a very faulty command of English; she, however, was small, delicate, beautifully dressed, charming and a real stunner. It was a day of great excitement in the school and I thought what an amazing turnabout it was for the nuns when their old student, Gemma Moran, came back to the school as a Government Minister—for Education of all things—accompanying the Crown Prince of Japan. The children in the school did everything well and performed really beautifully, but I would have preferred if the Crown Princess could have made the pretty speeches, since she was the Sacred Heart student in Japan. More gagging of women.

This was followed by a Taoiseach's lunch given for the Crown Prince in Iveagh House, but I don't like those State lunches very much, and couldn't wait to get back to the office.

All this formed a complete contrast to tonight's event, which was a big meeting of the Roundwood Fine Gael branch up in the cold sheep-farming hills, addressed by Paul Connaughton, Junior Minister for Agriculture. We had a long night on sheep, scab and dog control—most instructive.

145

Home after midnight to find a threatening letter ('We'll bomb you out') in relation to the Family Planning Bill, of all things! I get a lot of nutty letters and some of them would make you shiver they're so sick. We've started a file: 'nutcases'. Only the very occasional one gets referred to the Gardai.

There is one area which I find unnerving: that is when I have to put any complicated questions of policy to Government. I have no confidence at all in my powers of argument and tactical persuasion. I get thrown off balance by unexpected questions and tense about being challenged. Not that anybody is aware of all these feelings, of course, and because of them I do three times as much preparation before meetings as anyone else. At the moment my 'Ages for Learning' proposals, on which we have worked so long and so hard in the Department, are in Garret's hands. They represent a massive hurdle and cause me a lot of mental anguish in advance. I know that is all so stupid and I shouldn't let it happen but it does. The funny thing is that no-one knows about these feelings because I work so hard to hide them.

There are massive ructions going on about RTE and our decision to suspend the appointment of the new Director General until a new Authority is appointed. Poor Jim Mitchell; he is emotional under pressure, and his pressures on this from Labour have been devastating. Fianna Fail are in full cry on this issue, and I hear that Garret is making a statement tomorrow, which strikes me as being not wise because it might elevate it all out of proportion. But it has certainly scuppered Frank Flannery's chances of being the new Chairman of the RTE Authority—a pity— but even though Frank is an extremely good person indeed and would be outstanding, the Chairman has to be seen to be totally non-political.

Saturday
9
March

Eileen Flynn's appeal [to the High Court] was lost yesterday, after a big case about her being sacked from her teaching post because of being unmarried and pregnant. She is well and truly fired now; there has been a lot of fuss about it, which I've managed to keep

146

out of, not without a certain amount of confused guilt feelings: the law, no matter what I could do, would still have found against her on the grounds that a school has a right to its own ethos irrespective of what the teaching contract was. The case has a lot of significance for schools and teachers generally.

One of the big sessions I had last week was with Alan Dukes, John Boland and Ruairi Quinn, to try to find the savings in my pay vote. Among the suggestions flying around: moving the retirement date for teachers from September back to June would save £2.6 million. Do they think I am mad? I can't believe they understand how it would strike people: giving a 6% increase to teachers at work, but making the elderly ones, about to retire, pay for it. Anyway, industrial action would immediately negate the whole thing. Luckily the discussion was closed when I had to go to the airport to wave goodbye officially to the Japanese couple. Phew! Alan has to keep pressing for money savings. Why don't they face up to the Public Service pay issue?

| Tuesday 12 March | Yesterday, Monday, Garret called myself and John Harris to his office and we had a good discussion on the 'Ages for Learning' document, |

but he confused the whole issue by throwing in his ideas for the new National Matriculation Certificate, which we had already decided against.

| Thursday 14 March | Arrived in Miami for the St Patrick's week celebrations and seemed to be immediately surrounded by large American cops in plainclothes |

with bulges in their jackets.

| Friday 15 March | This is a very peculiar and extraordinary few days. We are driving in huge security cars. I am instructed by the chief detective always to sit on |

the right in the back, and if he calls me 'Gemma' at any moment, I must do exactly as I am told, principally throwing myself on the floor. They swivel their eyes and hover at my shoulder always.

I learned today that they have sent up to Washington

for a woman detective to come immediately to join the group, so I can be minded in the loo as well!

The first function today was a visit to Dade County Court House to watch a green stripe being painted on the road. Then lunch and a meeting with the school system superintendent and some staff.

After a brief rest we went to a reception in my honour on the terrace of a magnificent new Junior College. I was festooned by them with a massive orchid, with green ribbons and clay pipes hanging all over it, and I made sure to speak, and chat, and laugh with every single one of the people there, but, my goodness, it's tiring, tiring.

| Saturday |
| **16** |
| March |

We went to an amazing Mass in St Patrick's Church on the beach: the 'colleens' in strapless dresses bringing up the Offertory gifts, everybody in bright green and shamrocks, St Patrick himself greeting us (a Hispanic called Manuel), the Church nearly empty except for the people involved in the ceremony, mostly very old people there, me festooned with the biggest, ugliest confection of orchids, plastic clay pipe, green polka-dotted ribbons—Unbelievable!

We have now acquired a security woman called Maria and a blond man with a briefcase full of automatic weapons which he clutches, but which we are supposed to describe as a telephone to the White House!

The big parade: Derry and myself in a bright green open convertible, riding along Flagler Street, the main thoroughfare, being greeted and escorted to the reviewing stand. Lots of presentations to me at the most unexpected moments. Everyone in green—blacks, whites, Hispanics—lots of bands and colour, hot sun; I made some of my speech in Spanish which went down very well, and generally it was a very typical US St Patrick's Parade, with no sign at all of NORAID or any untoward incident.

We sat on the platform with Claude Pepper, an elderly and obviously revered Congressman, who is impressive and dignified and very interested and knowledgeable about Ireland.

Then we went to the elaborate Coral Gulf Chamber of Commerce Annual International Ball at the Hilton. I sat beside Mr Mixon, the Lieutenant Governor of Florida who was a nice, old, conservative gentleman, who knew absolutely nothing about where Ireland even was. But he knows now.

There was a long prayer at the beginning of dinner, when we all held hands with heads bowed and prayed not to be too materialistic . . . .

Sunday **17** March

I'm finding the security a bit pushy and intrusive, it gets between me and talking to people, but I suppose I can't really complain.

Tonight was the very big Emerald Society dinner. I had worked and re-worked my speech with Derry's help; it turned out well and was enormously well received. I was quite exigent and made sure that I got a podium, a light and a microphone in the right place, so I was able to deliver a sincere, slightly Americanised speech, with a strong political message about peace and about American support for us against the IRA. It got a standing ovation and a lot of requests for the script.

Friday **22** March

Back to work. We had a bad old journey home, after two freezing cold days in Boston with Liz and Bill Shannon, where we found ourselves attending a party given by the gentle and nice Seamus Heaney, at Harvard, and a quiet dinner with him afterwards.

Visited the Boston Fine Arts Museum, and had lunch in 'Jimmy's' on the waterfront, and then got a few moments to buy presents for the children. Liz had a few people in that evening to meet us—she's her usual vivacious, kind, energetic self.

Monday **25** March

I'm absolutely furious because my friend Senator Sean O'Leary has been so messed about over his re-admission to the Parliamentary Party, having been expelled for voting against us on the Criminal Justice

Bill—it's unbelievable. I just had a long talk with him on the phone. He walked out of a meeting of the 'special committee' on his re-admission, when Sean Barrett came on heavy. God, they're such fools. Sean O'Leary is so valuable to us, he absolutely cannot be spared and shouldn't be alienated.

Today I had Nick Scott of Northern Ireland down for a meeting. We had a few words privately first on the subject of the discussions going on with the British about the North—there is definitely an air of anticipation around, although the dramatic speculation in some papers is uncomfortable-making. After that conversation, which was really the important thing, we had rather an anodyne official meeting where nothing of real importance got said, followed by lunch in the Shelbourne. Alan Goodison, the British Ambassador, is an amusing and interesting companion—he is certainly very pro-Irish in his approach to the talks, or is he being just a superb diplomat?

Saturday **30** March

Ireland won the Triple Crown at Lansdowne Road today. Once again I was in the IRFU committee box in my capacity as Minister for Education and therefore Minister for Sport—did I ever think in my student days when I breathlessly made the tea and sandwiches for the UCD Rugby Club that I would see the day that I'd be sitting with the alickadoos in the committee box in Lansdowne Road on such a big occasion!

Thursday **4** April

One hell of a busy week with pressures building up for next week's Teachers' Conferences. Cabinet all day on Thursday, National Development Corporation discussion, Dick starting out very combatively, John Bruton surprisingly and rather nobly conciliatory, working out an NDC which would be near the Programme for Government. My meeting with Garret took place and was good and useful, despite all the enormous, long statistical questions he keeps asking. He says that Mrs Thatcher was so mild and co-operative in Brussels last week that they were all terribly taken aback.

| Sunday |
| **7** |
| April |

Today, Easter Sunday, I spent four hours on my speeches for the Teachers' Conferences, finding the bad spots, the awkward spots, things I don't understand, adding bits, rehearsing, taking out bits, phone calls to Peter Baldwin, Finbarr O'Callaghan, Assistant Secretary of the Department, practising the Irish, boning up on the background — all in the basement of the house downstairs, doing a Virginia Woolf on it, locking myself away while the family very nobly coped with supper and everything else.

| Monday |
| **8** |
| April |

Left home at 7 a.m. I have spoken to about 1,000 INTO people today, in addition to another 700 or 800 ASTI. The hours of rehearsal, the thought, the work paid off and I was well, if somewhat sullenly, received in Waterford by the INTO, and almost warmly in Killarney by the ASTI, to my surprise.

1.10 a.m. and I have just come up from a pleasant night at the ASTI dinner, sitting between the very sweet Henry Collins, the current President, and Kieran Mulvey who is of course charming when he wants to be.

I broached the subject of teachers' bad image with Henry, because he is so reasonable. He confessed to a great worry about it and said that it is a constant sub-theme which is not spoken about publicly at ASTI meetings. Of course their problem is that the really good, concerned, highly motivated teachers are not necessarily the ones who are the Union activists.

To my astonishment, I was groped disgustingly by a drunken Donegal teacher after the dinner, who wanted me to get on the dance floor — I considered slapping his face and then thought better of it. Luckily, at that point I was rescued by the officers of the ASTI, and we all went off to a small room for a few drinks. The Secretary of the Department rather misunderstood who he was talking to when he was chatting to Sylvia Meehan and called her 'sweetheart', ruffling her hair. She took exception to that and I told him he should apologise, and that it was a mistake. I don't know if he did or not.

Tuesday **9** April

The TUI dinner in Cork. My speech, delivered to about 600 people, too well wined and quite well dined, was received fairly politely and it even got some applause for the bit on equality. There was some heckling from one corner but nothing serious. The Vice-President (who was even more nervous than myself) was less rude than usual, so all in all it wasn't as bad as anticipated. I was helped by familiarity with the scene and by my friends Paddy and Grainne O'Flynn, and I had Liam Burke TD beside me doing a great job as Lord Mayor in 'Cork 800 Year' which is really something. Tourism is booming in Cork.

I sometimes wonder after speaking to these huge hostile groups will anything ever frighten me again.

Tuesday **16** April

Cabinet today. Michael Noonan suddenly had a go at me on the closure of Ard Mhuire Special School in Lusk. He brought it up under 'Any Other Business'. I would never have thought of doing something like that to him, without warning him in advance. I will have to be more wary in future. Anyway, I hope to cool it on Thursday. Is it because I'm a woman that I expect that people with whom I have a warm personal relationship will not behave unpredictably? How can you operate for two years in close contact with someone, sitting beside them through thick and thin, supporting them, sympathising with them, without developing some sensitivity about their feelings? I am fond of Michael (and I hope that will continue); I'm also fond of John Bruton and Paddy O'Toole and Garret and Austin; even with Alan 'Cool Hand' Dukes. How could one not have a special relationship after the endless days and nights around that table, cluttered with papers, too hot or too cold, tense or laughing. The people whom I feel I really don't know very well, or who are rather indifferent towards me, are John Boland, Dick Spring, Barry

Desmond (but he's not cold), Peter Barry, Pat Cooney and Liam Kavanagh.

Thursday 18 April

An appalling day in Cabinet. Dick Spring behaved as strangely as I've ever seen him. The problem was that his people in the Labour Party won't buy the National Development Corporation, as agreed to a week ago, at any price. There have been behind the scenes problems resulting in Dick staying up all night alone, thereby getting himself into an exhausted condition. Understandably John Bruton was upset and we were all very depressed. It went on and on interminably, with no food. A formula was cobbled together somewhat uneasily, then we discussed illegitimacy, which under the circumstances seemed fairly easy. Finished at 7 p.m. and dashed home with a headache and depression, to change and go to listen to the theologian, Hans Küng, at Trinity College. As always, he was charismatic and admirable.

Sunday 21 April

We are in the home of Robin and Margaret Bailey, in Malone Park in Belfast, where we came yesterday. Robin and Margaret invited us ages ago for this weekend to stay with them. Robin is a former Industry Minister in Stormont. He is a liberal Unionist. Our fellow guests for dinner last night were Nick and Cecilia Scott, John Parker (chairman of Harland and Wolff) whom I found to be an impressive young man with considerable charm, George and Marie Quigley (he is a senior civil servant in Northern Ireland, she is an EEC person). It was, all in all, an interesting evening, not too much politics up front, but always there, of course, in the background. A great deal of worry expressed about Northern Ireland losing all its bright young people to England, but they don't want to try anything much with the Republic either. Robin resents the English but distrusts the Irish. However, many here are so London-orientated that they will find their identity there finally, as most of their children have.

Today, Sunday, there was a lunch for about 20 other people, a much more relaxed occasion and very nice people. They included Ewart Bell, Maurice Hayes the Secretary for Health, Lindy Burton a nice psychologist, and various other bright, interesting and mostly interested people of the Unionist persuasion—very useful to meet them in such large numbers and to have a good chat with them.

Monday	Horrible night, farmers roaring at me in Ashford,
22	dull old clinic in Arklow, worse in Wicklow,
April	everybody screaming for more spending and less

taxation; I'm fed up to the gills with that. Pressures and problems building up in Education, the Government doing badly, some media leaks about Thursday's meeting. I hate having to govern with Labour, although maybe I'd be crucified worse with cuts if they weren't there—such schizophrenia! If only Dick had leadership and authority. Maybe he's too young.

Tuesday	A long session with the Conference of Major
23	Religious Superiors (CMRS) in the office, a ring of
April	male clerics scrutinising me and being oh so polite

and oh so determined—as I am also. Two bishops, Flynn and McKiernan, the Christian Brothers' Superior plus Father Paul Byrne and Brother Declan, who did all the talking, with only the odd word from the impressive Sister Eileen Randles. We fenced around a lot of subjects and I made my strong statement on sex education, which I was pleased with and seemed to go down well, but I do find them very tedious and stiff. Bishop Flynn willingly agreed that the male religious orders had been totally remiss on sex education, said they'd been inhibited, and that it would have to be changed.

Friday	Geraldine Ferraro comes over next week to speak
26	to the Women's Political Association. I will be
April	meeting her a few times and I hope to be able to

get some of my close 'sisters' invited to dinner in Iveagh House. Peter Barry was concerned that I was treating her 'as a woman and not as a politician'. I explained to him that there are some people who are definitely both.

Today I started earlier than usual and tried to get

through the massive load of stuff which always seems to increase and never seems to get less. I toured the Equality Exhibition for schools in the RDS and opened a new Community School in Tallaght. It was a moving occasion with youngsters, who were born in the inner city slums and are growing up in Tallaght, singing and being generally cheerful and bright and happy. But I did feel oppressed again with all the religion and religious statements. The old but genial Bishop Carroll spoke about teachers' private lives, the head nun went on and on, and both she and the Principal listed things they want money for as we stood in the truly magnificent school which cost £3.5 million and is fully equipped.

I am working also until all hours of the night preparing reams of stuff about the 'Ages for Learning' document for Cabinet next Tuesday—I dread that contest but I'm delighted with the document.

| Saturday |
| 27 |
| April |

Reflecting on last Thursday's Cabinet: John Bruton was sort of depressed, and who could blame him? He recalled that when he received a seal of office for the first time, President de Valera had said, in the course of a rather rambling speech, that in a coalition every member of Government had to remember that their first loyalty was to Government, and only then to party.

One of my main worries at the moment is about Scoil Ard Mhuire and its closure. The reaction is building up and I fear there may be fierce pressures to postpone it, so I will have to talk at length with them to try and sort this all out. I got my Higher Education Authority appointments through Government with no hassle at all on Thursday; Dick didn't seem to notice. The pity is that there are only two women out of seven. It became impossible to do otherwise because of the constraints on who can do the nominating. However, it is a good list—Fr Enda McDonagh and Ailbhe Smyth being two strong liberals. I hope Ailbhe will get some stir going there; it will be a great thing if she can.

Monday
29
April

A day spent in Co. Meath, opening yet another splendid palace of a school and visiting very many others, speaking to a large number of students, getting a great response from most of the girls—the boys all seemed to me to be a bit sullen.

Wednesday
1
May

I was in a fit last night because we didn't take the 'Ages for Learning' document in Cabinet, and both Alan and Garret are messing me up on the third level capital programme. We had a long, tortuous session at Cabinet, between housing and farm tax, mostly dealing with things which seem to have arisen from a lack of forethought.

One very bright spark in the day: Rachel has got the Trinity 'Schol'.

Thursday
2
May

Had lunch and dinner today with Geraldine Ferraro, a small, slightly tired looking but sharp, lively person, relaxed and easy, first names coming quickly, very political style. Lunch at the US Embassy Residence, where I haven't been for so long. Dinner at Iveagh House—unfortunately rather boring, not a good meal and a frightfully dull guest list. Geraldine Ferraro found herself between Peter Barry and Pat Cooney at dinner—I don't think she was totally at ease in that company.

Cabinet all day, tensions abounding because John Bruton and Dick Spring are still colliding on the National Development Corporation. Peter Barry was chairing the meeting; at the end he refused to take the 'Ages for Learning' document because Alan insisted on challenging my figures. It was a mess. John Boland supported my attempts to have it taken, as did Michael Noonan, but to no avail. God damn it! As John Boland once said, one wonders what side we're all on; is it all the same side? Perhaps the looming Labour Party Conference is making us all tense.

Friday
3
May

Did my speechmaking thing today in Athlone. First at Our Lady's Bower, which seems to be a good forward-looking school. Bishops O'Reilly and Cahal Daly were there—and the usual worrying moment when I don't take Communion. Then another speech at the Vocational School. I'm getting really good at the off-the-cuff speeches. Mary O'Rourke and Pat Cooney obviously very present everywhere. Mary, because she is such a political animal, was very pushy and I didn't cooperate too much with that. I was worried, however, as I thought she looked a little strained and not too well. A beautiful sunny day.

Saturday
4
May

We had a WPA lunch in the Beaufield Mews for Geraldine Ferraro, and then she spoke at their big meeting in Jury's. She is competent and warm and witty. She hadn't worked on her script but charmed them with her informal answers, deftly dealing with apparent anomalies, such as her admiration for Margaret Thatcher. Anyhow, it was all quite interesting.

Friday
10
May

Went to Brussels on Sunday to attend a three-day meeting of the Council of Europe Ministers for Education. Returned home yesterday.

Derry has gone down badly with gastric flu and, most unlike him, is in bed. I left the house reluctantly at 10.15 a.m., having fussed, got the doctor and generally arranged the household for the day. Dashed off to the Shelbourne for the launching of a 'Life Skills' video and then a rapid drive to the noble pile of Birr Castle, where I was guest of honour at the launching of a photographic exhibition. The castle is beautiful but freezing cold inside despite a mild day. It must be hell to live in. The Earl of Rosse struck me as very earnest and hardworking. About thirty of us sat down to lunch in an amazing dining room. Then, after speeches we proceeded to the exhibition which was housed in the stables. It was very interesting and worthwhile. Anthony Armstrong-Jones was pleasant to talk to.

Garret is being criticized in the media for spending two

weeks travelling and speaking in the United States and
Haughey is fulminating about it. I suppose everything
can't be perfect in this world but I do wish Garret was
more of a charismatic, firm, strong leader. Our main
advantage seems to be people's fear and dislike of the
alternative—C. J. Haughey.

At the moment we are heading for heavy defeat at the
local elections, and annihilation further down the road in
1987. I could write two volumes on whose fault this is and
in reality it can't be laid at any one door.

Saturday **18** May	The lack of entries in the diary these days is an indication of the amount of work, hassle, exhaustion and sheer 'busyness'. What a week!

Main event by a long shot was the approval by Cabinet
of my 'Ages for Learning' package. John Harris and Sean
O'Mahoney had worked very hard to beat Finance people
into agreement and so we eventually did. I am absolutely
delighted that all our work, investigations, meetings,
discussions and plans have been successful at last. So on
Thursday morning we presented our document to the
waiting world at 10 a.m. and after some initial hiccups,
with John Walshe of the *Irish Independent* getting it slightly
wrong, the papers on Friday were wonderful in their
reception, especially *The Irish Times*. They're all particularly delighted about the six-year post-primary cycle and
the transition year.

At Cabinet there was some last minute soul-searching
and discussion over the four years school entry age, but I
kept my cool and spent a considerable length of time being
extremely reasonable and as a result smoothed over all the
difficulties.

Thursday was, I suppose, the culmination of one heck
of a week.

Having got home from the Dail at midnight after the
usual endless Wednesday, I left home on Thursday at 8.15
a.m. dashing to the hairdresser; then at 9 a.m. over to
Setanta building for a last minute briefing with Sean
O'Mahoney and John Harris; and at 10 a.m. the press
conference in G2, a not very glamorous room in Setanta.

The conference went on for about an hour. I recorded a television interview, did *Day by Day* from the Dail studio, recorded another interview for the 1.30 News; dashed out to the Burlington where I socialised, sweated and presented Texaco Art Prizes to 250 children and ate a horrible lunch and got a very bad pain in my back; back to the Dail, rushed through the final Ard Fheis script, received Nicholas Scott, the Northern Ireland Minister, at 4.15 p.m., attended a vote and dashed over to the Mansion House where I presided at the opening of the Ulster Games and made a speech.

Got home at 6.15 p.m., lay down on my bed for three-quarters of an hour and then entertained 100 people from the constituency until 2.30 a.m. That party, which I regularly do the night before the Ard Fheis, was I hope a great success. All my Wicklow people are a nice bunch.

John B. Keane from Kerry arrived at the party, from where I'm not quite sure, and I seem to recall him very late at night singing Jacobite songs in a very gentle voice on the sofa in the sittingroom.

| Sunday
19
May | Yesterday was the big Ard Fheis day in sunny Cork, moving around between different venues. My session went well, not exactly bringing the |

house down but then, do I ever? However, it was good and solid. A lot of media attention and interviews.

The Neptune Stadium, where Garret's speech was given, was awesome: wonderfully organised crowd-wise but the acoustics weren't the greatest. He took me by surprise by launching into Irish when he came to the bit about Education—and Garret never sounds happy speaking in Irish because his way of jumbling words sounds even worse. As usual I find it very hard to judge what the leader's speech is like; that's because I'm too close to it. If I was giving that speech I would have to spend a considerable number of hours at the microphone really getting everything right. It is, after all, an acting performance, and one for nearly a million people when you come to think of it. Afterwards, the large group which we had organised went to the Arbutus Lodge for dinner. The

Noonans, the Birminghams, the O'Learys, Nora Owen and Mary Banotti and Mark Mortell. It was a very pleasant occasion, if somewhat expensive.

Tuesday
21
May

Yesterday was hectic, marred alas by another one of those chest pains, which could be indigestion or could be . . . what? Anyhow, it caused a slight drama. I left my slightly startled office and went to the doctor; now I have to see Dr Risteard Mulcahy.

Clinics in Bray and Kilcoole, launching of the Bray Directory where I ad libbed my speech, and finished my night in the RDA Hall in Rathdrum facing a huge packed hall of fuming farmers, roaring and shouting against the Land Tax—I spoke to them and was at least listened to with some politeness, but it was nothing substantial. I can't help thinking about the health question. Have I finally allowed things to get so bad that my heart has become affected? The blood pressure is up anyway, the doctor told me yesterday. No doubt Mulcahy will have me starving, teetotal, non-smoking and depressed but I will have to do it. What a fool I am. And just now when things are beginning to go right for me politically.

This morning I visited three schools: the Church of Ireland school in Rathmichael near Shankill—a quiet visit, lovely children; St Patrick's National School (Loreto) in Bray—huge fuss and more wonderful children; Presentation College in Bray—extremely low key. Have the Brothers a problem with me?

Went back into Leinster House and had a long and difficult meeting with officials about the Curriculum and Examinations Board. I think there is a lot of sludge around, and veiled hostility to the concept of sharing power with the wider education world.

Worked and worked with Peter Baldwin trying to make an impression on the monstrous, ever-growing pile of files, letters, minutes, problems. A quick (healthy) supper with Paul Connaughton, one of my favourite people (he is funny, genuine, concerned and generous), Avril Doyle (elegant, voluble, funny) and Alan Dukes (charming and so calm that you would wonder where was the stubborn, relentless person I see at the Cabinet table).

Anyway, I finally got home around 8 p.m. and had a free night then. Isn't that a miracle?

Sunday **26** May	A lot of hassle this week, inside my head maybe, because I finished the week visiting Risteard Mulcahy.

I can hardly remember a thing about the week. Cabinet on Thursday spent a long time on a new RTE Authority. I was trying to get a feminist on to it. Garret was sympathetic—but is that enough? To my great alarm there was some effort by Labour to go back on the local water charges—horrifying thought. I will really have to fight that.

On Friday I went to Risteard as arranged and he indeed looks rather scrawny and peculiar himself, with a fanatic gleam in his eye about what he is going to achieve with me!

Later on Friday Alan Dukes came to do a constituency visit in Wicklow and put the heart across me by being nearly an hour late for the businessmen in Bray—my blood pressure, probably already up, was no doubt going through the roof! However, he was his usual cool, confident, civilised self. Then we dashed across the hills to Blessington for a slightly tense meeting with a whole lot of farmers, who were throwing all sorts of questions around but of course Alan was well able to handle them.

Saturday **1** June	After forty-eight hours of tests in Vincent's I had my big chat with Risteard Mulcahy, who was not a bit extreme but very sensible. All the tests on

my heart are all right; the problem appears to be a combination of weight and stress, related to blood pressure which goes up. The blood pressure came right down over the few days total inactivity in hospital. Since then I have been watching my diet, but all the recurring life problems are still there—late nights, dinners, hassle. I can't see how on earth I can control all this.

So Cabinet business this week for me involved grappling with the third level capital programme. It was very difficult indeed, but the real problem was because the North Dublin RTC was not on the list, and that caused some dismay and disruption from John Boland who fights his corner in an extremely up-front way indeed and I don't appreciate it at all.

After the Cabinet meeting, a few days later, I saw the Government decision minuted from the meeting. That Government decision has all sorts of peculiar things in it which I certainly don't recall having agreed to, the most alarming thing being the closure of a Teacher Training College which I don't think had ever been discussed. The thought of another very bloody battle over that leaves me limp. So I have to initiate moves to correct that inaccurate entry in a Government decision which I suspect was slipped in by Finance.

| Thursday |
| 6 |
| June |

Had one of those very tricky meetings with a Cashel deputation about my decision to put a Community School there. I met a roomful of very sulky, sullen-looking VEC members and the deputation included Labhras O'Murchu. The Oireachtas members knew that they were on a loser trying to get me to change my mind, so they were keeping fairly quiet. I got through it at length, trying to be a combination of wise, stern, understanding, exhortatory, all at once. Since one has to say *no* to the vast majority of deputations, and since the vast majority of deputations include people who know exactly what one has to do, it is rather like a set piece. The important thing is for the Minister to be firm and charming at the same time, and to save the faces of the local public representatives by treating them in a dignified way.

Garret reported to us again this week on Northern Ireland, which is a very difficult scene indeed. The British are baulking at various suggestions and Garret confessed to me a great worry about it, saying that he goes to sleep and wakes up thinking about it. We had a long talk about all the implications of the negotiations.

Saturday 8 June

Today, I had my first meeting with the new National Parents' Council. Despite all my fights for them and my work at getting them set up, there they were, a crowd of people looking suspiciously at me, and only some of them are friendly. We had a reception followed by lunch in the Gresham, and three speeches.

My announcement of £20,000 for them went down like a ton of cement; Fergus O'Gorman (chairman of the National Parents Council) was looking for about £100,000. The CSPA [Catholic Secondary Schools Parents Association] delegates were peering frostily at me. Well, all I can say is that I hope they get down and do the work for which I set them up, and that they realise what an amazing parent power they could have if they stopped worrying about what the Minister has or hasn't given them and started building on their structures. I've told them so many times that now that they have structures, 5p a week from every parent would make them a very rich and powerful body.

We went to the National Concert Hall to hear the National Children's Choir. This involved making a speech on stage with about 500 youngsters behind me and more than 1,000 people in the auditorium, but it was such an inspiring occasion I managed it fine. It was all very pleasant—beautiful massed children's voices singing Bach and Britten; the excellent Sean Creamer from the Department of Education has inspired so many teachers. Then we came home to find an empty house and watched the astonishing fight between Barry McGuigan and Pedroza, McGuigan fierce, and dogged, and winning, but as a sport you can have it—it should be banned.

Thursday 13 June

On Monday we had a very long and testing day indeed: Garret's visit to the constituency. Everything was going fine until he put salt in his tea in the DART cafeteria in Bray and of course that made the headlines next day.

The worst part, however, was a sour, tense meeting in

Arklow which Garret found difficult—not that Arklow is ever easy to handle. I think perhaps that he was extremely tired and of course the Taoiseach shouldn't have to get involved in touring constituencies for local elections when he really has so much to do at national and international level.

There was a funny scene during the constituency tour also: in Arklow, Councillor Vincent McElheron arrived into the hotel meeting room holding a huge ray fish, which we all assumed was dead. He proceeded to proffer it to Garret and then it suddenly began to jerk violently. Garret's face was a study of horror and annoyance and the photographer caught the moment, which duly appeared in the *Wicklow People* captioned 'Arklow's Ray of Hope'. I fell into bed (as usual) at 1 a.m.

Thursday 21 June

The funeral for Alexis FitzGerald earlier this week was beautiful and dignified, huge and emotional. Poor Barbara, the quiet serene presence behind two men both lost to her. Fr Enda McDonagh spoke wonderfully well of 'the great quietness of death' and also quoted a letter of Alexis' when he was Government adviser: 'I am—disgracefully—more interested in the questions of Christology than the crises facing my country'.

Saturday 22 June

Feeling dispirited again after a long defeating day (yesterday) watching Fine Gael being decimated in the local elections all over Wicklow, particularly in Bray and Arklow. As the votes got worse and worse and Fianna Fail crowed more and more, and our people looked sad, dismayed and shocked, I mostly felt anger. Anger at the total apathy of some people who stayed at home and anger at my own stupidity in thinking that my hard work and attention to Bray and to Wicklow generally would help our candidates.

Nationally it was the same, worse in Dublin North and Central. Now we have to pick up the pieces and get on with the job which has to be done and must be done for the next two years. This morning I will go on the radio and soldier for the Government.

Later: that radio interview went well; one finds resources to sound chirpy, confident and reassuring. Then I went and spoke to the Catholic Primary School Managers in Drumcondra that went well too.

Monday
24
June

Last night having given supper to various relations plus Mark Mortell, I went to the Fine Gael 'Victory Dance' at the Wavecrest in Bray. Despite the casualties all over the place, there was a very good attendance, which says a lot for the spirit of the organisation. Heard today, however, that there were all sorts of dramas taking place at the function unbeknownst to me — quarrels and insinuations and boiling, and I think it is better to let everybody simmer down because there are a great many bruised egos around. And there was I, being all cheery and oblivious.

I am worried about leaks of Leaving Certificate examination papers which seem to have happened in the Department and Christina Murphy appears to have the proof but, under my new personal rules, I am not allowing myself to get upset or uptight — we will just have to do the best we can. All through the Leaving Certificate exams we have tension every day because it's such a huge operation in every part of the country and we wait for some awful problem to arise.

Another international disaster is the crash yesterday of an Air India Jumbo jet 250 miles off the south-west coast of Ireland — a bomb suspected and 329 killed — what horror.

Sunday
30
June

On Friday after a five-hour flight in the Government jet with President and Mrs Hillery, we landed at Reina Sofia Airport in Tenerife to be greeted by a gale force wind, blinding sun, fluttering flags, bands and soldiers and the entire Spanish Royal Family.

We were there because of the official opening by seven Heads of State of the European Telescope complex on the top of a mountain in the Canaries. Since the President is representing Ireland and must be accompanied by a

Government Minister whenever he officially travels out of the country, I was chosen to accompany him on this visit, because the Dublin Institute for Advanced Studies is involved and they're under my aegis.

Throughout the visit we stayed close to the Hillerys at their request—I'm not quite sure what people thought I was because, of course, all the other accompanying Ministers were men and the only accompanying women near the Queens of Spain, Denmark and the Netherlands seemed to be ladies-in-waiting. How do you manage not to look like a lady-in-waiting?

The first stage of our journey home involved a trip of half an hour in a tiny Piper Navajo aircraft over to Gran Canaria, with just the Hillerys and ourselves and two pilots. The heart was put sideways in me when the pilots insisted on the President taking the controls. So we bumped our way through the clouds over to the Gran Canaria Island and Paddy Hillery actually landed the plane, to my considerable but bottled-up consternation. I can't believe I've travelled on every conceivable type of aircraft and survived it all!

| Saturday 6 July | A rather strange week. There were lots of clinics all over Co. Wicklow, lots and lots of long Dail sessions and continuing Cabinet worries and |

crises over the Radio Bill. One of the Cabinet sessions went on until 2 a.m. over the problems that Labour have with some of their people threatening to vote against it (Toddy O'Sullivan, Frank Cluskey) and then next morning it all appeared to be sorted out, but it wasn't, because yesterday Frank Cluskey stood up and torpedoed it with accompanying threats about other legislation. With that kind of thing going on, it now seems inevitable that we should plan for an Election. How can we govern? The whole Radio Bill is sick-making. It has been a mess from the beginning.

As well as the portents of doom in the Radio Bill, we are dealing with massive ICI problems, Irish Steel soaking up money like a sponge, growing unemployment figures, and behind it all but sort of overshadowing it is the North, the IRA, the Sangster threats, the Anglo–Irish talks. Garret is very ebullient and brisk at the moment—I wonder how he does it?

Thursday 11 July The Dail Adjournment Debate. Garret gave an almost entirely unscripted speech, which turned out to be very good, except that we were all worried that he would lose his way permanently among the many bits and pieces of paper scattered over the surface in front of him. I sometimes watch the Press Gallery as they observe Garret. Looking at their faces I feel that some of them regard him fondly, while others are less benevolent.

Saturday 13 July There is the most fantastic and wonderful thing happening on television: *Live Aid*—non-stop music and performances for Ethiopia, simultaneously in many parts of the world, coming from the US and London, Dublin and lots of places, all organised by Bob Geldof, who is in a perpetual frenzy to help. Everything is geared for people to pledge money.

Tuesday 16 July The *Live Aid* marathon turned out to be a sort of major world event, with Ireland leading the way in generosity and as I write we have reached £4 million. It makes one think all sorts of thoughts after one has admired the guts and single-mindedness of Bob Geldof, the lad expelled from Blackrock College, who has now raised more than £45 million worldwide for famine relief. Garret went on TV and announced a contribution of £250,000 from the Government (at my suggestion) and people have mixed feelings about the rightness of doing that. However, I have to admit that I sometimes wonder how come—in this 'depressed' country where you are laughed to scorn if you dare to be optimistic—there are all these millions lying around in one twenty-four hour period, and this on top of about £9 million raised already in the last few months.

This evening I had quite a chit-chat with Archbishop McNamara, who was attending the launch of a new Adult Education project for Wicklow. The actual reception was in Mountjoy Square. Anyway, I had to speak last of several speakers and had no script. I think the speech went very well; he certainly thawed out greatly under my opening few flattering words. It's a funny thing that I feel it is important to charm him, but I do. I suppose that's not surprising in view of the differences between us and the fact that I need his, at least, benevolent interest and support in a lot of Education matters. He is quite a nice man once you get going on the small talk, and responds quite warmly if you keep it up. I think he's shy.

I am worrying a bit about second daughter, Ruth, who has gone off to London to work. She rang tonight, sounding a bit despondent and rather young. What a worry it is to have youngsters on their own in a place like London.

| Wednesday |
| **17** |
| July |

Tonight I hosted a big reception in Kilmainham for the 'European Reading Association'. It was a very international gathering and so I made a short tri-lingual speech and circulated among 500 people; and think I had a talk with nearly everyone of them. I'm proud of Kilmainham at times like this.

| Saturday |
| **20** |
| July |

The weight loss is going so well, I don't dare to mention it in case I go off course, but I'm really delighted. I am doing my early morning four-mile walks at 7.30 a.m. and eating sparsely.

| Thursday |
| **25** |
| July |

Just home at midnight from a two-day Cabinet meeting at Barrettstown. In many ways it was as unsatisfactory as ever, but in some ways better. I felt that my contribution was a strong one; I have no idea at all what anyone else thought of it but at least it was there, clear and thought out.

Barrettstown is a lovely, smallish house, the surroundings are beautiful, the lawns and rolling fields, horses in the distance, small lakes, swans, pleasant meals, but it's so weird to be sitting in the same room for the long, long meetings, which went on for about eight hours yesterday and ten hours today. We had the customary trawl through Departments looking for money, my heart in my mouth about the usual Finance list of cuts, but I defended calmly and, I hope, logically and anyhow they all seemed to understand. The bad financial situation is stark, the parameters are now non-existent, the challenges terrible. I'm giving anything I possibly can; I hope they know it.

One gets to know one's colleagues, though many of them are complex and unknowable. I have no close relationship with any of them, but I think there is a certain amount of mutual respect and I am glad to say that Garret is remaining cheerful, even ebullient.

Saturday **27** July

I think Garret will do some kind of a re-shuffle, when and if the Northern Ireland Agreement gets done. That Northern Ireland question is exciting, dangerous and carries the possibility of a great break-through or unthinkable chaos. We discussed it at some considerable length on Wednesday and I got some changes made to upgrade the economic side of the document. The possibility of a very good foreign fund is quite dramatic and could be a great help in getting people to accept the Agreement.

Friday **9** August

Spending two days in George Birmingham's rented house in lovely Dingle. It stormed and poured a lot last night and also this morning as we walked around the town, which is really lovely except for the unfortunate muzak blaring from loudspeakers on lamp-posts. This afternoon Derry and I did a very long walk to beaches near here; the bright sun is now shining with a strong wind. George and Myra are very nice people.

Sunday **11** August

Before we left Dingle last night, we were joined for dinner by Michael and Florence Noonan in the 'Half Door'. To my surprise Michael wasn't as relaxed as I expected he would be. The Special Branch 'heavies' are everywhere around him; maybe that's why.

Monday
19
August

A rather depleted, brief Cabinet on Friday covered a lot of ground in a short time. John Boland announced guidelines of a pay freeze for twelve months in the Public Service and I asked the Cabinet for a combined approach, and that there should be general support of speeches made, but they're not really convinced of the need for it. So a speech of mine goes out tonight and I wonder if it will get any coverage or will it just be old, predictable, conservative Mrs Hussey doing her thing as usual, provoking people into reactions. Rumours—apparently true—that Hugh Geoghegan (Public Service Arbitrator) is going to award a further 10% to teachers, on top of the general Public Service increase. The millions that would cost will make a nonsense of Budget figures.

It is nice to feel that there are no local disasters and hassles just at the moment. The constituency is as quiet as death, but clinics tonight in Bray and Kilcoole. I'm desperately worried about the pay Arbitrator's proposed award—£170 million!

Wednesday
21
August

There certainly was a strong reaction to my speech about pay—it caused uproar. I went on *Morning Ireland* and did a very long interview. I think there may be considerable reverberations from that because I used the word morality when discussing teachers' demands for £170 million more in pay, on top of the Public Service increases that they've got already. I suppose I am also a bit annoyed about the threats to picket John Boland's and my constituencies—penalising children just because they happen to live in a particular area. The teachers are making a great deal of noise and I wonder if they will really go ahead with strike action. I have had a very critical *Irish Times* editorial and at the moment I feel like saying 'to hell with them all', the Government as well—I am fed up with the lot of them. How can the country find an extra 10% which the Arbitrator has just awarded to the teachers, when we're desperately trying to control spending? But is the word 'morality' only to be applied to sex?

170

Today I visited the office of the Athlone Examinations Branch. It went well and I hope to do that more often. There is a sort of flat, hostile feeling there, but we had a general meeting and I spoke to them all in the canteen and I think the applause might be described as warm rather than merely polite. There is a very good civil servant called Johnny Bracken in the Examinations Branch—he has a great spirit and a sense of humour and pride in his work, work which is very well done despite the out-of-date manual methods for which I'm battling to get the money to computerise.

| Tuesday |
| **27** |
| August |

This was the first full-day Cabinet, with Garret back again and in a resolute humour. Chatting in the coffee room before Cabinet, he was complaining about his increase in weight and I brightly suggested that he should come with me on my four-mile fast walk at 7.45 every morning, at which his face registered horror and he said 'Absolutely not'. The meeting went on until 7.30 (despite assurances at the beginning that it would end at 5 p.m.) as we completed the Public Service White Paper, which is John Boland's very good and intelligent document about a new way of running the civil service, mainly concentrating on giving people more motivation and separating different areas.

Last night in Wicklow I had a very busy clinic, as usual in the old-fashioned Royal Hotel on Main Street, 'a good Fine Gael house'. After Cabinet today, I spoke at considerable length to Alan about a particularly difficult case of a third-level grant for a boy whose mother is dying, and he did make some optimistic noises that we might be able to help. Please God we can—what a disaster for the family.

The teachers have decided on one-day strikes, county by county, then a one-day national strike. Obviously they can't be allowed to win that battle; the money implications for the future are absolutely horrifying.

| Tuesday |
| **24** |
| September |

Back to work after two very quiet and peaceful weeks on holiday, mostly spent in small villages in the foothills of the French Pyrenees. Because the French air traffic controllers were on strike, we had to drive to Bilbao to get a flight to London on Wednesday last. As soon as I reached London, I went straight to Oxford to attend a conference on the new Irish studies area organised by Garret's daughter, Mary FitzGerald. My partner and fellow speaker at the conference was Sir Keith Joseph, 'the Mad Monk', Thatcher's Education Minister. He is an exquisitely polite, saturnine, old-fashioned sort of gentleman. He was most affable and nice to me during the dinner—while I was eating nothing at all and drinking occasional sips of water because of a tummy bug picked up in Bilbao and he was eating a kosher meal because he's apparently very orthodox Jewish. All the other people in the impressive Oxford dining hall were tucking into roast beef and two veg. and no doubt thinking we were a right pair of oddities.

In the course of my conversation with Sir Keith, he registered considerable shock when he heard of the extent of my involvement with my constituency and with the party nationally, in addition to Cabinet responsibilities. He told me solemnly: 'Thirty years ago when I was first selected to be the Conservative candidate for the North Leeds constituency, I solemnly undertook to visit the constituency at least once a month and I have faithfully kept that promise'. I told him what would happen to an Irish Cabinet Minister who adopted that attitude towards his or her constituency!

His affability and agreeableness at dinner, however, didn't extend to his speech which was all about the question we were there for—the Irish studies area. He read his non-committal speech like an automaton. Despite bad tummy and not feeling very well, I had given considerable attention beforehand to my own speech and I believe that the large Irish contingent had good reason to be proud of their Minister compared to the British one. Mary FitzGerald, who was the moving spirit behind all this, looks extraordinarily like Joan FitzGerald. She is

172

pregnant and apparently has a leg very badly in trouble.
She was very warm and charming towards me. A strong
character like her mother.

| Thursday |
| **26** |
| September |

Back in full harness, running helter skelter from
here to there, lots of activity, various openings of
schools and seminars and receiving Curriculum
and Examination Board documents (they are working
away so well and show such promise). Quite a lot of
publicity—even some remarks for my slimmer self—some
moans in Bray, gloomy politics, Cabinet today fairly
aimless, School opening Masses attended, talking again to
the dry old Archbishop, and daughter number 2 bounced
home this morning from her wanderings around Europe,
brown, disorganised, happy and sweet, thank goodness
in one piece but lots of adventures behind her.

| Tuesday |
| **1** |
| October |

There has been a disgraceful neglect of this diary
in recent days, which is a measure of considerably
heightened activity and increasing late night exhaustion—including a very busy weekend distributing my
Newsletters by hand in Wicklow all day Saturday, opening a fine school in Inchicore on Sunday (surrounded by
the Jim Mitchell mafia, which he has so amazingly well
under control), entertaining old folks, being nice to all Liz
Shannon's visiting American group of women, seeing
Sean O'Mahoney off officially, although he's coming back
to work with me, entertaining all those American women
in Leinster House and pushing the boat out for old
Ireland's sake, going to hear the Washington Orchestra
(and a superb Shostakovitch piece), meeting with the
ICTU [Irish Congress of Trade Unions] Women's Group,
who exuded hostility at me across the table, (why don't
they realize that with a woman Minister for Education,
who is also a feminist, it is their best chance ever of
achieving something for women?)—extra Cabinet meetings re Insurance Corporation of Ireland. Not much time
this week for thinking, planning and reflection.

173

Friday
4
October

Today I went down to Limerick for the opening of the new NIHE buildings. It was, as one would expect of Ed Walsh, all beautifully done. Garret was the main guest and flew down with Michael Noonan, but I funked the flying and flew down in the car! I told them in my speech that I was going to set about investigating giving University status to NIHE Limerick and NIHE Dublin and of course they are all over the moon about that. Yesterday, by contrast, Cabinet was dreadful all day and then we had more Cabinet this morning, all on pay and other things.

The teachers' campaign has become very personal and somewhat vicious and is not helping me to keep in a calm mood. I have to go on *Saturday View* again tomorrow morning and will get a big briefing from Peter Prendergast, who always picks out the improbably positive things! I am often on *Saturday View* these days with Brian Lenihan, I suppose because he also lives within fairly easy reach of RTE. He is a very funny man and arrives quite frequently looking appalling, and downing cups of black coffee and rubbing his eyes. However, as soon as he's asked a question he launches into this long spoofing spiel which is very entertaining, but it all sounds very serious over the airwaves—in the meantime he rolls his eyes round the table as if to say, 'this is all a game anyway isn't it?'

Thursday
10
October

As usual, once a year when I distribute 20,000 or so of my Newsletter, the clinics on the following Monday are always extremely well attended, with long queues and taking a very long time indeed. One does become oppressed at the end of several hours by the worries of the world and I'm inclined to forget that the vast majority of people don't come to clinics, because all you can see are problems about bad houses, damp walls, sick babies, unemployment, feuds with neighbours, planning permissions, third level grants, bullies at school, school transport problems . . . the list is endless.

There is increasing tension over the pay issue at Cabinet, we're not looking strong, and it is infuriating. My position is always that we must take a firm and public lead so that people will feel we're in charge and that we can show that in the whole pay area we are facing up to the seriousness of the country's situation.

On Tuesday night I had to collect money at the doors in Bray for the Fine Gael National Collection and found not a bad reaction. But understandably it is very hard to get the party workers out to do it so I must give a lead. Is it worth the night's work when you only get about £20? At least it's contact, and waving the FG flag.

On Wednesday I officially visited St Gerard's School in Bray: the ASTI members of the staff were very pleasant and welcoming despite the teacher Unions' announcement last week that I was 'to stay out of Wicklow schools'. What lengths they go to. . . .

At the Parliamentary Party meeting this week Liam Skelly attacked me very strongly, but that might be a good thing! In fact I got quite a bit of praise from other members of the party (and I was the only Minister to be praised).

Last night I dashed off again to Greystones and collected in a huge new estate there called Hillside, with some of the very faithful party members. We did very well and it was all very successful on a fairly pleasant evening.

| Saturday |
| 12 |
| October |

At Cabinet this week there were very long talks about pay generally. I sometimes feel I am seen as tiresome and rigid. There are various members of the Cabinet firmly on my side, but I feel that there needs to be a general stiffening up; otherwise I'm afraid there will be too much giving in for the sake of eventual peace, with all the financial implications that has for borrowing next year.

Deputies at the Parliamentary Party meeting, understandably, are doing a fair bit of moaning. Maurice Manning criticised the rather bludgeon-like tactics of Jim Mitchell, saying 'He's like some kind of Rambo . . . no doubt you've seen that film, Taoiseach'. Garret very innocently and unsuspecting, said quite seriously and in a concerned voice 'No, I'm afraid I haven't', the Parliamentary Party collapsing in mirth.

The Anglo–Irish talks are at a very crucial stage and are dragging on and on; as they come towards conclusion things are tense and difficult. We're all on edge; it's like treading on eggshells. Our discussions are solemn, we search the documents for ambiguities, hostages to fortune; but it's astonishing how far we've come in a year. All the time we wish there was some way of involving Unionists, but they've blocked every single avenue.

Sunday **13** October	Attended the SDLP dinner with Derry last night and I was very pleased at the nice compliments I got about my weight loss. Isn't it funny how that

can be important? I felt that there was definitely a positive feeling at the dinner, John Hume and all of them showing themselves to be in good humour, forward-looking. God, what they've been through . . . our problems fade into insignificance. Hume is obviously bullish about the Agreement.

Tuesday **15** October	Today is the day of the Public Service general strike. The editorials in all the newspapers have generally condemned it, even using the same

language as I did in the speech of 21 August which caused all the trouble—and even using the word 'morality'. And in *The Irish Times* there was a very despairing article about this Government which was described as 'on a withdrawal phase,' saying exactly, alas, what I feel.

I have realised that one of the main things which keeps me in this Government is the Anglo–Irish Talks/Agreement. I obviously can't do anything that could weaken them and I can't be disloyal to that effort. But when it's all over, there won't be that constraint.

Tuesday **22** October	How, how, to convey the comings and goings, the complexities, the endless days and nights, the return of Garret this morning from the US,

slumped, hoarse, a back problem, dropping with fatigue, buffeted by blockages in the whole Northern Ireland package for crunch meetings tomorrow; my meetings, deputations, clinics, the portrayal of me as 'insulter of teachers', the frightful bad temper and bickering at the Fine Gael North Wicklow district meeting in Bray last week, occasioning an angry riposte from me—and the continual effort to keep calm and keep the stress level down.

Wednesday 30 October

Early morning: today is the day that my Green Paper *Partners in Education* is going to come before the Government. This has been a great, long battle to try to come to grips once and for all with the daft disparity in so many different kinds of second level schools which causes all sorts of problems, particularly in provincial towns. I am suggesting a whole new system of Local Education Authorities to bring them together, as well as a system of autonomy for RTCs. Part of the long countdown to finally getting it into the Cabinet room was having facilitating meetings with Alan Dukes, Ruairi Quinn and Liam Kavanagh. We are now down to bed-rock—the principle of majority political representation on the LECs (Local Education Councils), which I am against.

Divorce has been the big issue this week; Michael O'Leary has behaved extraordinarily, and has been pushing his two Divorce Bills himself. The Parliamentary Party had a long, detailed, but not bitter, discussion on it. Garret was good, positive and clear on *Today Tonight*.

Sunday 3 November

Yes! Yes! I got my Green Paper through Cabinet with some very small changes but the principle intact—a minority of public representatives. I had strong support from John Boland—*mirabile dictu*! The Labour Party didn't like the question of the size of the political representation and were joined by Alan Dukes, but I wouldn't be surprised if he did it for the sake of avoiding the party line decisions. I am pleased with myself today because it is a very significant Green Paper and I'm delighted to get it through—now the fun will start!

The divorce thing goes on and on and gathers momentum, the Labour Party trumping Michael O'Leary by deciding on their own Bill, confusion reigning.

As usual one is well into the wars at this stage of the week. I am at this point feeling under siege because of the teachers' strikes beginning to-morrow and a feeling that most people believe that I'm personally responsible, particularly Ruairi Quinn, who said so directly as we argued about whether or not to make a statement.

We had a great deal of Northern Ireland talk at Cabinet today, analysing the final stages of the Agreement—it continues very tense leading up to the Agreement. Garret is obviously annoyed with me over the pay question, although he thought my appearance on television was very good ('You got away with murder') and he was snappish over the third level discussion paper, which he says has all sorts of wrong/contradictory figures in it and he has to discuss it with me before it can go any further. He wants to revolutionise the Universities but not to talk about the immediate problems.

So I may have blown my excellent progress with what are described as indiscreet remarks on the Arbitrator's Report and I will go down as someone who 'lacks judgement'. This pay thing—however—has a long way to go—sometimes I feel I could kick myself, other times I feel that what I said was the right thing to say and it has been echoed by lots of other people, even in all the newspapers. Will no Government ever face up to the Unions?

When I ask how we could justify massive disimprove-ments in standards of education (like increasing class sizes, cutting grants, increasing third level fees, cutting out equipment, in-service training) all to give big increases to already quite well paid teachers, no-one seems able to answer me, except people like Austin Deasy, who is horrified at the implications of pay awards.

Wednesday 13 November

The long gap in this diary writing has been because of the illness of my parents, because of the huge work to be done on the Green Paper reactions, because of all the meetings we've been having on Northern Ireland. We move this week towards the Anglo–Irish Agreement, an air of anticipation, tension, as the Cabinet discuss it in its final stages: nearly impossible to judge what the reaction will be. Garret, naturally, is totally absorbed in it—it must be the most fulfilling thing for him. My worry (at least one among all the other worries) is that he will be very emotional about it on the day, which is Friday. Haughey meanwhile fulminates against the whole thing; John Hume is strongly supportive. I ask myself if there will be violence following it? That's on all our minds.

On Monday this week I launched my Green Paper, to a very big reaction—and I must be doing something right because I got general condemnation from all sides; the bishops have yet, however, to pronounce. All the interest groups are fiercely protecting their own patch of the garden and nobody is prepared to give an inch; and it is precisely that kind of attitude on the part of the VECs and the Churches that has got Education to the confused state it is in now. The Joint Managerial Body (in charge of voluntary secondary schools) said 'We asked her for bread, she gave us a stone'. I couldn't believe my eyes when I read that.

Saturday 16 November

The day after the Anglo–Irish Agreement. The launching at Hillsborough went extremely well, except that Haughey has categorically and immediately rejected it in the strongest language. He, Blaney and the Provos are on the same side and the Unionists are rejecting it equally strongly from the other side. It has been, however, a marvellous success for Garret. Thatcher behaved herself perfectly, well almost perfectly—the whole international scene is good, but the Unionists are going bananas altogether. Thank God there has been no bloodshed or sign of it yet. That is our greatest worry.

179

Some of us were given the task of briefing various
people before the news actually broke yesterday. I found
myself briefing Tomas MacGiolla at the last moment. I
just gave him a rundown on the whole Agreement and
some hand-written notes in my quiet office in Leinster
House at 1 p.m. He was mild, curious, unsurprised and
quite supportive. Then, with considerable pride, I
watched all the doings from Hillsborough on television.
Thatcher is undoubtedly the sharpest thing out, she
looked very well (how can she be 60!), quite feminine, but
totally in control and totally on the ball. Garret, while he
will never be as authoritative or clear-spoken, obviously
knew exactly what he was at; every word was carefully
chosen. Then I made my way to the airport where we all
greeted Garret and company as they got off the planes;
general muted satisfaction and handshakes all round—he
must have a great feeling of achievement and
apprehension.

Watched a feast of television all night; the slit-eyed
Haughey condemning it, Gerry Collins spitting out words
he couldn't defend, Austin Currie appealing for support.
Most people, in fact, were like Currie—supporting. It's all
very historic and exciting but in the back of our minds is
the dread of a possible violent backlash.

Friday 22 November Drama on all fronts during the past week. A
magnificent reception here and in Britain and
abroad for the Anglo–Irish Agreement, the Unionists simmering and hollering and buffeting Tom King,
Haughey and company doing verbal athletics to retrieve
their unpopular position—its unpopularity was confirmed
in an opinion poll today.

The Dail debate on the Agreement was opened by
Garret with an excellent analytical key speech, closed by
Peter Barry with a fine script very badly delivered. I
managed to get my few words in too. (It's a pity Peter
Barry makes such a mess of the best scripts that any of us
are supplied with—we all envy him the Foreign Affairs
speechwriters.)

Mary Harney finally had her moment of truth and voted with us in the Dail. I think George Birmingham's years of friendship with her must have meant something after all — they are real friends. That was a brave decision of Mary's.

We are still worrying ourselves sick about the Unionist reaction but thank God, thank God, there hasn't been violence. The whole Unionist community is obviously bruised — but we did try for so long and so hard to get them talking about anything.

I organised champagne for the Cabinet after the Dail passed the Agreement yesterday. I can't understand why nobody else thought of it, but anyhow Garret seemed pleased by the idea and so did several others and we had a quiet glass of champagne in the little ante-room, with some solemnity because we all look on this as a beginning, not an end.

I went to Carlow for one of the major Fine Gael meetings on the Agreement. There were about 400 people and there was a great reception for my speech, which I had spent hours and hours writing myself (Barry Deering, a good strong supporter of mine, said to me at the end of the meeting 'Gemma, that was a great speech. Did Derry write it?').

Tuesday **26** November

Just after midnight — so tired, so hassled, so worried. Endless Cabinet and Estimates, tensions, bewilderment, Department not backing me up, meetings, Arklow, Wicklow and Bray, pressures and never at home, worrying about the children, worrying about never seeing Derry. What's the point of having a nice home if you're never there to enjoy it. But why do I let the pressures build up, what on earth does it matter — but how to stay calm and how to rescue some life back again for myself and family? How does Garret stay as sane as he is? Could you blame him for letting things get on top of him sometimes? Another pressure point: my Dail Questions (again!) on Thursday — I hate that, I'm not good at it. I haven't had time to see my father, who is ill.

Saturday
30
November

The end of a very busy week. Cabinet several times, functions every night.

A further pressure point was Dail Question Time on Thursday, but I think I did alright.

We have asked the teachers to talks—will they come? What will we say? What can we say?

Monday
2
December

Gales, rain and grimness this morning as I attended the appallingly sad funeral of two women, an aunt and niece, who were murdered in their farm in Wicklow last week. The tiny Barndarrig Church in the hills was packed. There was a palpable air of bewildered shock about the whole thing—these very good, plain country people contemplating two very ordinary women, their neighbours, raped and strangled by some man as yet unknown. Two plain coffins, the whole thing very simple, sad and just stuns one into silence. The priest, Fr Murphy, was very calm but obviously under stress. How can one possibly answer the questions on an occasion like this? I didn't attempt to go to the graveyard; the chaos was unimaginable in the grey downpour.

Then, as is the nature of things in politics, I did something completely different and dashed in to open an Antiques Fair in the Shelbourne Hotel and toured around it. What a contrast.

Wednesday
4
December

My big task this week has been clearing most of the Curriculum and Examinations Board Bill through Cabinet in various facilitating meetings. Alan, however, is obdurate. The facilitating takes place in the Cabinet ante-room, over several cups of tea and coffee, with the calm presence of Sean Barrett and with Sean's secretary the faithful Colm Butler, taking notes, while those of us round the table wrangle over various details—which I find very pressurising. Anyway, the Bill by this stage has almost the all-clear. It will be a really historic piece of legislation.

Tom King, the British Northern Ireland Secretary,

uttered the most appalling gaffe in Brussels yesterday, saying that Garret had 'accepted partition in perpetuity' in the Anglo–Irish Agreement; an unbelievable foolishness which will undermine our position and strengthen Haughey's and generally cause mayhem. What a fool! Is it perfidious Albion? It certainly wasn't off the cuff.

| Friday |
| **6** |
| December |

I was in Brussels this week for an EEC Education Ministers' meeting. It was much more interesting than usual because there was disagreement between Peter Sutherland and the German Minister Wilms. The argument was over money/power really, not subjects that usually trouble EEC Education Ministers' meetings. Peter is ebullient, on top of the job, clever, aggressive. I told him he should persuade Garret to stay on as leader of Fine Gael until Peter was ready to take over; I think he was secretly quite pleased—though he immediately said, 'You're leaving yourself out too readily'. Anyway, I had to leave, to travel as fast as I could back to Cork. Long, double flights, quite bumpy, frightening, and got into Cork on time for my meal with the Vocational Education Committee (Dick Langford is, as usual, clever and amusing). Then I went to a very high standard concert by the Cork School of Music orchestra in the City Hall. They were great, enthusiastic, lively.

Fell into bed at 11.30 exhausted.

| Friday |
| **13** |
| December |

The usual pre-Christmas late Dail sittings which kept me away from Roundwood, and a very heavy fog on Monday which kept me away from Tinahely.

Garret looking worn out all week, but all the same I'm fond of him even though he drives me mad. A very late and pleasant session with colleagues in the Dail bar on Wednesday night—unusual for me—some good crack with Avril Doyle, Nora Owen, Fintan Coogan, Alan Dukes. They all feel the teachers have gone over the top; they report solid support from their constituencies for our position.

I got my Curriculum and Examinations Board Bill through Government on Tuesday with no bother at all and won the point on getting the grant-in-aid to the new body as well. Also, I hope I got them to think again on the teachers' pay, to consider starting talks at four quarters for payment instead of at three thirds. This is against John Boland's wishes, but then I think he's too givish altogether and would land us with paying out too much too quickly.

We had a very busy night on Wednesday with the Senate motion on teachers' pay, followed by Senator Michael D. Higgins on the question of the Catholic Primary School Managers issuing their guidelines about having only practising Catholics as teachers—I was furious about that, they really are mischievous at best, malicious at worst, or maybe just plain stupid? If we weren't all under such pressure I could get John Rogers to think carefully about the Constitutional implications of it. Fianna Fail, as usual, called for the pay increases to be given in full and immediately; their Senators are a carbon copy of their TDs.

Sunday 15 December

Hilary Pratt rang me at 8.30 a.m. yesterday to enthuse about Joan FitzGerald, who apparently was on the *Late Late Show* on Friday—'She's won the election for you', and apparently Garret who joined her later was very good too. So that is generally a cheering-up thing. I forgot to ask 'what election?'

Saturday 21 December

Dessie O'Malley's new party, the Progressive Democrats, was announced today. Michael McDowell is the chairman. Will it hurt Fianna Fail more than us? It is depressing that Michael did this; it must be hurtful to Garret.

Once again went down to RTE for their *Saturday View* programme, which was a sort of adjournment debate. I'm so frequently down there I must have a path worn to it.

Anyhow, I think I did very well and find, as usual, that the key was careful preparation. Brian Lenihan was getting quite steamed up after lots of black coffee, Maurice Manning was mild and low-key and Ruairi Quinn was masterful, if a bit long-winded as usual.

THE FOURTH YEAR

TO

DECEMBER 1986

*Government discussions begin in January with the teachers'
Unions and other public sector Unions on Public Service pay
issues — The first public opinion polls taken since the foundation
of the Progressive Democrats show them gaining strength rapidly
with 19% of first preference votes — The Dail votes to amend the
Arbitrator's award to teachers so that it will be paid over a longer
period without retrospection. Fianna Fail and the Workers Party
oppose the motion — Mary O'Rourke, opposition spokesperson on
Education, announces the closure of Carysfort in the Dail while I
am engaged in private discussions with the College authorities
and preparing to make the official announcement — Garret Fitz-
Gerald announces a restructuring of the Government and then a
full re-shuffle and I am moved to Social Welfare — Jennifer
Guinness is kidnapped and released, her bravery being admired
throughout the country — The United States bombs Libya — The
Government offers the teachers a £35 million cash deal in an
effort to avert a strike. This offer is first rejected and later
accepted — 46,000 women get increased Social Welfare benefits as
phase 1 of the EEC equality directive is implemented — Teachers
threaten to boycott the examinations. The Government rejects
mediation by the Church in the on-going disputes — I announce*

new Social Welfare schemes over the summer: part-time work allowance, educational opportunities allowance, anti-fraud measures and the pilot 'Jobsearch' schemes—Joe Bermingham resigns from the Labour Party—A prolonged Dail debate on the 10th Amendment to the Constitution (the removal of the ban on divorce)—The Referendum takes place and divorce is rejected by a majority of 63% against, 36% for, with a poll of 62.5%—King Juan Carlos and Queen Sofia of Spain arrive for a four-day State visit—At the launching of An Post stamp series on distinguished Irish women, I make a speech on the ordination of women—I make a speech on Northern Ireland and the Anglo–Irish Agreement at the McGill Summer School in Glenties—On the night of 25/26 August hurricane Charlie strikes the East coast causing considerable damage, particularly in Wicklow—Garret FitzGerald dismisses Eddie Collins as Junior Minister for Energy—The Government announces that there will be £180 million overrun on the budget deficit—Considerable upheavals within all political parties over the implementation of phase 2 of the EEC equality directive. The Government makes several adjustments to the package which had been agreed in the Dail in July 1985—The Dail votes to spend £18 million on the Christmas bonus for Social Welfare recipients, instead of £21 million—Violent scenes outside the Royal Hotel in Bray, while I am holding a clinic there—Alice Glenn resigns from Fine Gael—The Extradition Bill is passed by the Dail—The Government wins the Adjournment Debate in the Dail and Oliver J. Flanagan makes his last appearance in the House.

Wednesday
1
January

I've been trying to make contact with John Boland in order to have preliminary discussions with him about tomorrow's meetings, but I haven't had any success in finding him. This is intensely frustrating. In the end we drew up a list of questions for him, got it over to the Department of the Public Service, and the Secretary of my own Department rang me up with the answers today. What a peculiar way to carry on! I keep telling myself not to get steamed up about it.

Thursday
2
January

I presented myself in the Department of the Public Service and then went with John Boland into the big conference room where we faced Gerry Quigley, Kieran Mulvey, Jim Dorney and accompanying persons. John was quite polite before the meeting. He handles meetings well, though I feel that I could do it quite easily myself, because there are certain formulae. I do think that the Public Service Ministry is considerably easier than Education, because he doesn't have all the big policy headaches and all the very small problems simultaneously.

All during the talks everybody was scrupulously polite and on the teachers' side Gerry Quigley did all the talking. We had arranged in advance that John would do all the talking from our side, so as to have general cohesion and consistency. So John did the usual introduction, which we all have to do, on the full economic background and I added a few back-up remarks. At this stage we seem to have progressed to the point where they are going to talk about everything. The meeting started at about 10.30 a.m. and ended around 1.30 p.m., so really after all my worry it was all quite mild.

If nobody says anything publicly about the talks, and if we abide by that agreement to say nothing, then something might be achieved. But the more I think about it the more indignant I am at the thought of teachers getting 10% on top of all the other Public Service increases. If we had really strong Government they couldn't possibly get it, certainly not without major productivity arrangements. But in reality, looking at the national figures, of course

everybody including ourselves should be taking a freeze
or a cutback in pay.

Saturday 4 January

Dessie O'Malley's new party is making great
waves politically, mainly Fianna Fail waves, and
making people sit up and think. Anything could
happen really.

Tuesday 7 January

A long Cabinet session, assembling a bit like
reluctant school children facing a difficult term,
prolonging the tea and coffee session in the ante-
room so as to put off the difficult moments. My main
worry was the question of Barry Desmond, the VHI and
the new private hospitals at Blackrock and the Mater. It
does seem as if there is a great ideological problem for
Barry in relation to these two new hospitals; Garret seems
to be instinctively against much private medicine and I
raised the question with some trepidation but at least got
a little discussion going. Sean Barrett and myself had a
long chat with Barry Desmond afterwards and he has
agreed to see the people from both hospitals tomorrow,
but I'm not really hopeful of a result. He sets his face and
gets very stubborn. We also had our first gallop around
the Budget figures, which imply a gap of £200 million at
least, without any hope of tax easing for anyone, Barry
pronouncing that he won't make any more cuts, and that's
final, he says.

It would seem that there will have to be cuts in the areas
of Health, Social Welfare, Environment—all Labour Ministries. That's ominous.

Sunday 12 January

A great deal has happened since last Tuesday.
More sessions with the teacher Unions, which
have all gone very smoothly, very calmly, and
Kieran Mulvey doing the talking at the very long second
session.

Monday 13 January

Midnight, after the third session of talks with the
teachers, which went on since 5 o'clock this
afternoon. They were more difficult but at least
we adjourned them and didn't break them off, which

seemed to be a strong possibility at one stage. They have homed in on retrospection, which is out of the question and may well be the breaking point, and then the fun will start again, only now we are approaching examination time. The demands for more money seem to be insatiable.

Yesterday, after a Bray Wanderers football match, in which I was heartily, if good-humouredly, booed by the Bray Wanderers cheer section, I did a big cook-up for various elderly relations.

| Wednesday |
| 15 |
| January |

Between preliminary Budget meetings and the meeting with teachers today, things are very tense. Cabinet yesterday indicated the gap that has to be bridged, and the meeting with the teachers was suspended to let them report back to their Executive. It culminated tonight in their decision to hold special meetings on 8 February and to consider further industrial action — this has the look of confrontation and severe danger and is profoundly depressing. It is hard to see an outcome which will do anything other than wreck a lot of what I have been trying to achieve, and of course will damage me severely in the process. So it's back to the pressure cooker and the lid which blows off may well be me. How can they hold out for £110 million on top of the already extra £60 million on the Education pay bill? But no doubt there will be divided views among my colleagues on this.

| Friday |
| 17 |
| January |

Just back in (at 1 a.m. on Saturday 18) from Cabinet on the Budget. Yesterday, I came home in shreds of tension because of the threatened pupil/teacher ratio attacks on my Education Estimates. Such a prospect kept me awake (which is unusual for me), tossing and turning with a headache, finally coughing and coughing and a few hours fitful sleep before I was up telephoning various bodies to work out my defence strategy. The problem is that I could not really do that to Education, and would have to resign rather than do it, but I must work so hard to try to convince colleagues.

Anyway, we had a long afternoon and night at Cabinet getting nowhere. We found £26 million on Current Expenditure and about £30 million on Capital, with a possible £38 million Current on Pay Related Benefit. I was tense and anxious, having held meetings in the Department on all the problems this morning. Finbarr O'Callaghan, the excellent and highly intelligent Assistant Secretary, was as tense and anxious as I was. All this is happening against the background of the first opinion poll since the foundation of the PDs—putting the new party at 19%, 22% for us, 41% for Fianna Fail. O'Malley is really a rolling force; he has caught people's imaginations without actually saying what he is going to do. How very frustrating when we're in there grappling with the impossible. Anyway, at the very last minute I raised the question of my discussions with Alan etc., and my impassioned plea and offer of finding alternative cuts made them agree to drop the pupil/teacher ratio thing. The relief I felt was washing through me. I had worked myself up into a quiet, internal frenzy over it. Garret at these times is compassionate—I think he understands the emotion of educational cuts. Anyway, I think there'll be a lot more difficulty before we're through.

Tuesday
21
January

I'm still in bed at 10 a.m. because Cabinet met until 4 a.m. this morning. How can I describe the cold light beating down in the large Council Chamber, the thin stale air, the coughs and snorts, the occasional nervous hilarity or high spirits when things seem to be falling into place and the silent despondency when it turns out to be worse than expected, the chicken and chips eaten out of brown paper bags at night, wine out of a tea cup (we only have drinks very late to keep going).

John Boland produced a scheme last night which looked for a while like our salvation, occasioning hours of examination by his experts and Department of Finance experts, but eventually producing a fraction of what we hoped for. Garret manages to keep going through it all, how I don't know. Meetings have been going on non-stop for days and it seems like forever.

| Wednesday |
| **22** |
| January |

Yesterday we only started Cabinet at 4.30 p.m. and ended at 12.30 a.m., relatively short as our meetings go. But now at last there seems to be a Budget taking shape; uncertainty hangs around because I never know if there will be a change, but I don't think so now, the shape of it is peculiar. A 7% rise in spending— that's debt service and social welfare (not unemployment, mainly rises in the rates of social welfare)—a deficit of £1050 billion. Garret says that is the absolute outside maximum, a raising of taxes on Insurance and Pension Funds, 23%–25% VAT, all going to finance £100 million of income tax relief.

Labour fought great battles in every area and won some of them. I was somewhat inhibited for part of the time because of my anxiety not to have some awful cut imposed on Education. Garret told me privately that Labour were particularly annoyed by my successful defence of the pupil/teacher ratio—which made me indignant since I had given up equivalent savings! The group dynamics are fascinating: John Boland, clever, sharp and highly political; Alan, intellectual, sarcastic, ploughing his way calmly through the maze of figures; John Bruton, hair askew, a mixture of clever, honest incisiveness and originality but very frustrated; Peter Barry (only there for a day) is political but doesn't seem intellectual at all.

| Sunday |
| **26** |
| January |

Yesterday I did a marathon—drove to Tralee with John Harris, working all the way, and delivered the John Marcus O'Sullivan Lecture to about 300 people from the Education world, in Tralee RTC. It was an hour-long speech, written mostly by John Harris and myself and concentrated entirely on the main ideas in the Green Paper. It was the first such very long lecture that I've delivered, but since it was given to people who are really interested in Education, it went down well and was very carefully listened to. I had a cup of tea with various dignitaries (Sean McBride, the Principal of the RTC, was beside himself with joy) and then drove back to Dublin and joined some friends very late for a curry, which would have been lovely if I wasn't so exhausted. Eight hours work in the car, three hours in Tralee.

Des O'Malley's new PD bandwagon rolled into Bray last week. That's all a bit worrying, to put it mildly.

The Budget, however, is all in place. There are several severe cuts in my area which will be sensitive to deal with, but when I think how much worse it could have been . . . .

The strangest event for me this past week was the visit of the Minister for Education from Qatar. He was a dark, quiet, small Sheikh (the Emir's brother). I seemed to spend the whole week sitting beside him at endless meals, struggling to communicate through his interpreter, making speeches to him and finally waving goodbye at the airport at 4.30 p.m. on Friday as he went off with his entourage in the brother's Boeing 707. Despite the Arab attitude towards women, he proffered very warm invitations to Qatar for Derry and me, but I can't imagine myself actually going. I got landed with the entertaining job because the College of Surgeons had invited him to visit — they have 34 students from Qatar and I gather that he is important in the Arab world.

|Friday|
|**31**|
|January|

Alan delivered his Budget speech two days ago, coolly and well, but he totally undersold the tax relief element in it. So the whole thing fell rather flat, to the chagrin of a lot of us. I could kill him for missing the opportunity.

Late on Budget night, in the bar, Austin Deasy confessed gloomily, sotto voce, to myself and Pat Cooney that he was very upset about the way the Budget had gone and felt that too many easy options were taken. He said that when he looked at the children going to school at age seven and eight, with their little bags on their backs, he felt he was letting them all down. So we confessed that there were a lot more who felt badly about it, but we all had different reasons for hanging on in there. And we reminded him that Haughey had done and would do much worse. We have to do the best we can.

Long, long days and nights. I worked away at a lot of things at my desk across 'The Bridge of Sighs' in Leinster House, including mainly the development of strategy on teachers' pay. Apparently John Boland had words with Garret very late at night over some newspaper reports of increases in politicians' salaries etc. However, considering that John was responsible for a great amount of money found for the Budget, he does deserve a lot of credit. But I couldn't trace him all day yesterday, he seems to go to ground occasionally. I had extremely urgent business to transact on Thursday and had enormous difficulty getting at him at all.

My relations with him have progressed. He had an awful letter from a purported Fine Gael woman ASTI member accusing him of using foul language throughout the teachers' negotiations. I composed a reply telling her how very wrong that was and how untrue, and he was very grateful to me, nearly emotional, about it. What a complex character. Like myself, he must have all his own self-doubts inside.

I had Dail Questions on Thursday and managed to keep calm most of the time—a new approach, despite the impossibility and indignant excitement of Mary O'Rourke.

There has been a big set-back on the pay issue. Mary Robinson has advised Greg Maxwell on the Public Service Union side that they can't agree to alter any Arbitrator's award, so back into the melting pot with the whole thing.

The teachers' quite vicious campaign against me continues.

| Tuesday |
| **4** |
| February |

Am well and truly in the wars over the Carysfort closure. Mary O'Rourke somehow got wind of the decision before I had time to make the public announcement, leapt up in the Dail, and announced it to an apparently horrified world. Despite the delicate steps we were taking in order to break it properly to everybody concerned, the education world, led by Fianna Fail, has now gone into a paroxysm of hysterical indignation. Mary Harney has joined in the emotional bloodbath and the Sisters of Mercy are describing me as hard-hearted, insensitive etc. Oh the hypocrisy of it all! Between that and the impending teachers' pay debate and subsequent strikes, the important thing is to keep the cool and battle on. I would like to be able to persuade my colleagues to let me re-appoint the Arbitrator, but John Boland is completely against it. Several meetings have taken place.

Friday	It has been one of those weeks . . . culminating
7	yesterday in the Dail with the teachers' arbitration
February	motion, while the Carysfort storm developed

apace, but I am keeping extremely cool, presenting to the world a calm, reasonable and firm front, I hope. I feel, of course, that the Department has let me down severely on the Carysfort question once again, and that we could have had a longer lead-in to it—not to mention the fact that the Government wouldn't listen to me when I told them the implications of doing this. So all day yesterday in the Dail the teachers gathered and the speeches flowed and I think I dealt with the closing shouting match on my feet in the Dail coolly and well; my colleagues certainly were happy with me and congratulated me afterwards.

I did a great many media interviews, including one in *Today Tonight* which led to a considerable hassle with Joe Mulholland over the format. I was quite firm about the arrangement which I had made with them about going on by myself for a final interview. There were awkward moments when I arrived at RTE, because they wanted to change it; I stayed firm and for a while the programme looked doubtful. Mary O'Rourke was there but had the sense to realise that in fact RTE were trying to change an already agreed format. Brian Farrell weighed in, trying to make me change my mind, but I was quite adamant and then I went on and batted well enough, I hope, with Brian Farrell. I didn't need all that hassle before a very important interview—Mulholland and Farrell pressurising me while the make-up girl tried to iron out the ravages.

Now the problems in Education will really start because

the chief bottlewashers in the Unions, who are also extremely political, will have to try to get some kind of vengeance on me because of the vote. The PDs finally voted with us. I suppose they really couldn't justify any other course of action considering the enormous extra amount of money implied. Nobody (except me) seems to put it to Fianna Fail that they are behaving totally cynically in voting against the motion in order to give the teachers even more than the huge increases we're already giving them.

Liam Skelly even voted with us, having attacked me on television and radio—his most hurtful comment being that he 'never approved of token Ministers anyway'. That greatly annoyed my colleagues. Nora Owen, with great rage, issued a condemning statement.

| Thursday |
| **13** |
| February |

I'm a bit stunned today. There's a re-shuffle going on and I am to be Minister for European Affairs. I spent last night thinking and talking over it because I was worried at the beginning that it would look like a souped-up Junior Ministry. Garret is adamant that it's a full Ministry, but then he's not me.

This comes right in the middle of ongoing hassle and chaos over Carysfort, which has escalated to being a political disaster of amazing proportions—as I had warned. The PDs have swept the boards in the latest poll, leaving us behind. The Parliamentary Party is in a fit and now Garret has set his re-shuffle in train. It may, however, be too late to save us and who will he have to blame? I am desperately trying to protect myself and I hope I succeed.

More media exposure last week. I am trying not to notice the tide of personal abuse. My instincts about this over the past few months turned out to be right. One of the most hurtful things was a telegram from someone I thought was a very old friend, over the Carysfort issue. The telegram read simply 'High-handed and cruel'. What good friends to have in a crisis!

The pressures have been much worse than I thought possible, but on the whole I have kept, I hope, an outward cool.

As part of this re-shuffle Alan is going to Education; the mind boggles—God help them, they'll have a fit. I think he will be very good indeed.

Friday
14
February

I am in black depression. Garret has made the most appalling mess of the re-shuffle and I am the victim to expediency and am now Minister for Social Welfare. I have spent some of the time privately in tears and had seriously considered resignation, but Derry called in our very close friends and we had an in-depth talk about it and they were absolutely against resignation. The Fianna Fail people, naturally, are calling it a total botch-up and have put down a vote of no confidence next week.

Alan Dukes is now in Justice—he has been badly treated too. All the sordid details of Barry's refusal to move from Health and Social Welfare are well exposed in the media, leaving me described as being thrown to the wolves, demoted, sacrificed etc. together with various assessments of my performance. If Garret had thought I was a bad Minister for Education, surely he would have had the guts to tell me?

Today has been quite an ordeal: going up to the Phoenix Park, keeping a tight and cheerful control, saying goodbye to all the officials in the Department of Education and all the great girls who have been helping me so much in my Setanta office with constituency matters. It is extraordinary and quite mind-boggling how one can be so rapidly moved from a Department without even time to think.

Shocked messages are pouring in from all over the country and from all the parties, including an extremely warm note from Mary O'Rourke, which caused me some emotion. I'm astonished at the warmth from literally hundreds of people.

This morning I found it difficult to look at Garret at all and had to avoid the sympathetic signals from John Bruton and Michael Noonan.

Tonight I face the Multiple Sclerosis Ball and I think I might die in the middle of it! But of course in the middle of all this disillusion I have to pick myself up and get stuck in, because I'm damned if anyone is going to see me down.

Garret went on television last night and spoke a whole lot of soothing nonsense to try and calm the situation.

Saturday
15
February

I'm writing this full account of the whole re-shuffle today because I feel it's important to get it down accurately while it is fresh in my mind.

At about 6 p.m. last Wednesday (12 February) Garret called me down to see him. I was at the time in my office on the second floor of Leinster House, surrounded by about fourteen people representing staff and students of Carysfort College, working through the fall-out from my announcement about the closure of the College. The phone rang and it was, unusually, Garret on the other end saying 'Can you come down to my office?' I said 'Could I come in about half an hour, because I have some people here from Carysfort?' and Garret said 'No, I would like you to come down straight away'. So I apologised to the people and explained I had to go down to the Taoiseach's office and if they would like to wait I would be back as soon as I could.

So I went down into Garret's office and he quite hurriedly but cheerfully told me, to my astonishment, that he was beginning a major re-shuffle and had decided that it would be right for me to leave Education because it was damaging me in the constituency particularly, and that he had decided because of the Northern Ireland situation to divide Foreign Affairs into two full Ministries and make me Minister for European Affairs and Development Co-operation. He mentioned that he felt I would do a very good job and that I had already shown a 'flair' for this area; he was pleased that I spoke two of the major European languages as this had been a big problem with Ministers for Foreign Affairs. I was quite stunned but I thanked him and said it was an honour that he was offering me this appointment and that I would work very hard at it. However, I said to him that I was a little bit worried that it might be seen as being second-in-command in Foreign Affairs, and I would be glad if I could think about it and see him to tease it out later, although I had very positive feelings about it and obviously would do what he wanted. He was extremely affable and said 'Yes certainly, some time to think but not too much', made some more flattering remarks about my work in Education and the prospects of this new job and patted me affectionately on the shoulder with a cheerful smile as I left.

By that stage the Carysfort people had left my office with a promise of a resumption of our discussions as soon as possible, and I had to dash over to the Senate to sit in for half an hour at an Education debate. I had a very quick sandwich in the canteen and then went over to the Parliamentary Party meeting, to find that Garret had just announced to them that he was embarking on a major Government restructuring next day.

Naturally, for the rest of the night rumours and stories abounded and Garret remained in his office with people going in and out. I rang Derry, who came in. I also asked a particularly close political friend of mine who is always very balanced, Senator Katharine Bulbulia, to come up to my office, and the three of us formulated the elements I'd need to have for this new package. They were both very positive about it, as I was, and pleased at my getting a whole new Department.

When I was down in Garret's office, I explained to him quite forcibly that I was not concerned about the enormous pressures or the personal unpopularity of my Education job, that I felt there was an undercurrent of support in the population, that there were a lot of things I still had to do in Education but that if he wanted to move me, obviously I would do what he wished, but hoped he would put someone in Education who would carry through what we were doing. I made it quite clear again that I didn't mind losing my Dail seat if what I was doing was the right thing. He responded warmly to this and made a remark about not too many people having such courage.

During the course of the evening, Garret called me in several times between 9.30 p.m. and 12 midnight, expanded on the new Ministry and answered various questions that I put to him, for example: where would the offices be? would there be a full Departmental Secretary? who would receive visiting European Heads of State (in the context of the forthcoming visit of the King of Spain)? All during these brief discussions whenever I said 'Garret I'm sorry to bother you with these questions' he always responded that I was absolutely right to raise the questions because it helped him to clarify his mind also on the new position. He repeatedly made it clear that it would be a full Ministry with full Departmental structures.

So I came home at half past midnight, very pleased, having fully accepted the new post, without many misgivings, leaving Garret apparently in good form. I rang my sister in Brussels to tell her to get the spare bedroom ready.

Next morning, Thursday 13 February (two days ago) at about 10 a.m. I was unaware that Garret had been up most of the night facing a major crisis, and I rang him with two more queries: first to clarify how we would deal with parliamentary questions in the Dail, and second, what we would do about conveying to Foreign Ministries of the EEC that I would be a full Minister so that they wouldn't feel they weren't dealing with the person at the top. He said that he really hadn't gone into that detail, but that he would consider it and that the Dail question area posed no problem whatsoever. He sounded distracted and tired, which puzzled me.

So then I went in to the Dail and found Leinster House a ferment of eddying and whirling currents of rumours — difficulties with Barry Desmond were among them. Changes to the scenario of the night before seemed to be happening; word of Alan Dukes for Education, Boland for Health and Social Welfare. My heart began to sink gradually and my fears were confirmed when at about 2.30 p.m. Alan Dukes came into my office and said, obviously under some stress, that the plan was changed and that I was going to be given Social Welfare. Alan obviously felt very awkward about telling me — I presumed he had been sent by Garret and my first reaction was to have a quick weep, to Alan's kind consternation. Then the phone rang and I was summoned down to Garret's office to be greeted by someone quite different from the night before, who was very brusque, tense, and said 'Really, with all this difficulty you're creating about who's going to do what, it appears that the whole thing just wouldn't work and I have decided to give you Social Welfare'. This was such an extraordinary volte-face from the entire attitude of the night before—the helpful approach to all the questions I had asked, the congratulations to me for thinking it out and asking them—that I was literally struck dumb. When I recovered I asked him if this change wasn't simply a result of Barry Desmond being troublesome and refusing to give up the Health side of his portfolio, necessitating a separate Social Welfare Department, rather than any other reason. I can't really remember his answer to that; he avoided it I think and went on and on about how the Social Welfare Commission's Report was coming out soon and there would be a great deal of policy work to be done. I pointed out to him that, on the contrary, Social Welfare would indeed be all cuts in the Budget and incredible difficulties, with no time for me to develop policies. He discounted that earnestly, saying 'there'll be no more cuts in social welfare', and assured me that the staff people in Social Welfare were excellent and, obviously under some time pressure, put me out of the office. One of the things he said was that all the Labour Ministers had volunteered my name for Social Welfare when it was decided to make it a separate Ministry. That news didn't cheer me up. He said Labour felt I would be 'caring'.

I stumbled back upstairs, deeply upset, but had dutifully accepted the situation.

At 4.30 p.m. a tense group of Ministers, hardly looking at each other, obviously shocked, assembled in the Cabinet room and Garret rattled out the list of Junior Ministries. We all rushed in to the Dail at 4.45 p.m. where he read out all the changes and uproar ensued.

Since then I have been terribly upset. It appears that the original restructuring which Garret had intended was that there would be the new Foreign Affairs Ministry, the amalgamation of Public Service and Finance, and Barry Desmond moved to Environment with John Boland in Health and Social Welfare. Of course, Barry's position of refusing to move wrecked all that and I got shafted!

| Sunday **16** February | I have recovered my calm somewhat but it has been replaced by anger mixed with despair of a kind. |

I had to go to a Ball the night after the re-shuffle, (St Valentine's Night 14 February, in the Mansion House) smiling brightly and being photographed in *The Irish Times* and described as 'radiant' at the dance. I suppose this is real politics. I was approached by Kieran Mulvey of the ASTI, who expressed 'great regret' that I'd gone and was amazed at the choice of my successor. More bright smiling for TV etc. was needed when those of us involved in the re-shuffle had to go up to the Park to exchange seals of office. I wore bright cheerful red and kept the chin well up.

My recovery was somewhat upset by an *Irish Times* headline story on Saturday (yesterday) which implied that it was all my own fault because I 'had refused the Foreign Affairs job'. So in my defence I felt I had to speak in confidence to some Sunday paper journalists and did so and told them the facts. I felt Peter Prendergast had fed that wrong version to them to defend Garret.

| Tuesday **18** February | Life goes on and things are reverting to an uneasy calm. I find the Social Welfare offices down in Busaras in Store Street to be depressing, brown |

and 1930s style. The whole subject of Social Welfare is almost a completely closed book and the constant, unremitting reminders of Education are painful. Dee has made the change with me — the only familiar face.

Cabinet today was — how would I describe it — peculiar. Garret was quite matter of fact, even throughout the discussion on his unmercifully foolish boob over 'accepting the resignations' of Junior Ministers Donal Creed and Michael D'Arcy, who publicly denied that they had resigned, causing yet another statement in the Dail.

I am bowled over by the huge number of kind people who have been writing to me and by all the TDs who have been approaching me very sympathetically, and I have been resolutely chatting, smiling and shrugging. Garret suggested conspiratorially to me that I should give him a list of things that I wanted to see done in Education, so that he could speak to Pat Cooney.

Last night I had to go down to Greystones and East Wicklow district meetings and I made my 'politics is about serving' speech which I had composed to meet all occasions. They were all very noble and paid handsome tributes to me and so I felt like someone who had actually died and passed away. All I can hope is that things will somehow work out. On the principle that a week is a long time in politics and that a dignified demeanour is the only course open to me, I will struggle on and persevere, but I will not give any cuts until I know precisely where I'm at in the Social Welfare Department.

One of the bizarre side-effects of this mess is the fact that Pat Cooney is in Education. When I heard about that rumour in the middle of the maelstrom, I asked Garret on the phone not to make the appointment, but he said despairingly 'it's too late now'. That was one of the things people found difficult to believe and I'm wondering what role did Peter Barry play in it? And in the axing of my European job?

Maybe I was a disastrous failure to mention 'morality' at all in this extraordinary country—apparently morality is only about sex—and maybe I should have defied the Government on the closing of Carysfort. Perhaps those words 'morality' and 'Carysfort' will both be written on my grave.

| Thursday 20 February |

I invented the flu yesterday and came home at lunchtime. This was caused really by the fact that so many kind people, Michael Noonan, Nuala Fennell, John Bruton, Maurice Manning, Madeleine Taylor-Quinn, Hugh Coveney, were all wanting to come and talk to me and tell me how they felt about the re-shuffle, and so much concerned niceness and kindness from people whom I like made me feel quite on edge, so I decided to clear out.

This morning's *Irish Times* leads with the teachers having 'courteous' talks with Pat Cooney and Enda Kenny—now Junior Minister in the Department of Labour and Education with strikes being deferred, Pat Cooney 'appreciating' their decision to run the Easter oral exams. All this makes it look as if a difficult woman, who was in Education, was the cause of it all and has now been got out of the way.

Bruce Arnold has an excoriating article on Garret in today's *Irish Independent*. It includes a scathing dismissal of Peter Barry, but they'll all say I caused him to write it despite the fact that I had nothing to do with it, and Bruce never mentioned it to me.

Derry is being extremely kind and supportive. He understands fully my reaction to the whole question. He is in a somewhat difficult position as he has to continually meet Garret and is doing so this evening on their strategy committee which Derry chairs.

The Cabinet has begun to close ranks again and of course I will do so as well, despite the traumas. I suppose one of the worst aspects of all this is the shock to one's self-confidence and the anxiety that one hasn't been a good Minister, that one has made serious mistakes and that maybe the teachers were right and that it was all my fault. That's a sort of a lonely feeling.

Thursday 27 February

Keeping going at full belt now, the equilibrium almost 100% returned, the prospects, however, still most unattractive. I had Social Welfare Questions in the Dail yesterday and seemed to handle them alright. I had a Combat Poverty Agency Bill in the Dail on Tuesday. In Cabinet I had a disability cuts crisis and have warned Garret repeatedly that I won't carry out £15 million cuts—which John Bruton, newly in Finance, is immediately demanding. John is glowering at me continually and I hope Garret has done what I've told him to do and has spoken to him about it so that there will not be this confrontation in Cabinet. I've reminded Garret of his insistence that Social Welfare cuts were 'all finished'.

This business has not done the constituency's morale any good at all and it will be up to me to raise their spirits by making them see that I'm in good spirits myself. That's a good joke.

| Saturday |
| **1** |
| March |

I toughed it out at Cabinet and more or less won the day, but not without considerable tensions. Poor John Bruton is under pressure. He feels pressure intensely. Garret's attitude was 'we made a mess of this £15 million cut and we'd better sort it out'. It certainly is a huge mess, that's for sure. So the Social Welfare Bill, with all its difficulties, is even further delayed while we wrangle.

Feeling rather low and dispirited, I had a chat with Garret, who just looked miserable and generally upset when I told him how I felt. He said that my position after the re-shuffle was the thing he was most unhappy about. But, as I pointed out to him, he didn't have any positive suggestion of any kind as to how the damage might be undone. It's a peculiar feeling to go around being regarded as the object of some pity, like a wronged woman, but it doesn't help the image or the status and is a bit of a death knell for any kind of personal motivation.

I'm worried about the Social Welfare Bill and all its manifest complications, the timing of it, next Tuesday's cuts meeting. I can't imagine how it will all work out.

At the Cabinet meeting last Thursday, I was totally calm and matter of fact, explaining that I was simply not in a position to go into the Dail with unexpected Social Welfare cuts. Despite John Bruton's problems, there was obviously no way around that. Garret later asked me to reflect and give at least one of the cuts. I wrote him a note later saying that if John Bruton took the responsibility of announcing a list of cuts on Tuesday night, including any Social Welfare ones, I would consider that. How John would explain it all is a matter which he can worry about.

There are gathering storm clouds in Northern Ireland,

with a general strike for Monday. The test of Thatcher is at hand on this issue. Garret is, I think, obsessed by it, and that's one of the problems which causes him not to think enough about other areas.

The divorce issue is gathering momentum too, but I'm glad to say he seems determined about a Referendum before the summer.

Monday 3 March

Peter Barry had asked me to go to address two important St Patrick's Day dinners in the United States, in Savannah and Atlanta, but now they turn out to be all-male. I was absolutely furious and said 'Really, if these people are going to refuse to receive a Minister of the Irish Government on grounds of sex, the rest of the Irish Government should boycott the dinners'. However, I reluctantly had to see his point when he said that we need the Americans more than they need us. It makes my blood boil—the Irish in America are even worse than the Irish at home.

Tuesday 4 March

All in all, things political are not cheerful on any front. Should Garret go? I think he wants to, but what about his replacement? And I seem to have been transformed in the public mind from a competent, achieving, firm Minister, to an unpleasant, intransigent, uncertain person. Garret feels very strongly about the teachers' issue but is not directing it hour by hour as he should. He is giving an impression of confusion.

Austin had a strong supportive speech about the Government's stance all ready to give, but he told me he was asked by Pat Cooney to say nothing at all. The whole scene is rather depressing. Ruairi Quinn and Pat Cooney (what an alliance!) are, it seems to me weakening the Government position. Some of my people in the constituency and the Parliamentary Party feel that we should have gone to the country the night after winning the Dail vote on the Arbitrator's award to the teachers; I'm beginning to feel they're right, Fine Gael would have a strong position of integrity and courage and a platform of 'who governs the country, Government or special interest groups?' But we've slipped away from the high ground already. They also feel that I should have done what Barry Desmond did, and refused to move from Education. That never entered my head for one minute.

Cabinet today was one long nightmare, when I stated my opposition to the whole range of cuts which they were proposing in Social Welfare—remembering meanwhile Garret's earlier assurance that I would not be required to make these cuts. I found the whole day most painful, soul-destroying and incredibly pressured. We finally broke up at 8 p.m., having started at 10 o'clock this morning, and I had conceded basically nothing except £2.1 million extra in tightening-up measures. I don't think Garret ever expected to find me so stubborn and certainly all the others were shocked by my attitude. I kept reminding myself that I didn't care. I resisted all appeals for reason or helpfulness. John Bruton was fed up and of course I don't blame him at all. Alan calmly announced that he felt I was behaving unacceptably.

I wish in a way that it had ended in crisis, with me being fired, because there is a bundle of trouble ahead. Understandably, John Bruton has had to identify the areas for cuts and he sees Social Welfare as full of wasteful expenditure. Of course, I didn't go into this job for crucifixion or self-destruction. I can't believe Garret allowed it to happen after the serious discussions I had with him, both on the day of the re-shuffle and on several occasions since, quietly pointing out the implications to him. The Labour Party sat quiet while all this was going on. When I staggered back to my office at 8 p.m. Mary McEntaggart (my doctor friend) was in my office; she exclaimed at my white face and prescribed copious cups of tea.

Northern Ireland erupted today in a lot of serious trouble—demonstrations and rioting. The Unionist politicians got it all wrong and couldn't control it. It's a very worrying situation which fills us all with concern, and particularly Garret. I do think he would be a lot better off if he didn't find himself spending eight hours in Cabinet hounding me for cuts which I had warned him about in great detail several weeks ago. To put it mildly, that sort of day is unproductive.

| Thursday |
| **6** |
| March |

Yesterday, Wednesday, the Fine Gael Ministers' meeting about the Social Welfare cuts was tense. John Bruton exuding anger; I'm blamed, of course, by everybody. I feel that perhaps something is being cooked up; I am not sure. So Garret's chickens are, alas, coming home to roost now and I will have to tough it out because going to Garret has obviously not worked for me in the past. I pointed out that if anyone had a right to sleepless nights, it was me. (Actually, I very rarely stay awake.)

Meanwhile, the Social Welfare scenario unfolds in front of me. It seems impenetrable and is hugely problematic, immovable, there is every possible anomaly in the system, there are Union problems causing continuous hassle. The new Private Secretary is very difficult to get used to, even though she's full of goodwill.

The closing of Carysfort is still a cause célèbre. There are lots of talks about appointing special bodies to find out other uses for it and Fianna Fail are still condemning the closure and making promises behind their hands about keeping it on with teacher training.

I'm a bit miserable, under a lot of pressure, very little enjoyment, if any, left in the scene, and it is small consolation that so many people think I was good in Education.

And behind all this I have a great deal of serious worry about the health of my parents and the continual need for contact and care.

| Sunday |
| **9** |
| March |

Today's papers carry a whole lot of rotten publicity about me, a particularly upsetting article in the *Sunday Independent* by Anne Harris (I wish these people would even come and talk to me), and Geraldine Kennedy's interview in the *Sunday Press* is totally different to what I expected, so that's a bad day. So what, so what—but it's hard, hard. Where would I be without Derry?

We have to go to the United States next Friday to do our 'representing the Government' bit. There will be at least a chance to think a bit on the long flights. I'm delighted to hear also that we are going with friends for a quick visit to the Holy Land at Easter.

I really hate political life at the moment, although the North Wicklow Fine Gael meeting on Thursday in Bray was well attended, good, cheerful. I don't like to think of the effect of all this negative publicity in today's paper on all my loyal Wicklow friends.

All in all, the depression and sadness about the political events have passed, but the lack of motivation and interest persists. I'm constantly able to rise to occasions and nobody would ever know that I have any problems; internally however I constantly suffer set-backs. The huge numbers of lovely letters from all over the country have been a great help, and some of them are very moving. My friends are unanimously furious about what has been going on, but already I am determined to throw myself back into this job 100%, determined to make it something, determined to come out of this strongly, and writing this diary is an enormous help and is one way of getting it out of my system.

| Sunday |
| 16 |
| March |

On Friday we flew out on that nine and a half hour marathon to Miami, met by last year's heavy gang plus all the usual top security, and also by Pat and Marcia Byrne from the IDA, who are both extremely thoughtful, relaxed and helpful.

The weather was scorching and the parade and all the functions in Miami were very like last year, but they seemed to consider me an old friend. We dashed from the parade to the airport and flew to Philadelphia through horrible rain storms and bumps all the way, to attend another parade and more functions.

We marched in the Philadelphia parade, which was a long and pleasant walk in the sun and the breeze. The parade was like any other I suppose. Having mounted the podium, I said all the right words at the right moments, left the stand and stood behind it when NORAID appeared, plus a band of youths from Antrim carrying crosses with Bobby Sands etc. all over them, youngsters with black berets and sunglasses looking extremely sinister and tragically young.

Monday
17
March

We emerged from our Philadelphia hotel on this bizarre day to find the efforts of our 'minder' had resulted in a huge white limousine arriving at the door. He had, apparently, phoned around to get a normal car but this monstrosity was the only one available. So we drove to an almost totally empty, large, side-chapel of the Cathedral. Another St Patrick's Day Mass, after which we repaired to City Hall where we all made speeches. Next was a lunch with the Friendly Sons of St Patrick. I did my sincere thing and it was well received. The food was cabbage, bacon and potatoes. In the evening we drove to Delaware for a big formal dinner where I spoke to a large crowd.

So, our official visit is completed. Philadelphia might be a very nice city indeed if we had managed to look at it at all, but it's been lovely to at least have had a few days away from the hassle at home.

Friday
28
March

All day on Sunday Fine Gael Ministers met in the Berkeley Court Hotel (upstairs in a very nice penthouse suite, where we can be totally private, with the very kind personal attention of P.V. Doyle). We had long, interesting and very challenging discussions.

This week I brought the Social Welfare Bill through the Senate in some considerable detail. It was very interesting and didn't give me trouble—indeed the debate helped me to clarify points.

Saturday
29
March

We are in Jerusalem for Easter and have spent the day touring the whole city with an extremely good guide. It was absolutely fascinating between the old city, the layers of archaeology and history, the Christian holy places, the Arab streets, the Jewish quarter.

Sunday 30 March

Today we set off very early and drove through the desert, the wilderness of Judaea, through dry brown hills and scrub, past Bedouin tents, and along the Dead Sea emerging through a haze on our left.

We visited Masada, an amazing place (reached by cablecar) where 1,000 Jews committed suicide in AD 70 after a 3 year siege. We met some Irish pilgrims who had been walking in the Holy Land with Donncha O'Dulaing—they were all in absolutely great form. Lunch at the Dead Sea, in which Derry swam, but I must say I was put off by the heavy sulphuric smell. On to Qum'ran, the site of the Dead Sea Scroll discovery, very dramatic too. All in all, another quite amazing day, full of unforgettable sensations, the ancient history and the modern conflict and tensions all rolled into one. This is a sad and tragic land. What a world. It puts my troubles at home into perspective—a mere spot on the huge history of everything.

Sunday 6 April

Home to a very familiar scene. Teachers threatening sabotage on the exams—what else is new! But the economic indicators are looking slightly better. Northern Ireland, unfortunately, is looking bad, we are afraid the loyalists may be turning to violence and intimidation of RUC men and women. The office is as demanding as ever, with a huge amount of problems to be tackled.

Sunday 13 April

Criticism and isolation of me on the teachers' pay issue, Fine Gael very low indeed in today's IMS polls and Michael Keating has gone to the PDs. That's not a real surprise.

Wednesday 16 April

Garret finally spoke out last night and went on television to be strong and definite on the teachers' dispute and the huge retrospection they are looking for. He was very good.

A Fianna Fail motion on appointing a mediator is causing some tension, Labour vacillating again, problems about the vote.

The whole country delighted this evening at the release

211

of Jennifer Guinness, who was so cruelly kidnapped recently. She has been astonishing the nation on television with a perky, humorous press conference.

In Sunday's papers I came in for more heavy criticism. We plummeted in the polls last Sunday, at 25% and Fianna Fail at 45%. I wonder what you have to do to get popular in the country?

Austin Deasy is disgusted with the attitude in the Cabinet towards teachers, although his anger doesn't quite extend to sticking his neck out. He feels we're vacillating and not strong. But the general feeling around that table is fear of what the teachers can do to us. That's why we have short school days, short weeks, short years, and general anomalies in the system, all caused by weak Governments caving in like [John] Wilson and Haughey in 1980–81.

On the international front, Reagan has finally blown his top and the US has bombed Libya, causing desperate world anxiety, to put it mildly. If the pictures of the women and children and innocent dead are true, then I don't know how one can fail to condemn it. Gaddafi has gone to ground. We discussed it at Cabinet yesterday; general fury with Reagan but some feeling that Gaddafi is up to a good deal of no good.

| Thursday |
| **17** |
| April |

We won the Dail vote on the Fianna Fail motion easily. The PDs found a way to vote with us because of some ambiguity about a mediator and bringing the Employer–Labour Conference into it. The occasion was used to criticise me more heavily, even on television. Goodness! as if I was half as devious as the teachers' Unions.

The conciliatory statements that were made by Pat Cooney and Ruairi Quinn during the Dail debate this week on the Fianna Fail motion have very much defused and confused Garret's strong television statement of a few days ago. It seems to me that the confusion stems from Garret's failure to apply his mind to the whole question and to direct firmly the way we are going. He said to me on Wednesday night 'I should have spoken weeks ago.' I refrained from saying 'I told you so', despite the severe provocation.

Today at Cabinet we started our serious discussion on divorce.

| Thursday |
| **24** |
| April |

The divorce proposals were launched on the world, to a largely welcoming reaction. We discussed them at length over a few days, I had a considerable input and I'm quite pleased with them—I fought particularly to have included clauses providing for the financial protection and reward of full-time spouses in the home, which has always been my worry. Pat Cooney is very unenthusiastic on the divorce question, as is John Bruton, but John is reasonable; it may well be defeated.

| Friday |
| **25** |
| April |

Today, Fianna Fail have announced that they won't oppose the Bill in the Oireachtas and will leave it to individual TDs to campaign or not. I'll believe that when I see it!

| Friday |
| **2** |
| May |

I continue my constituency work, my delving into Social Welfare matters; continuing frustration and my lack of motivation must be stopping me making too much progress. My public profile obviously plummets and I'm not getting very much exposure except hostile harping back to Education. So I'm feeling quite sidelined and out of the way. An element of this is also the uncertainty about the future. There is uncertainty about the life of this Dail, a nervousness about, a real feeling of something unstable, a considerable uncertainty about my seat in Wicklow, though losing it would solve an awful lot of problems. But I have no intention whatsoever of going out of politics that way. When I go, 'I'll do it my way'.

Teachers' talks all week. We offered them a final £35 million but this morning I heard that at 7 a.m. after all-night talks the offer was refused and the issue is back to square one. I am getting a constant hostile barrage from teachers in Wicklow—they really seem to hate me. On the other hand, I've joined in the Fine Gael national collection in Bray quite a lot in recent days, knocking on doors and

213

looking for money for the party, and found it interesting
and not actually as depressing as it might have been.

Today it transpired that Ruairi Quinn and Pat Cooney
took a decision at 7 a.m. this morning to issue the
statement agreed by the Government yesterday, but without the key paragraph (which we had agonised for hours
over) saying where we got the money—which was basically from the special pay on graduate/non-graduate pay
rates and not additional money. Garret hotly attacked
Ruairi in the Whip's room at 10.30 a.m. I heard him saying
very crossly that he was going to issue a full statement
himself. But, to cut a long story short, the rest of the
statement was never issued because the TUI are meeting
about possibly taking a position independent from that of
the other Unions; so Garret's credibility is still falling. I
kicked up a row about it and demanded a Government
meeting (and failed), when Garret rang me to explain that
the TUI were delaying the matter anyway. It is becoming
increasingly clear to me that Ruairi and Pat, who are clever
operators, are quietly trying to fix this whole issue, giving
as much money as they possibly can to the teachers and
trying to bring Garret along at the same time, leaving me
totally isolated—again.

| Friday |
| **16** |
| May |

The divorce debate began this week in the Dail
and Garret started to get worried about the Social
Welfare implications, demanding instant solutions from me. That threw some panic into the Cabinet,
who didn't like the slightly vague inclusion in the speech
which I delivered at 6 o'clock yesterday evening, having
listened for one and a half hours to the extraordinary Dail
roaring and ranting of Padraig Flynn—who really couldn't
be serious about three-quarters of the things he says,
surely. It is extraordinary how Fianna Fail, having said
that they would not vote against the Bill in the Dail, have
now started to make endless sickening speeches, all about
the sad effect on women and children, and generally
trying to have their cake and eat it.

Next week I go to the United States because I want to
look at the 'Workfare' programmes and related schemes,

probably with Ruairi Quinn; if he can't come Enda Kenny, Junior Minister in the Department of Labour and Education, would come instead.

| Wednesday |
| **21** |
| May |

Arrived in Washington last night, accompanied by Enda Kenny and officials from the Departments of Labour and Social Welfare. We have spent a very busy day seeing officials in downtown Washington. As usual they were very kind, enthusiastic, informative. What's emerging is that there are a lot of parallels and also a lot of differences between Ireland and the US in the Social Welfare systems. Here there is a national unemployment figure of 7%, which gives the whole thing a slightly different perspective from the Irish scene.

After lots of meetings in Washington, we flew down to Charleston, West Virginia.

| Thursday |
| **22** |
| May |

The usual early American start at 8.30 a.m. when we went off to meet the people in Human Services. The Commissioner on Human Services is Shirley Lord, a stunning-looking woman, who's forty, looks twenty-five, and is interested and charming; we also met Governor Kane, a cute old bod to the right of Genghis Khan but bluff and all-American too. Their 'Workfare' programme is compulsory and therein lies the difference; and the other difference seems to be something that they constantly mention, which is a strong emphasis on the work ethic.

We met several people who were working on the programmes, and had the opportunity to speak to them privately without the American officials near us.

Most were pleased with their activities though disgruntled at not having a 'real job', but all said in one way or another that they preferred to do some work in exchange for their welfare payments. Mind boggling! They get paid at the rate of the US minimum wage, which is 3.25 dollars an hour, so a married man with a couple of children might be getting a couple of hundred dollars a week, and will work quite a number of hours more than the unmarried mother of one child who will be getting less. It makes considerable sense.

Sunday **25** May

Flew through the night via London, and now I'm back at home to the usual life, politics in full spate. I've done a *Morning Ireland* interview on the 'Workfare' programs, and the 'Job search' concept, to reactions which varied from interested and encouraging to horror and disgust.

Friday **30** May

On Tuesday I had the new US Ambassador to Ireland, Margaret Heckler, and six of my very active, prominent and lively women friends to lunch at home. I wanted to welcome her here, because she'd had a bad press. Unfortunately, the lunch didn't go very well. Margaret seemed to think we needed to have her ideas about Ireland and didn't seem to be very interested in what we knew or thought, and that gave a generally bad impression. She is certainly not another Liz Shannon or even Bill Shannon. The food at the lunch was very good and all the friends, who are such active and lively-minded people themselves, found it interesting to meet her even though they felt she wasn't particularly interested to meet them. Mavis Arnold says she was more or less told to shut up twice. What a pity that Margaret has missed an opportunity to hear a lot about Ireland from some very interesting and achieving people. Ah well, I tried.

It has been a long, unsettling, worrying week. Garret visibly not in control of the party—which is depressed, worried and somewhat detached from us. I veered between killing myself working and worrying, and simultaneously trying not to care. I am making as many strong positive speeches in public about the Divorce Referendum as I can possibly fit in, and tonight I went out with a good Greystones group and collected money as well as canvassing.

Fine Gael's divorce campaign was launched today—a disappointingly desultory performance by Peter Barry in one of those rooms in the Shelbourne, and the whole press conference was cut short suddenly when we all had to go back to the Dail for a vote—I thought it was lacklustre and barely decent. I think Peter wishes he had never heard of the subject. He seems more interested in keeping the party together than in motivating them all to win this Referendum.

Finance is once more putting the heart sideways in all of us with bad news about the half-year figures and more lists of cuts—it's very scary. And I'm determined to bring in dental and optical benefit for dependent spouses. I am thinking carefully about this and about how to work it out. I'll certainly have to put the arm on Garret.

The first half of the equality measures in Social Welfare went into operation this month, not that any of the 45,000 women getting more money seemed particularly pleased. Any announcements were greeted with silence.

| Sunday 1 June | The middle of a Bank Holiday weekend. I have done some very active walking, visiting of old folks, a great deal of cooking, 'walking-about' in |

Bray and now I am engrossed in a whole lot of preparations for my divorce speech on Tuesday. Derry says I mustn't be confrontational—everyone says I have a bad image—and if I was to pay a great deal of attention to all that, I'd be so milk and watery that I'd do nothing and say nothing and be nothing. I pointed out to Derry that the progress, such as it is, that I have made in politics has been made by being direct on issues on which I feel strongly. However, I've toned down the speech a bit, after all that!

| Monday 2 June | Bank Holiday Monday. We paid one of our infrequent visits to the races, which was all very much clouded over by the fact that there was a |

frightful fire in Loreto Convent in St Stephen's Green, last night. Six poor nuns died in the fire, most of them very old. I called in to the convent this morning to sympathise. Garret and Joan were there too. What a grotesque and macabre end to a long and good life. What sense is there in it? The Loreto nuns were, of course, being brave and religious and resigned 'to God's will'.

Saturday
7
June

I didn't manage to get out to Bray on Wednesday to speak at the Divorce Action Group meeting, which was just as well, because I discovered that my brother who's very active in the Charismatic movement, was going to speak against divorce—that would have been awkward and would have been manna for the media.

Monday
9
June

Yesterday, horror of horrors, Pat Cooney had a full page in the *Sunday Independent* fulminating against divorce. I'm furious at the whole injustice of it, at the thought of him being Minister for Education and causing this trouble. Anyway, I sent Garret a brief note saying that I thought that Pat's escalation of the divorce split in Fine Gael was putting the Government in an impossible position (the first note, torn up, was a scorcher), and Garret rang me back sounding very fed-up but saying that Pat had observed the letter of the arrangements he'd agreed with him. He also said that if Pat was removed from the Cabinet he would be considered to be a Christian martyr around whom the anti-divorce campaign would revolve.

I am trying to diet again, not very successfully—but I am managing my walk at 7.15 in the mornings. This morning I met once again one of our neighbours, the very sweet and polite Church of Ireland Archbishop, Dr Donald Caird. He was striding along in his Aran jumper, jauntily swinging his stick, while I strode in my sweatshirt and anorak, miniature radio in my ear and Socks, my lunatic dog, trotting along beside me: a lovely blowy, mild morning. These early morning brisk walks are very good for the general mental health!

Wednesday
11
June

Yesterday, Tuesday, I went to the elegant Italian Embassy in Lucan for a stately lunch with President Cossiga of Italy. I sat beside Garret and no one would imagine that there had been any problem to hear us talking to each other. I couldn't believe it when he told me how he 'would square up to Pat Cooney' when it's clear he won't. I said mildly that if he was going to square up to Pat, and if Pat had to go, well then I'd like my job back—gales of laughter and then 'Now that the teachers' thing is out of the way, you could go back. I felt it would drag on and on and pull you down . . . '. Anyway, on the way back to the farewell ceremonies for the Italian President at the airport, I heard that Joe Bermingham from Kildare was resigning from Labour and going Independent; that certainly upsets the apple cart for Fine Gael and Labour in a big way.

Sped off like the wind to Drogheda for a divorce speech, accompanied by Deputy Brendan McGahon who represents us in Louth. He is an interesting, shrewd character of some complexity. He decided he was going to give me some advice, and he told me to speak out and do my own thing altogether. The divorce issue, despite all the work I am doing on it, is considerably worrying. One feels that there is a lack of dynamism in the direction of the campaign, to put it mildly.

| Sunday |
| 15 |
| June |

The Divorce Referendum campaign is deteriorating badly: the 'antis' are concentrating only on fear, mainly stirring up the fears of women, trying—and succeeding—to make them feel threatened, and despite a fairly good opinion poll today the general forecasts are not at all good.

The Social Welfare Department, in a fit of great stupidity, gave the Commission on Social Welfare Report to the Dail and Senate Library before it was officially released. I was astonished that this could happen. As a result, Michael Bell welcomed it heartily, gave bits of it to reporters, and the rest of the press don't even have it. This is quite an unbelievable act of nonsensical thoughtlessness and, of course, who gets blamed for it?

| Thursday |
| 19 |
| June |

Yesterday I finally told Garret the size of the problem I have and the reasons for it. I had an appointment with him and I went into his office. Garret was inclined to have a good chat about how the

219

Divorce Referendum was going—I had to cut that short. With some trepidation I set the whole problem out for him—the cul-de-sac I was now in with Social Welfare, and how it is impossible to do anything at all because of economic and political barriers. He, as usual, heartily and humbly agreed that it had all been a mess, that he had made the mess himself, that I had been very damaged, that it was all very difficult—but he had no solutions. An interesting side comment: when I suggested that Pat Cooney should be put in Social Welfare and me back in Education—I wasn't really serious—Garret said 'The only one thing wrong with that is it would mean me admitting that I'd made a mistake . . . '; this was said with a smile. He went on a bit about the basic income concept which he's studying ('could be a major radical new structure') etc.; would I be interested in running with that ('but it mightn't of course get through the Government or the party'). I laid out the things I saw as necessary to make something of the job and to do something good in policy areas—dental and optical benefits for spouses, proper staffing to deal with the fraud problem, money for the widespread computerisation of the system, accommodation improvements in all the unemployment offices, which are in such a shocking state, as well as new schemes to let people work part-time, or to study while they're drawing the dole, and the 'Job search' scheme to sort out who's really looking for work, and to help them. The 'Workfare' idea is too sensitive at this juncture to be pursued.

Saturday **21** June — I felt better after the session with Garret, although there were no solutions.

We're all so caught up in the divorce issue that it dominates everything. The latest ruction was because it seemed that Pat Cooney had agreed to appear on a very big 'special' on divorce that they're having on the *Late Late Show*—as a witness against divorce. We found this out and it came up at a sparsely attended Cabinet meeting on Thursday. Naturally I reacted very sharply, as did Ruairi Quinn. Garret was trying to get agreement that other people's recollection of Pat's most recent undertaking not to say anything was the same as his. Anyway, it appears that Peter Barry and John Boland were sent to talk to Pat later on Thursday, working on him to withdraw from the programme. I rang Peter Barry (rather, he returned my call) at about 7 p.m. and I told him that Pat's actions were making it extremely difficult for people like me to continue to be fully loyal and stick by Cabinet instructions. So, as we might have known was inevitable, it all broke in the papers on Friday afternoon and I saw Garret on television denying that he had put any pressure on Pat Cooney, which strictly speaking was true.

Since I was in Bray yesterday, I watched the 2-hour RTE television divorce special in Mark Mortell's house—it was fascinating and not conclusive. The pro-divorce witnesses were much better than the antis (Sean McBride spoke for the anti-divorce team; he has only just spoken up in the campaign and seems rather confused about it) but the summing up on our side was weaker than the direct, emotional, clear call of the other Senior Counsel, Nugent. I'm not sure what effect that programme will have on people generally.

It was time for Social Welfare Estimates in the Dail yesterday and at the beginning I had a slight exchange with Haughey over my minor supplementary estimates to get my schemes started, but I explained that Sean McCarthy, his spokesperson on Social Welfare, had already agreed with me on Thursday, so the row subsided. McCarthy told me later that C.J. ate the face off him afterwards, using the usual colourful language.

Sunday	
22	
June	

Down to RTE studios again yesterday for the *Saturday View* radio programme, which was on divorce. Mary McAleese (fast-talking, Belfast), Bernadette Bonar (tight-lipped fervour), Fr Martin Tierney (clever) plus two lawyers, one from the Divorce Action Group and another, a Senior Counsel called Clark. I think—and hope—I kept the cool and made the points calmly, but is anybody still listening? If it's narrowly defeated, Garret and Fine Gael will be severely damaged;

the campaign has been nothing short of lousy and half-hearted.

I'm generally feeling a little bit detached at the moment because I can see so many stone walls around me and I don't know how I'm going to get over them. However, I don't think people in general know this.

Tuesday 24 June

The big item of the day is the latest divorce opinion poll to be published tomorrow, showing a huge drop in support and it certainly looks strongly like defeat. So there is a lot of worry and despondency about; it's such a damn shame that Fine Gael so grossly mishandled the campaign. There will be a great deal of bitterness among the Divorce Action Group about Fine Gael's lacklustre campaign, and probably severe divisions in the party. Pat Cooney will be a protected species, no doubt for fear of a party collapse; it will all be about rallying cries for unity, Fine Gael together, together. Fianna Fail have behaved utterly disgracefully and without principle all during this campaign and will come out unscathed, while people like myself, who have been totally loyal and severely damaged, will be considered to be sour grapes if we say anything at all.

Wednesday 25 June

Parliamentary Party and then lunch with political journalist John Cooney. I also had a pre-arranged personal meeting with Peter Barry. He was quite cool and despairing of being able to do anything at all. John Cooney told me he is absolutely convinced that it was Peter who stopped Garret from dividing the Department of Foreign Affairs at the time of the re-shuffle and that the top brass in Foreign Affairs helped to scuttle it too.

Friday 27 June

A shocking reversal on the Referendum, a resounding *no* vote, the outcome very similar to the Pro-Life Amendment in '83. The reverberations are rolling around (like a sudden violent thunderstorm this morning). Yesterday, polling day, was a beautiful, warm, sunny day and I spent it mostly standing around polling stations, urging people and wondering, but the signs were unmistakably there, the zealots and the fearful and insecure women all trooping in, nuns coming from convents. The blame being flung around will be flung at Garret in particular. I've started and torn up several notes to him, a mixture of sympathy for him and anger at disloyal colleagues, but it's very hard to sound anything but bitter.

This awful news is somewhat offset by the fantastic news about Rachel, who has got another 1st Class Honour and several prizes in her law studies at Trinity.

| Sunday |
| 29 |
| June |

A black weekend generally for the Government, with the awful Referendum result sitting there like a large coal lump in everybody's mind, an insurmountable reality.

I finally did send a note around to Garret and why wouldn't I, and I hope it was nice. In the note I suggested that he should make some definitive gesture to assert his authority; I said that his friends need his support now and his friends want to support him, and things like that. He should know that the reason I write him all these notes is that there are various points of view and I suppose mine is as valid as anyone else's—only since I'm never asked, I have to keep giving it unasked.

Tomorrow, Spanish royalty arrives. It would have been nice to be Minister for Europe.

| Monday |
| 30 |
| June |

Just home from a State Banquet for King Juan Carlos and Queen Sofia of Spain. It was a very splendid occasion in Dublin Castle, except for the appalling music—a violin and piano not well played. All sorts of side currents going on, Fianna Fail being their usual pushy selves, I gather.

| Tuesday |
| 1 |
| July |

Cabinet this morning for three hours and an afternoon of work, only remarkable for a long lunch 'à deux' with the depressed and depressing Michael Noonan.

Tonight there was another State Banquet for the Spanish royalty, to which I was asked again (in order to speak

Spanish). Before the dinner I had a chat in a small group
with the King. This conversation was distinguished by Jim
Mitchell asking him in his round Dublin tones 'Tell us,
how didja handle Franco?' Juan Carlos gave the already
well-publicised answer that as a young man he had asked
Franco if he could sit in with Ministers to see how the
business of running the State was done. Franco had said
no to him because 'the Spain that you will take over will be
a different Spain.' He also told us about the famous night
in '81 when there was an attempted coup by some Army
officers. He had rung up all the generals around the
country and had some difficulty persuading the Government that this was essential. He called his young son
Felipe into the room to be with him all during that night so
that he could see how this crisis was handled. When he
rang the seven relevant regional generals, they had indeed
been waiting to hear from him what they should do and
they could have gone either way. John Boland was very
forthcoming at the dinner and we had a pleasant conversation, the nearest to a consensus that we've got. Somewhat to my surprise, Garret kissed me warmly twice on
leaving.

There is an air of impending crisis about—Fianna Fail
only counting the days.

| Thursday |
| 3 |
| July |

Yesterday we had a thorough blood-letting on
divorce at the Fine Gael Parliamentary Party. I
foolishly interrupted Alice Glenn as she got into
her stride in an enormous diatribe. She started giving out
about our slipping in the polls. At that point I said 'with
your help Alice'. Alice shouted across the room at me
'your day is done Madame'. There was mayhem when
Alan Shatter started a heated exchange with her. We were
all saved by the division bell.

To nobody's surprise, it is all in the papers today.
However, we got it sorted out and Garret made a fairly
good fighting response, which was greeted with some
relief by people who are starved of leadership. So we have
survived that day, which might well not have happened.

Saturday **5** July	Sitting, tidying, walking, thinking, phoning, worrying about next week (cuts, cuts, argument, hassle) lots of constituency matters, continual

feeling of hostility/indifference towards me hard to take. Cabinet hassle was dreadful over my staff allocation. I ended up with 193 which is a fraction of what we need but John Bruton went on and on and on, doing the job he has to do.

Thursday **10** July	Derry and all the family are doing a rota of bedside vigils with Dorrie [his mother] who has been very ill all these days.

Grainne O'Flynn of the Teachers Union of Ireland came to see me because of a letter Pat Cooney sent to the Curriculum and Examinations Board on which she serves. The members of the Board felt that the letter was terribly negative and dismissive of their work. I said I'd try to get Garret to speak to Pat.

Derry didn't come back from his bedside vigil until 5 a.m. and so we slept fitfully.

Tuesday **15** July	This evening Derry and I went to the US Embassy for a very elegant dinner in Garret's honour. We had some premonition in the back of our minds

about the condition of Derry's mother. Towards the end of the dinner he was called to the phone and I knew exactly what it would be; so we left and went out to the Nursing Home.

Thursday **17** July	Obviously these days have been completely caught up with family and obsequies. Garret very kindly came to both the removal and

the funeral, which was an exceptional gesture on his part.

In the middle of it all, I had an absolutely unavoidable obligation, which was to turn the first sod for the new Protestant school in Wicklow town. It is an historic building because it is going to be the first second-level school built on a green field site for the Protestant community since the foundation of the State. It was a lovely occasion; I was surrounded by endless clergymen of different denominations—although I don't know if I saw a Catholic one there—flags, marquee, the Hallelujah Chorus and Donald Caird as well. Sun and songs, goodwill all round, and I'm proud of that school.

Saturday 19 July Yesterday morning was yet another nightmare, as the Cabinet started again on Social Welfare cuts. It was the usual dreadful hassle, reducing me to a fraught state, so much so that at lunchtime, before I did a taped interview with Monica Carr for radio, I found myself having a private cry. I sent Garret a note saying that perhaps he'd better ask for my resignation at this point. Having cleansed my soul with that note, I then did a cheerful interview with Monica Carr. If she only knew!

Garret sent for me and told me that there would be no financial discussion in the afternoon. He said he couldn't see a Budget being put together and we should perhaps consider Fine Gael parting company from Labour at some stage during its preparation. He also chided me for not letting Labour veto all Social Welfare cuts, which he knows they would have done. If Garret had some strategy worked out for avoiding Social Welfare cuts because of Labour's opposition, he should have told me about it. He didn't seem as cross as I feared or as he had a right to be with me, but perhaps that's one of his problems. Really, what can you do! Anyhow, there is yet another fearsome list of cuts for the 1987 Budget figures, with apocalyptic implications.

Thursday 7 August A long day yesterday, mainly the launching of the Commission on Social Welfare Report. I had the entire Commission in for drinks and for lunch, to thank them for their great work and I did several interviews with papers, also for the TV News. Their Report is undoubtedly an amazing document, full of extraordinarily good, well-meaning, well-researched recommendations, but the financial implications of the central recommendations are absolutely mind-boggling. Of course I am taking considerable public criticism from every single organisation involved with working with the poor for not promising to fully implement the recommendations in the Report.

Saturday 9 August

We have had a very sociable week, Italian, German and British Embassy parties all crowded together and a lot of the same people going, but since I ignore them for the rest of the year and it is only these few weeks I can go to them, I am making up for it now so that they won't think I'm rude.

The media seem to have decided to stop condemning me at the moment and, to my surprise, I've had a great many compliments both on Education and on what I'm trying to do in Social Welfare as regards new schemes. As Monica Barnes said to us last night 'You'd be mad to start believing in your own publicity—it changes so much all the time . . .' But I feel I'm gradually rehabilitating myself, which is a relief.

Tuesday 12 August

Yesterday, 11 August, I entertained John Bruton (at his request) to lunch in the Department of Social Welfare—which means we get a cold plate of salad sent up to us in my office. He was in good form, ate up his food and had his glass of wine, and discussed where we're going politically, with considerable 'sang froid'. He thinks an alliance of some kind with the PDs is absolutely necessary if we are to avoid total disaster at the next Election. We got on extremely well and I told him my personal position and why I had to be so 'bolshie' at Cabinet. John is a bit of a Jekyll and Hyde; he's an attractive character if he wasn't so volatile. He is quite intellectual and I have no doubt that he is a genuine patriot. It's hard to help liking him. He also gave it as his opinion that Garret was planning a November Election.

Sunday 17 August

Dashed over to Connemara for a weekend and when we went out on a boat to visit Inishbofin I was immediately approached by residents of the island to see if I could organise a pier which they want. The trouble with any break in Ireland is that you get no peace.

Wednesday
20
August

It is a year to the day since my 'morality' speech. This week has been very hectic. Moving around clinics, speech writing, going to see Michael Lillis in his heavily secured retreat in Delgany to talk about Northern Ireland in preparation for my big speech in Donegal at the McGill Summer School. Michael is very clever and laid back and very firm in his resolution on the Agreement, but far from optimistic on the future for the North. The fact that he is heading up the Maryfield team must be terribly tricky and very hard on his wife Jane, although she is a strong character. He told me what he thinks of Thatcher: she's a highly intelligent, shrewd, well-briefed, generally very able, but difficult to deal with lady, at least publicly. I have heard from other sources that Thatcher thinks very highly of Michael. He is a realist about Garret but admires the way he has handled Thatcher, to the point where she is if anything more adamant than we are on the Agreement and on dealing with the Unionists.

The first draft of the Northern Ireland speech—on which I've been working with Michael—is excellent and I'm sure will be just exactly what will be needed in Donegal. But I had great difficulty getting a final error free version out of the Department. This conference in Donegal is quite a challenge, maybe a bit tricky in terms of the kind of people who will come over the border to attend it. The north is sizzling away; a hopeful sign today is that workers are being united with each other against intimidation from anyone in Lisburn, but it is an awful, awful scene. The speech hits violence, from all sides, and praises Thatcher for courage.

Yesterday I spoke at the launching of the *An Post* stamp marking Irish women's achievement. I was very strong on the question of women priests and caused a good old furore and all the expected reactions. It was in fact a low-key dignified speech, but it seems to have touched a very raw nerve. I wonder will it be seen as a big mistake or as the right thing to do. I really couldn't care less—I thought it was the right thing to do. Joe Jennings, in the Government Press Office, didn't like the speech and tried to stop me doing it. Some Fine Gael TDs have screamed blue murder (Michael Begley, Alice Glenn). The *Irish Press* carried a cartoon depicting me as a plump Cardinal Hussey.

| Sunday |
| 24 |
| August |

I had a 'succés fou' with the Donegal speech (delivered with slow intensity as befitted the subject and the quality of the script) and particularly with the very long question and answer session afterwards, which was tough, full of Sinn Fein and Provos in a large group which, to my astonishment, I was able to deal with slowly and deliberately and toughly. I was inundated with congratulations afterwards. So I hope that the evening did the Government and myself proud and may have helped a little bit in the Northern crisis. Such a fulfilling night takes some of the misery away.

I spent Friday night listening and absorbing, so as to be able to judge my audience. They're a mixture of Dublin academic/slightly left and a whole lot of decent Donegal people, Protestant and Catholic, a sprinkling of people from across the border. The negativism has to be countered; my whole approach was to stress the absolute need to press on and persevere with the Agreement for the sake of peace. Last night, I ended up singing 'The Zoological Gardens' at 2.30 a.m. with a happy crowd. Derry doesn't like it at all when I sing, and I don't blame him.

Funnily enough, the flak from the 'women and the priesthood' speech is still flying around. There was a strong defence of me in the *Sunday Independent* from Anne Harris, who has stuck so many daggers in me in the past. Various priests have supported me, but Brendan Comiskey grumbled on the radio that I'd never mentioned the question to him 'in our social meetings'—such arrogance.

| Wednesday |
| 27 |
| August |

A hurricane struck the East coast on Monday night causing devastation and chaos in Little Bray, also causing huge criticism of the Government, but I've tried to deal with it as fast as I can and keep in touch. I never saw anything like it but no one was hurt or killed, thank goodness. I waded in the floods early on Tuesday, getting abuse. God.

The reaction to the women priests speech has exceeded anything I could have imagined and has uncovered a lot of strong feeling, mostly supportive I'm delighted to say.

Apart from the hurricane, there are gathering political storms: Garret coming back for a Cabinet meeting tomorrow, and half the country seems to expect millions, both for farmers and for flood damage. Frank Cluskey threatening, Joe Bermingham threatening, talk of votes of confidence, By-Elections, and I am trying to keep quite calm.

Saturday 30 August

Yesterday Garret toured the Bray flooded areas. It was the kind of occasion I have come to dread and it was exactly as I thought it would be. People screeching at him, demanding everything they can think of. He kept going resolutely, listening patiently, never getting fussed. I was impressed, I must say, but I was not a bit proud of many Bray people who seemed to consider the Government personally responsible for the hurricane. So all of us, officials, myself, councillors, wended our way in and out of the houses in Little Bray, the houses all upside down and the people working away, the Army active in clearing work. I thought it would never end, but end it did after three hours.

Thursday 4 September

A few days ago, Sean Donlon sent me a telex to tell me that the British Government have widely circulated my Donegal speech in the US, describing it as 'official Irish Government policy'. He seems annoyed about that; I can't imagine why. It was inspected by Foreign Affairs (not that I would have changed anything anyway). So I didn't react to the telex.

The week, in full working spate again, has been full of political speculation, Cabinet sessions, aftermaths of floods, a very long and successful conference on anti-fraud measures, great and continuing worry about the state of my father's health.

Monday was cruelly busy, culminating in a Bray

Chamber of Commerce meeting about all the businesses that were damaged in the floods. One long demand for money to compensate people who weren't insured and the whole thing has been very politicised. I was exhausted and disgusted. Of course there are other demands from people who have been really ruined: fish farmers and the turkey farmer who lost everything and others who deserve help. Cabinet was less than givish on the subject and you can't blame them, but the hysteria in Bray is rising, whipped up intensely by every Fianna Fail member plus the Workers Party, and with Garret's constituency visit scheduled for tomorrow I don't know what's going to happen.

Today in the Department I had a meeting which was politically important: with Joe Bermingham, at my invitation. He ambled in agreeably and chatted nicely to me over cups of tea. He has, I think, a certain sincerity and he says that the media have put him into corners which he didn't actually mean to get into. But he's quite a cute old fox and maybe cuter than I thought. Anyway, it was all very low key. He told me that he is not going to run for election again and he doesn't want to bring the Government down. So we parted the best of friends.

| Saturday |
| **6** |
| September |

I am 'hors de combat' with a stretched tendon in the calf of my leg, acquired when disembarking (as *The Irish Times* has it) from Arklow lifeboat yesterday morning. We had Garret's big visit to the constituency yesterday and it went much better than I thought it would. We started with St Catherine's Day Care Centre and School for the Mentally Handicapped in Newcastle and we ended with the much-prepared-for barn dance and barbeque at John Leeson's. There must have been a thousand people being deafened by the music, sitting uncomfortably on hay bales, but it was a fantastic success as far as the organisation and the spirit were concerned and must have made a fortune for us. Garret could have really motivated that huge crowd; instead unfortunately the speech was not strong. It didn't even thank John and Rosemary Leeson, or mention Godfrey and myself—what can Katherine Meenan, who is supposed to advise him, be thinking of? Anyway, I was in some considerable pain at it, hobbling on a stick with a terribly painful leg.

| Friday |
| 26 |
| September |

The end of an eventful week with all the signs pointing firmly to collapse of Government. Poor Eddie Collins was finally fired after a summer of speculation about company dealings. Katharine Bulbulia has been feeling intense heat in Waterford as a result. The special Cabinet meeting on the Collins case was grimly interesting; a lot of people were defending Eddie strongly; Garret was rather depressed I think, because he felt that the Government didn't approve of what he had decided he had to do about Eddie; but I couldn't understand how they could think any differently from Garret, considering the questions in the Dail, past and future. Anyway, outcries and murder going on in Waterford. Eddie being dignified at first, but a little over the top later. Katharine (because of PD pressure on her) being suspected of plotting against Eddie, me giving Katharine sanctuary in my office on Wednesday during the storm so that she simply wouldn't be available to the press.

Cabinet yesterday was not good: Garret refused to allow the dental/optical benefit memo to be taken at all, but he said that it must be postponed until the Budget. So that puts it firmly in an election setting and, as I pointed out passionately, it takes all the value out of it. I will work out a way of refusing to allow it to be an election promise, but will have it put firmly into the Budget figures. Fianna Fail, if they're going to be in Government, couldn't possibly take it out, so it will be achieved. I warned the Cabinet again about the equality issue and brought up the Christmas bonus, but all I get is glowers and frowns.

During the meeting, when Garret was temporarily out of the room, having told us that Richard Bruton was being made a Junior Minister to replace Eddie Collins, John Boland said 'I wonder how Richard will feel about being asked to become third mate on *The Titanic*'. When he was mock-chided for this he said 'Well, how about first mate on the *Lusitania*' and then 'Well, perhaps gunner on the *Graf Spee*'. All you can do is laugh helplessly. When I recount all this to Derry, it drives him quite mad: he believes we have to bring forward a major plan for growth and wealth creation, along with the budgetary solutions.

As each day goes by and the political boat gets more wildly rocked, it damages the country and the Anglo–Irish Agreement and all of our chances electorally. And Garret doesn't—perhaps can't—take control. Fianna Fail quiet as mice, ready to pounce and oppose every measure Fine Gael will put forward as a solution to the country's problems.

| Friday |
| 3 |
| October |

What a week. All weeks are 'what a week'! Why should this seem so? In many ways it has been less pressurised than usual, but yesterday (Thursday) I got that peculiar chest pain with a vengeance, so Derry insisted on bringing me down to our GP who decided it was a bunch of muscles in the chest area which I'm tensing up, because of stress. So I tried to believe him, and set off to Bray to various meetings.

At 8.30 a.m. on Tuesday we had a two and a half hour Cabinet to finalise the announcement of the £180 million overrun on the Budget and the reasons for it. Garret very preoccupied and quite cast down, I thought. We had a totally inconclusive discussion about the Christmas Social Welfare bonus, which, as is usual with every Government apparently, has been unprovided for in the Budget. Both John Bruton and myself wanted to force them to make a decision on it, but of course they didn't because it is one of those major flashpoints. So we stagger on with the uncorrected situation in that area, which, after all, is indefensible. The equality issue is a no go area any time I raise it, which I frequently try to do nowadays.

Education worries the life out of me. Nothing at all is happening there, but nothing. I prod and poke at Cabinet, but they're too worried about everything else.

One of Garret's big worries this week was the Extradition Bill and the British quid pro quo—three-Judge

Courts—a crucial step which we're working for in the Agreement process. He's been putting a lot of pressure on Thatcher personally. So we wait to see. According to Garret the British are unaware that five of the ten Northern Ireland Judges are either neutral or favourable towards the proposal. But if no progress is made, where does that leave us on extradition?

On Wednesday I chaired a huge mass meeting (about 600 people) of three South Dublin Fine Gael constituencies. It was addressed by Garret. Everything went extremely well, there was no hassle at all, indeed I worried about it being far too mild, almost reverential, which would not be a reflection of the real situation.

Joan FitzGerald made a point of offering to attend a big coffee morning for me when the General Election comes—she did so fairly modestly, to give her her due, and it was nice of her.

Thursday **9** October

I had a very important meeting this week with Godfrey Timmins and the central people in the constituency (Harry Cullen the Chairman, and Michael Tierney the organiser) with Finbar Fitzpatrick, the General Secretary of the party, to discuss the possibility of dividing the Wicklow constituency between Godfrey and myself, but Godfrey is very much against it. So it won't happen and I warned of the consequences.

My mind is in a spin. I believe the political situation is spiralling downwards and can't be controlled. Interest rates are going up today, continued talk about Government inability to govern and considerable worry about the deficit and borrowing. Against all this, the impossibility of getting Labour to agree to the cuts that are needed and the certainty that Fianna Fail will vote against them. All this has the potential to finish me off politically altogether.

Saturday **11** October

Everything has changed utterly. Yesterday the Fine Gael Ministers had an all-day meeting with the key strategy people, and discussion of the latest qualitative survey which shows, among other things, that unemployment is the key and overriding issue. This survey was done at the end of July and beginning of August, before the Budget overrun and the deepening financial crisis. Later, we Fine Gael Ministers went to Garret's office, where John Bruton and Garret put the suggested scenario.

The plan is to part amicably with Labour over the Estimates/Budget on 22 October, bring the Budget to the Dail the following week, which is the soonest possible legally, and then go to the country on a tough Budget, challenging Fianna Fail and the rest with: 'Okay, it's awful, but what would you do that's different?' The Estimate Books and Budget were laid before us by John and contained horrific cuts, the worst and most horrible in the Social Welfare area—in that nearly everyone in the PAYE sector as well as general recipients are touched. There was a sort of semi-stunned reaction. Despite all the terrible elements of it, my own reaction was one of relief with, however, a dreadfully sinking feeling about my personal position. The main reason for all this is the financial damage that is happening the country daily, fuelled by the political uncertainty. I pointed out the three Social Welfare areas where we might lose Dail votes— equal treatment, fuel schemes and Christmas bonus—and no one could answer my contention that we couldn't carry all three, certainly not the Christmas bonus one. After all that, we rejoined the strategy committee for what was a slightly unreal conversation, given their state of ignorance about what we had just been discussing.

Since then I have been reflecting a lot. I went to see Garret at home at 6.30 p.m. yesterday and had a conversation with him beside the fire in his downstairs sitting-room, with Joan there on the other side of the fire. I still feel quite a strong rapport with him. Having discussed the situation, we talked about leadership. Alan would appear to be the favourite for leader, since John Bruton feels that this Budget will finish him off. When I was leaving, I said to Garret at the door that, even though I'd like to be in politics for the next ten years, if I have to go out it would at least be for the good of the country. He was warm in his reaction to this and I hope it helped a little with all his worries.

All in all, these are exciting times politically. God knows where we're going, but the country must get back on the rails some way.

| Tuesday |
| **14** |
| October |

A month today since Daddy died and I am constantly thinking about him.

Fine Gael Ministers meeting quite a lot; rather a strained Government meeting.

I have put my closest confidants among my staff on alert making election preparations. I am not really clear if Garret is resolute enough just now; John Bruton certainly is and so am I. I made a very strong speech attacking Haughey and Fianna Fail hypocrisy last night and I got very good coverage — to my surprise John Bruton sent me a congratulatory note about it.

Now at 11.30 p.m. I'm in bed worn out, phone ringing, people calling and planning going on in the house — my campaign manager is taking holidays from his job to manage the whole campaign. I'm leaving lists of big and small things for everyone to do. I think we will have to get some of the items changed on the horrific Social Welfare cuts list when people's minds clear a bit. But I am afraid that the Cabinet will baulk at the whole shebang and the Government will collapse rather than facing the crisis up-front and, as they say, 'going for it'.

| Saturday |
| **18** |
| October |

Cabinet on Thursday was very odd and strange, with John Bruton and Garret pursuing the issuing of the statement about the actual Budget targets. I demurred (I couldn't for the life of me figure out what actual plan they were following, if any) and as a result of my urging we met again after lunch at 3 o'clock. So the statement was issued, and tremors beginning to be felt. John Bruton ate the head off me for causing the delay in the statement, so I ate him back for following no plan at all. What do they think they're at? It all reminds me of 'wars and rumours of wars'. If they have a plan, either they've failed to explain it or have excluded some of us from it.

| Monday
20
October | Garret's Ard Fheis speech was very good, mine went down alright but was delivered to a sparsely filled hall (but live on TV). The Fine Gael organ- |

isation was very good as usual, but there is still an awful lack of plan. I don't know what's in John Bruton's mind or in Garret's mind at the moment at all. I rang both of them today but I've heard nothing back.

| Wednesday
22
October | Opening day of the Dail. I started off the day by performing the ceremonial function of accom- panying the President in Aras an Uachtarain |

while the new Luxembourg Ambassador presented his credentials. I found the ceremony fascinating. In the informal conversation with Paddy Hillery before and after, he talked mostly about education. Quite correctly, we didn't touch on the impending political crisis. He loved being in Education.

Then I dashed into the Parliamentary Party meeting, which had a very self-indulgent discussion on interest rates. There didn't seem to be a sinking feeling around. However, the first intimations of trouble surfaced in a call from Garret at lunch-time—Joe Bermingham had announced that in order to vote for us tomorrow he wanted assurances about a particular group of people who live alone on unemployment assistance. He spoke to me in August about this, so I instructed the Department to get me the figures.

I passed on the figures to Garret. It would cost about £4 million to give about £5 per week to that group. I warned Garret that there shouldn't be any decision on this matter without a Government meeting.

The writ for the By-Election was defeated by one vote and Joe Bermingham wasn't there—to Garret's shock—but Liam Skelly voted okay.

Labour are kicking up murder about the equality pro- gramme, as I had warned and on which I have tried in vain to get the attention of the Cabinet for several weeks now.

Friday
24
October

Last night's Dail vote was alright: 83/81. In the end we had to make no commitments to anyone. Liam Skelly was brought on side by a promise of an early decision, Joe Bermingham by saying that we would give priority to a certain group of older people – aged forty-five plus, living alone, on unemployment assistance.

Spent all day at Cabinet where the worry actually was Skelly and not Bermingham. I insisted that the Cabinet would re-affirm its position on the equal treatment issue because there are all sorts of doubts and tremors surfacing on it. The Labour deputies are growling, despite the fact that it was all Barry Desmond's decision and Barry Desmond's legislation last July which they all passed in the Dail. And there is a Fianna Fail private members motion next Wednesday. I've been told so often in recent weeks that the Equality directive is already costing £18 million to implement and that there is not one penny more available; but I have this sinking feeling about it.

We ended the meeting by getting a copy of the draft Budget and I really can't imagine how I could survive against that picture of cuts in Social Welfare; try as I might, I can't find any other cuts that would make sense or be fair. So my mind is in a bit of a whirl as I write this. Am I a mad woman or am I Joan of Arc about to be burned at the stake? – but then maybe Joan of Arc was a mad woman.

I had an interesting and frustrating tussle with Pat Cooney on the Curriculum and Examinations Board Bill on Tuesday. He wanted to clip its wings even further and calmly denied that there was any hostility to it or blocking of it in the Department. I know much better than that. To my surprise Pat insists on personally opening the Dominican Convent in Wicklow, which of course is bad form. John Harris has been to see me; he is quietly despairing because nothing at all is happening in Education since I left. Pat apparently is in Marlborough Street much less than I was and rarely talks to John, so the old mechanism of keeping things moving has stopped totally.

Today, Friday, I spent a great deal of time on the equal treatment crisis and constituency work. As the Election approaches, my seat looks very much under threat; even people who don't know about the threatened Social Welfare cuts (and that's everyone) think it's a toss up whether I'll be re-elected, so I must consider my position delicate. If I am defeated, I would go back and fight for the NUI seat in the Senate but Austin Deasy tells me that Maurice Manning will be looking for that, so it would be some fight.

One of the things that happened this week was an agonised phone call from Peter Sutherland in Brussels about the Single European Act. He was all steamed up about it, so I will have to look into it and see what I can do. He feels it needs enthusiasm and speed, that otherwise we'll be damaged in Europe.

| Wednesday |
| 29 |
| October |

After a day when everything happened just as I had predicted. I am disgusted and depressed about the cave-in under pressures from Labour on the equal treatment business. There was a horrible Parliamentary Party meeting, horrible twelfth-hour Cabinet meetings, horrible tensions, and just plain messy. So I realize that nothing and nobody can be relied on any more.

Part of the scenario was a special Parliamentary Party meeting which was uncannily similar to the one nearly four years ago on school transport. People giving out hell about me, everybody whining and moaning, some people putting eminently reasonable points of view, but Monica Barnes, Nora Owen and Katharine Bulbulia, all turning up in solidarity for me. But in my new calm and detached frame of mind I refused to let it get to me and kept a reasonable and reasoning attitude. I didn't know at that stage of course that I would be forced into a concession half an hour later, because Dick couldn't get Michael Bell and company through the lobbies. So I stormed out of that Cabinet meeting at 6.55 p.m.—the Dail motion starting at 7 p.m.—and told them as I left that I was utterly opposed to this kind of governing. The immediate reaction to the climb down wasn't as bad as might have been expected. Perhaps we undeservedly got away with it. Barry

Desmond certainly sowed the seeds of trouble on the whole equal treatment regulations last year before I ever went near Social Welfare. I never saw such messing and of course I'm left to justify the unjustifiable. The new concession involves revising the supplementary welfare scheme to provide further help for families where both spouses are on social welfare. Where's the money suddenly coming from which I was told was not there at all?

Friday 7 November

Today I went out officially to Darndale despite advice not to go. I had been warned that it would be very unpleasant but in fact it was much better than expected. I got on well with the people there, feeling really bad inside about not being able to offer them much more hope. How anyone could have awarded that huge estate a prize for design is beyond me; it is such a depressing place. There are a lot of brave spirits out there, as well as a lot of fairly hopeless ones. We had good meetings and discussions.

Saturday 8 November

Last night we went to the Wicklow Cheviot Sheep Owners dinner dance in Blessington. What a night: a semi-edible meal which was more or less thrown at us, not a drop of wine during the interminable dinner and even more interminable raffles for fertilizer and sheep dip. Then I was totally ignored while Liam Kavanagh was invited to speak. So all in all it was a messy and unsatisfactory night and I wish I didn't have to go, not to mention poor Derry. Of course their chairman, Jim Norton, is a law unto himself, highly amusing, bluff, sharp as a razor, and I'm told he's Fianna Fail to boot.

Cabinet this week—which I expected to get to grips with things— was desultory. Michael Noonan said to me that he thinks there is a tacit agreement not to come up to the wire yet. I have circulated material to Cabinet about the Christmas social welfare bonus—that has all the characteristics of another disaster. The Darndale people referred to it constantly yesterday and our crazy system means that contributory pensioners, thousands of whom may not be in any need at all, will get it just like poor families with lots of children; short of means-testing hundreds of thousands of contributory pensioners, there is no way of distinguishing them. There will be holy war over the cut we're proposing and I wish it could be better.

| Wednesday |
| **12** |
| November |

Cabinet yesterday dealt with the question of the Christmas social welfare bonus and after some discussion they decided to spend £18 million on it and make it about three-quarters of last year's. I've been having strong second thoughts about it and will try to have it reversed tomorrow because I believe it's a daft decision. We will offend half a million people by a tiny cut on each of them to save £3 million, which could be found within Departments without affecting the Budget over-run. It really isn't on to do this because we could never win in the face of massive Fianna Fail opposition, so I really will have to get it changed.

| Saturday |
| **15** |
| November |

Spent Thursday between the Dail and the Cabinet; all sorts of ructions and tensions at Cabinet because I re-opened the Christmas bonus issue. I reluctantly gave in under all the pressure. But at least they now know the gravity of what they are doing and when the balloon goes up they can't say they weren't thoroughly warned and briefed by me, which was the whole purpose of the exercise. It was a nasty and tense-making session; I tried not to get angry but I am certainly not going to be anybody's doormat ever again.

The Community Welfare staff are all kicking up about the new implementation plans for the equality legislation and it may not work. That could be a disaster and I'll be blamed again—no solutions no matter which way I turn.

| Thursday |
| **20** |
| November |

Neither myself nor the Government have a shred of reputation left. Yesterday a new storm blew up over the equality directive and gathered momentum all day. I calmly fielded questions all morning at the Parliamentary Party meeting, following precisely the Cabinet decisions, with Garret sitting beside me. But by the time I got back from an obligatory visit to a function attended by Maeve Hillery out in Bray, the Government

241

had changed its mind and agreed to 'review the decision in the context of the 1987 Estimates'. I fought against it, warned them about climb-downs, reminded them of my constant pleas for courage, but all to no avail. So my nose is bloodied again, I'm humiliated and so are they. The ground shifts all the time under me.

And the private members motion on the Christmas bonus comes up next week in the Dail, Fianna Fail being totally opportunistic again. If there is a change on that I will resign next morning and say why.

A storm of media condemnation and disdain today. There are uniform 'Climb down' headlines and bad comments, as I warned. Appalling, I'm in bits—my stomach churns, my skin flakes and stings and last week I had a severe chest pain again. But the calm and smiling public exterior continues.

Tonight I did a television recording on Social Welfare and the equality directive, calmly and coolly, for Olivia O'Leary. It's all so reminiscent of the teachers' crisis and here I am again in the hot seat.

| Friday |
| **21** |
| November |

I've been through one of my worst weeks, with a finale in the Dail at 3.45 p.m. yesterday, when Haughey and I had a head-on confrontation on his private notice question on the equality package. I went at him all guns blazing and made it very political indeed, reminding him that he had designed the directive himself as Minister for Health–Social Welfare in 1978. And I asked him was he too busy plotting then against Jack Lynch to pay attention to what he was doing? He had called for the removal of 'this unfortunate woman' on the Order of Business. I'm in a maelstrom of conflicting feelings. I just had an anonymous phone call from an admiring woman and a very beautiful note yesterday from Mary Harney, but mostly it is total condemnation. Am I a complete fool? Can I stick it out? Stress symptoms abounding but keeping a bright, calm image to the fore. I had dreadful blatant hostility on a visit to Bray this morning, where a community hall was being started, but I also get friendly vibes

from some people, like Mary Banotti. I had assurances
from Garret that there will be no climb-down on the
private members motion on the Christmas bonus next
week. But on past experience, can I be sure?

Monday **24** November

Garret is all het up about the personalising of the
attack on me, which doesn't impress me at all. We
have run into the predictable stone wall on
Budget/Estimates cuts—I gave my four big Social Welfare
ones but they won't be accepted by Labour. I explained
calmly that I will not cut areas specifically attacking poor
women.

Wednesday **26** November

At 9 o'clock tonight in the Dail, the Government
finally faced up to one difficult decision. After
three days of knife-edge stuff during which I
made it plain again that any U-turn would be done
without me, we finally made it through the Christmas
bonus vote, but not without announcing yet another new
package on the equality treatment, greeted today as yet
another U-turn, but I had to do that, to show willing, in
order to get them through the lobbies tonight. Michael
O'Leary was the big problem in the end. He had a sudden
and mysterious crisis of conscience and was only got
through the *Ta* lobby, shepherded by Peter Barry and Pat
Cooney, to cheers from our side. So I sat in the Dail,
almost alone (except for Nuala Fennell beside me) listening to one tirade after another against me (things like
Padraig Flynn shouting that the cut was 'only a gin and
tonic' for me, Michael Bell patronising me). I felt a sudden
surge of emotion when the vote was won, but it was more
rage than anything else I think. Enda Kenny said to me
quietly that 'some members of the Cabinet at least had
some balls', including me. Austin Deasy raised his glass to
me in the bar later, but not a word or a sign from the
others. The further concessions on the equality thing have
given the whole process a sort of unreality; I'm numb.

Now the damage limitation will have to begin, to try to
rescue some of my reputation. I intend to do it, and how!

Monday
1
December

Rising tension, with Alice Glenn unwittingly insulting all the Churches, failing to get a Dail nomination, trying clumsily to climb down. Continuing full-scale criticism of Government. Not surprisingly, I'm at the centre of a lot of it, particularly from Anne Harris and Emily O'Reilly—why do they seem to hate me so? I don't know them at all, but I must have struck some kind of a wrong chord with them. Anyway, I am battling on, trying to present the world with a brave face and hiding the sinking feeling I have inside. I was shouted at in the street in Bray on Friday night and I hear there are plans for a big demonstration against me tonight. I got a cold reception at a Chamber of Commerce function in Bray but a warm reception from 500 building engineers earlier on Friday night when I spoke to them.

At the WPA Seminar on Saturday afternoon, the main speakers were Olivia O'Leary and Kathleen Kennedy-Townsend from the United States. It wasn't up to the usual WPA standard at all. I met Ms Kennedy earlier in Iveagh House. She's nice but very unimpressive, for the daughter of Robert, and obviously is quite unaware of the relatively sophisticated political women she was dealing with in Ireland. Olivia, to my surprise, gave a very folksy and down-market address.

I'd prefer an Election to happen and an end to this tension because I'm in the eye of the storm. Anything would be better than the present situation.

Tuesday
2
December

Yesterday was a long day. It included a live phone-in on Social Welfare with Marian Finucane on RTE, which went well enough. I had it all carefully prepared and planned, and no messing. I kept my end up calmly, perhaps even strongly. Marian gives an impression of slightly breathless chaos but knows exactly what she's at.

I had a sort of sick feeling about what might greet me in Bray and there was a nasty violent scene and demonstration as I was leaving my clinic in the Royal Hotel. The crowd was very small when I went in, but all during the clinic I could hear it building up on the street outside, chanting and shouting. A crowd of Sinn Fein activists from Little Bray, not the ordinary people of Bray at all, were pushing, fighting and shouting, and I had to be escorted through a protective cordon of Gardai to the car, being squashed and buffeted and cursed at, keeping a totally calm and expressionless face. I've never really felt the hot breath of rank hostility, the violence of physical confrontation before—if only one could reason with them. The manager of the hotel wanted me to leave by the back door, but I said 'no way'—I was going 'to go out the way I came in'. How could they imagine I'd slink out?

I got a very warm reception later from the Fine Gael Branch meeting which I attended, with lots of compliments about my courage, etc. I think I am far more damaged than they, in their kind loyalty, think. And I don't believe it was a question of courage; after all, what choices did I have?

Saturday
6
December

A stormy week but I'm all in one piece. A lot of sympathy on account of Monday's thuggery in Bray. The Gardai were roughed up, I'm sorry to hear. I sent them warm messages of thanks.

Thursday (just when I thought it was safe to go back in the water) Michael Bell cut up rough in the Dail about equality again—a case based on his brother's situation. I was trying to mollify him and talked nicely to him afterwards (he brought it up in my Estimate in the Dail). I called Barry Desmond in to deal with him; after all he's a member of the Labour Party and I hope he won't make waves. Felt quite sick at the thought of more trouble as the Dail situation is already bad. Michael Bell was lousy to go public in the Dail without coming to see me beforehand, which would have been the normal, decent thing to do.

I am disappointed with some of the civil servants in Social Welfare, who have not sufficiently briefed me, who have not seen trouble ahead, who have not delved into the details of the situations, who don't seem to have much interest or motivation in suggesting initiatives. I can't believe that neither Barry Desmond nor the Department foresaw this trouble when the Dail and Senate passed the

Equality Bill last summer without opposition; and then, the refusal to listen to me in October when we could have headed off the trouble.

Monday
8
December

I was almost reduced to tears this evening—in private of course—by a bureaucratic block on Combat Poverty money. I wrote a note to Garret, who would be horrified to think there was any hold-up on the poverty money and would blame me if I didn't alert him.

The IDA are being appalling about Arklow. Their new French factory now seems to be only offering thirty-five jobs after all the build-up about eighty jobs. Michael Bell is still threatening me, and the building programme for schools in Wicklow is being held up in Education. What kind of life is this? Dragging off to Greystones and over the Gap to Dunlavin—all decent people there, but I can't spare the sort of time it takes to attend all these meetings and functions, and they don't understand if you're not there.

Monday
15
December

A sort of gloom has settled over us all. An opinion poll yesterday had Fine Gael at nearly its lowest ever—about 24%. The impossibility of getting a Budget together stares us in the face.

We have about 14 hours of Cabinet this week, the rumbles are that John Bruton wants still more Social Welfare cuts, but the ones that are there already are quite horrific—have they lost their reason?

Long Dail session, Cabinet meetings that get nowhere and I'm getting sympathy from all sides (apart from the hostility or impatience that I don't personally have to deal with). I'm beginning to think it would be a miracle to keep my seat. Do I want it? Yes I do. After all these years of crucifying work and ill-treatment, I certainly do. Teachers are threatening again that they're going to issue 'electoral lists' about the further £75 million they want. Fianna Fail are, apparently, saying behind their hands that they'll give it to them.

Sunday
21
December

High drama in the adjournment debate in the Dail on Friday. There hadn't been too much tension around because the vote seemed safe. Garret spoke in the debate, not from a prepared script, and spoke very well and with conviction. Then, ten minutes before he was to conclude, all heads turned up to the lobby and there was Oliver J. Flanagan, being helped in by Tom O'Donnell and Brendan Griffin on a walking frame. He looked appalling, poor man. Five minutes later David Andrews was wheeled in (but he was looking elegant and healthy, just a bad back). So everyone felt very uneasy indeed, I suppose because we all knew we were in the presence of death, not to put a tooth in it. Anyway, we all filed solemnly past Oliver and shook his hand (he thanked me warmly for my recent nice letter) and we all felt rather shook. Tom Fitzpatrick paid a nice tribute to him at the end, to prolonged applause. The lobbies were full, galleries full, the Press Gallery very full and Oliver J. hauled himself to his feet, leant on the rails and raised both arms to the whole gathering with a smile like a Pope in St Peter's. In the event, the adjournment was won by one vote.

The rest of the week was numerous Cabinet meetings, with a lot of reluctance to come to grips with the bottom line. People—John Boland et al— not wanting to meet at all really. We haven't come to the crunch yet—the Social Welfare crunch. I announced the new schemes I have designed, to some praise (but the *Wicklow People* doesn't carry them at all). And I spoke on the adjournment on Friday morning, before Charlie Haughey, who had to sit through my speech and disliked intensely my references to his book *Spirit of the Nation*—I said it made me cringe.

Spoke to David Moloney about the NUI Senate, 'if the worst comes to the worst'. I don't think he's pleased by my intentions.

Tuesday
23
December

The last Cabinet before Christmas. We finally got around to Social Welfare but the gaps remained. Garret was plaintive, Dick stubborn, and finally some of the lads came up with bright ideas to get out of our problems, like selling Irish Life. I left a little early as nothing more was going to be done about Social Welfare and because I had to host my Christmas party for officials at the office.

| Sunday |
| **28** |
| December |

I am feeling more and more detached. I suppose there is quiet anger inside me all the time, while I'm publicly grinning and bearing it, not saying the things that I would love to, and all the pundits are forecasting my defeat in the election.

The Single European Act has been challenged in the High Court, and an interlocutory injunction got. I hope John Rogers hasn't misadvised us about it, it would make you see red that it's had to be delayed. Peter Sutherland going spare.

Nearly every day now there is some unfavourable Social Welfare item in the newspapers or RTE. In vain one repeats the list of improvements in the last four years, the big increases in rates, the new fund spent on voluntary bodies, the new schemes for education and part-time work—everything good is lost in the constant war about things that should be better, all led resolutely by Fianna Fail, the Workers Party and the Labour left and skilfully done too. I never got Fianna Fail to answer the question 'How would you have implemented the equality directive?'

I am also reading Noel Browne's fascinating book, *Against the Tide*. I empathise with a lot of it, but of course he was a loner from day one. He was very kind to me in 1977 when I was a new Senator.

JANUARY 1987

THE FINAL WEEKS

TO

MARCH 1987

The final Cabinet meeting of the Coalition Government—The Labour Party withdraws from Government—Fine Gael publishes its Budget Estimates and Policy Documents—The Department of Labour is added to my Social Welfare portfolio—The General Election is called—Polling day—Fianna Fail Government is formed with C.J. Haughey as Taoiseach.

Sunday
4
January

Back several days now. Cabinet all day Friday and several fraught moments for me as they tinkered momentarily with other cuts, but I kept calm because I think I'm feeling somewhat rested. We got a great deal done however. I can't see Labour wearing the decision that there may be no Social Welfare increase because it has been so far ahead of inflation every other year. Labour will insist on the increase. I'll be very glad of it.

I am working away very carefully at setting the scene for getting the dental and optical benefit for women. I have been very emphatic about it at every meeting, and will keep up the pressure.

The tacit agreement to part company is becoming more obvious and up-front; we're all going through the motions, knowing that the end is just around the corner. Some are angry, some sad, all apprehensive. I'm a mixture of all three.

Thursday
8
January

A sort of uneasy calm before the storm. Home all day Sunday. Worked at briefcases and planning and on Monday got a great deal done, mainly constituency matters. Tuesday, Fine Gael Ministers met at 6.30 p.m. with the Strategy Committee in Garret's office. The scenario was discussed and developed, the conclusion being that we would never get to 21 January let alone 28 January, and how can we let it go as far as possible to give us time—time to prepare the wider picture. Then we had some market research people in telling us about poll analysis, generally saying that things are not as black as they seem. So finally we got down to the Fine Gael Ministers' meeting, a long session looking at all the possibilities. We finished up at 1.30 a.m. with drinks in Sean Barrett's office, a sort of nervous gaiety about; and as we gathered all together for Cabinet for most of Wednesday, there was a tacit and amicable understanding between Labour and ourselves that we're coming to the end and a desire to continue to be friends after all we've been through together.

I still feel as if I am about to throw myself off a cliff

without a safety net, and I wonder if any of the Fine Gael colleagues perceive this or are they just bloody relieved it's me and not them.

Friday 16 January A great deal of shifting and movement going on, the most dramatic thing being the sudden snow and freeze-up all over the East and South of the country, causing chaos.

A sad Dick Spring spoke at the Texaco All Stars dinner that we went to—he is fed up about the whole mess but can't see a way out of it. Derry and I had agreeable chats with Ruairi Quinn and Liz; we all feel terribly regretful at the way things have turned out.

The Social Welfare area is somewhat less appalling than at the outset. There will be an increase this year after all and pay related benefit is halved, not abolished. And the big, exciting and good news is that the dental and optical benefit for spouses is in there too as part of the Budget and I am absolutely thrilled and proud about that.

Bruce and Mavis Arnold won their case on the phone tapping and Geraldine Kennedy did too—she's joining the PDs in Dublin somewhere.

Sunday 18 January It appears that Ciaran Murphy in Bray, who left Fianna Fail to join the PDs, has now had a row with the PDs in Wicklow and is pulling out, so they're all in a mess down there. And I also hear that they're losing their other candidate, Susan Phillips from Ballyfree Farms. Not sure why, but all this gives me some comfort, as least someone else is in as bad a mess as I am.

Thursday 22 January Well, the Election is on. Our final Cabinet on Tuesday was slightly strained and obviously very hard for Dick. We took a formal vote at 12 noon and then Dick handed over his prepared letter of resignation. There was a session of slightly sad, slightly emotional handshakes (a warm embrace for me from Barry and Ruairi). We were a very subdued bunch. Some of us then went off to Aras an Uachtarain (Garret nearly forgetting to notify me formally of my appointment as Minister for

Labour) where we accepted our new seals from Dr Hillery, who was inclined to delay us by chit-chat. None of us felt in the humour for chit-chat. Wish I'd been given Labour last February instead of now.

We had a Government meeting of the remaining Ministers, then a very big, public, formal presentation of the Estimates and Budget in Iveagh House and John Bruton did the whole thing extremely well. The Budget is tough, well-designed, and constructive, with realisable targets.

I'm working now on trying not to get strained or tense; when Elections start it's hard not to.

Sunday **25** January

Fine Gael has published Estimates, Budget policy documents, the lot. The pattern so far has been slagging matches on all the programmes, our side demanding simple, precise answers to all the figures, Fianna Fail saying mostly that they don't accept the figures at all and will put their own forward when they're in Government. Anyway, all the organisation and groundwork for the campaign goes ahead apace.

We did a big leaflet drop in Wicklow announcing the dental and optical benefit scheme (which got no publicity, no welcomes from women's organisations, after all these years of striving for it). People don't believe anyone in politics.

One of the worries is that if this Election is indecisive, we'll be back at this operation in another few months — although if Fine Gael finds itself in the Dail with Fianna Fail doing the things we said had to be done, why would we bring them down? A sort of National Government? Anyway, there's a lot of water to go under the bridge before that would crop up.

The PDs in Wicklow have replaced Ciaran Murphy with Aidan Murphy and have added a man from Arklow and a dentist from Greystones. All these men wanting my seat!

Saturday **31** January

Well and truly into the campaign, it is difficult, dreary, cold, dark, tiring and worrying. The atmosphere is quite different from the heady days of four or five years ago; I suppose that's politics and pendulums—and the dirty tricks brigade is out in strength. The population is testy, disgruntled and understandably mixed up. There is a great deal of hostility to me on the doorsteps, particularly vicious from the teachers, who are being terribly strong against all our canvassers. So, after week one, I've given considerable pep-talks to groups of canvassers and have led the teams into the housing estates to show a bright, cheerful and resolute face. The campaign is as difficult as I thought it would be for me; it's sometimes as much as I can do not to lash back at the rudeness and jibes. Fianna Fail are doing the predictable thing, fudging the whole issue, no precision except promising more on Social Welfare and saying that they would certainly do a great deal more spending on Education. Their campaign slogan is 'There is a Better Way' and they have very striking posters about health cuts, emigration, etc. After the violence of December the Gardai insisted on providing plain-clothes minders when I went into Fassaroe to canvass.

Joan FitzGerald came, as promised, to a big coffee morning in Bray, and was very impressive with everyone. She feels very bad about my awful troubles of the last year. Everyone loved her in Bray.

Wednesday 18 February The whole campaign is over and the count has started; I'm waiting for a call from the organiser in Wicklow with the first indications of the tally. The campaign finished with two leaflet drops, distributed by my wonderful teams of women and young people. The canvass on Sunday and Monday was desultory and winding-down. Mary Banotti canvassed all Saturday and Saturday night, Jim Dooge came down, Katharine Bulbulia came, Mary Muldoon appeared—I had a great crowd of people helping me.

What are the doorstep impressions of this campaign? One of the strongest was the venom of teachers towards me, their narrowness, their rudeness; my God what did I ever do to them? They got such huge money! And another impression—the hate from people in places like Fassaroe Park, who have been told by so many people that there are massive Social Welfare cuts (the opposite is the case except for the equality directive fiasco which only affects very few of them). They all seem to despise me; they are being told all the time by Fianna Fail that everything will be much better and that 'There is a Better Way'.

The wonderful large teams of canvassers going out from my house in Bray every night, their cheerfulness and team spirit, the desperate battle to win back PD voters who are disgusted with Fine Gael, usually because they were squeezed for tax and all worried about unemployment, the warm encouragement from other people who are generally supportive. Yesterday, polling day, the long, freezing day at the polling booths, wind whistling, thrusting leaflets and names at the voters, demoralized a little by huge, expensive PD buses, but cheered by our own troops' enthusiasm, such kindness, such activity—and the feeling, it is always inevitable, that I could have done much more, that I could have got more people, that I could have knocked on more doors, the worry about the other women, Avril, Nora, Monica, Nuala losing their seats as well as myself.

The amazing Fianna Fail campaign, with huge banners and posters 'Health cuts hurt the poor, the old, the sick . . . there is a better way' has alarmed everyone. How could the people buy it?

Friday
20
February

As it turned out I won the seat and Godfrey Timmins lost. This is not a good scenario, but it is an example of what can be achieved against terrible odds. There was a very tense first half of the day until the tally at about 3 p.m. showed me safe enough and Godfrey in trouble. It was a very trying day because while my people were jubilant, we had to be very subdued because naturally Godfrey's camp got more and more bitter in their disappointment. As usual the count went on until all hours, the final speeches not being made until 2 o'clock in the morning. It was one of the most difficult speeches I have ever made because it had to be low-key and very regretful. If only Godfrey had agreed to divide the constituency he'd still have his seat. Godfrey remained the perfect gentleman he has always been, all through the count and speeches.

But now I am trying to recover and feeling satisfied that I beat all the pundits and overcame all the gloomy forecasts. So after all the speculation, worry and wondering about the future, here we are facing a hung Dail. Charlie with his eighty-one seats; we're down to a catastrophic fifty-one. But some of the women won through, the biggest battle being Monica's against the Cosgrave forces and she just made it after a re-count, Avril survived and Madeleine Taylor-Quinn, but Nora Owen and Nuala Fennell lost out. The good Hugh Coveney lost and Fintan Coogan and Maurice Manning—some of our best. What a cruel game this is.

Today I am trying to rest mostly in bed but I didn't get any sleep, with all the phone calls. Garret rang me expressing great relief at the news of my election but feeling desperately sorry about Godfrey.

Wednesday 25 February

The political post-election atmosphere thickens amid a shower of congratulatory messages and cards from masses of people and a major effort to write thanks to so many people. I'm discussing and debating the whole situation.

Ventured into Leinster House today for lunch. There is shock and simmering anger and resentment in the party.

Cabinet yesterday with a lot of Fine Gael people in very bad humour.

Monday 2 March

The political situation gets more uncertain by the minute. Tom Fitzpatrick wants to be Ceann Comhairle, and hasn't accepted as yet the Fine Gael Cabinet's decision (which was divided anyway) and so there's a Parliamentary Party meeting to discuss that on Friday as well as the Senate.

I am disappointed that the Government went ahead and arranged a farewell dinner for tomorrow night in Barrettstown despite my being unable to go. Now I'm thinking of

re-arranging everything, but it may be too difficult—there
are about twenty people coming for a post-election 'thank
you' at home. How can I put them off?

| Wednesday 4 March | Garret rang me urging me to come and join the dinner at Barrettstown, even if it has to be later, so I set off for Barrettstown really very late, |

through storms and rain. I found them all in fine order—a
general mellow air but Garret looking worn out.

I suppose it was just as well that I made the effort to go,
however late, they all seemed to appreciate it. So I drove
back home in Garret's car in order to facilitate the drivers
and we talked about Haughey's attitude, Tom Fitzpatrick's position. Garret rejected emphatically any suggestion of Fine Gael abstaining on the Tuesday vote for
Haughey. He acknowledged my note which I'd sent
around earlier asking that if he was appointing a front
bench in opposition and I was on it, not to give me Social
Welfare or Education, but something completely different.
I also suggested that he put Avril Doyle on the front
bench.

Garret paid for the evening in Barrettstown himself. It
was a kind gesture.

There is a lot of unhappiness in Wicklow about Godfrey
losing his seat and a certain amount of blame on me,
which is understandable. Our bloody political system
leads to such hostilities among political allies!

| Monday 9 March | Home after a long, tense meeting of Fine Gael Ministers about tomorrow—a meeting which I had asked Garret to have, after a conversation |

with John Bruton yesterday, because I felt that we were all
floundering about in some kind of a fog. It was complicated and it's hard to know what the motivation of a lot of
the people is. John Bruton was in a peculiar frame of
mind. It was decided that we vote against Haughey
tomorrow, taking the risk that Tony Gregory would vote
for him and that Haughey would immediately go to the
country. But if there is a stalemate, Paddy Hillery may
decide that he doesn't want Garret to ask for a dissolution

but to resign and then have a second go at solving the problem: so Garret will try first to get the PDs and Fianna Fail together, then to achieve a Fianna Fail/Fine Gael arrangement, finally a National Government and then, if all else fails, an Election. But what would the Fine Gael platform be? We adjourned, as we often have done, to Sean Barrett's office for the final session of drinks.

Tomorrow looms, uncertain and worrying, and I'm supposed to go to the US on Thursday to address an international conference on 'Women and Leadership'— Geraldine Ferraro is one of the organisers.

The old Fine Gael loyalties, Pat Cooney, John Boland and Peter Barry with Sean Barrett in the enigmatic centre, John Bruton on the high ground somewhat isolated, Alan Dukes being agreeable but not really one of the boys—it's all fascinating and I wonder what they all really think of me, but as Derry would say, what does that matter?

All this pressure isn't a bit cool. I wish it was all clear-cut. Garret was definitely looking for consensus today, a clear direction about what he should do, and he got it.

Tuesday
10
March

Well, the brinkmanship worked and there is now a Fianna Fail Government, albeit a minority one. At least C.J.H. hasn't a free hand to get back to GUBU.

The Parliamentary Party meeting today was mercifully brief and uncontentious, mostly because it was clear to them that the Cabinet had a plan and also that secrecy is impossible if we talked about it. So high drama ensued, most of us thinking that we were into another Election situation, causing some tremors. Anyway, Tony Gregory made a long speech, a bit convoluted, but abstained, so the casting vote won the day. There was a strange degree of consensus after that, everyone saying conciliatory things. Garret committed Fine Gael to support for Fianna Fail if they do the right thing.

Now I'm at home, a Minister no more, and feeling glad, glad, glad.

Abbreviations

AnCo	An Comhairle: The Training and Apprenticeship Board
AONTAS	The National Association of Adult Education
ASTI	Association of Secondary Teachers in Ireland
CBC	Christian Brothers' College
CIE	Coras Iompar Eireann
CMRS	Conference of Major Religious Superiors
CSPA	Catholic Secondary School Parents' Association
DART	Dublin Area Rapid Transit
GAA	Gaelic Athletic Association
GUBU	grotesque, unbelievable, bizarre, unprecedented.
HEA	Higher Education Authority
ICI	Insurance Corporation of Ireland
IDA	Industrial Development Authority
IMF	International Monetary Fund
IMS	Irish Marketing Surveys
INLA	Irish National Liberation Army
INTO	Irish National Teachers' Organisation
IRA	Irish Republican Army
IRFU	Irish Rugby Football Union
IVEA	Irish Vocational Education Association
JMB	Joint Managerial Body
LEC	Local Education Council
NCEA	National Council for Education Awards
NDC	National Development Corporation
NIHE	National Institute for Higher Education
NUI	National University of Ireland
NORAID	A fund-raising group in USA with Sinn Fein/IRA sympathies
PAYE	Pay As You Earn
PDs	Progressive Democrats
PLAC	Pro-Life Amendment Campaign

Abbreviations continued

PMPA	Private Motorists' Protection Association
PRSI	Pay Related Social Insurance
Provo	Provisional Sinn Féin or IRA
RDS	Royal Dublin Society
RTC	Regional Technical College
RUC	Royal Ulster Constabulary
SDLP	Social Democratic and Labour Party
SPUC	Society for the Protection of the Unborn Child
TUI	Teachers' Union of Ireland
UCC	University College Cork
UCD	University College Dublin
UCG	University College Galway
UDR	Ulster Defense Regiment
UNESCO	United Nations Organisation for Education, Science & Culture
USI	Union of Students in Ireland
VAT	Value Added Tax
VEC	Vocational Education Committee
WPA	Women's Political Association
YEA	Youth Employment Agency
VHI	Voluntary Health Insurance

Index

Index

Index

Index

Index

Index